SBA Microloan and Specialty Loan Handbook

SBA Microloan and Specialty Loan Handbook

Patrick D. O'Hara, Ph.D.

John Wiley & Sons, Inc.

New York • Chichester • Brisbane • Toronto • Singapore

Copyright © 1996 by Patrick D. O'Hara
Published by John Wiley & Sons, Inc.

Library of Congress Cataloging-in-Publication Data:

O'Hara, Patrick D.
    SBA microloan and specialty loan handbook / Patrick O'Hara.
      p.   cm.
    Includes bibliographical references (p.).
    ISBN 0-471-13915-7 (alk. paper). — ISBN 0-471-13914-9 (paper :
alk. paper) .
    1. United States. Small Business Administration. 2. Small
business—United States—Finance. 3. Loans—United States—
Government guaranty. I. Title.
HG4027.7.O432 1996
353.0082′048045—dc20   95-53995
                                                CIP

Contents

Section One

1 Introduction

This book is written with the express purpose of providing information about the many specialty loan programs available through the Small Business Administration (SBA). The SBA has a general loan program known as the 7(a) program, which most business people are aware of and is covered in detail in the book *SBA Loans: A Step-by-Step Guide,* also published by John Wiley & Sons. But there are many more special programs that many people are not aware of. This is because the SBA administrators and Congress may see a need for a specific program and create it, but there are virtually no funds provided to advertise them.

Section 1 covers the current administration's activity with the SBA and gives brief explanations of the various specialty programs, eligibility requirements, loan terms, and how to apply. This allows the reader to make an informed decision as to which program is most likely to approve the loan application.

Section 2 covers the dynamics of the SBA and gives the reader a sense of the political climate surrounding the SBA and its loan programs. The aim is to help the reader develop an understanding of the SBA and how its programs are initiated, and to demonstrate that patience and persistence are necessary when dealing with the SBA—or any government agency, for that matter. Also covered here are some of the most frequently asked questions about the SBA programs.

Section 3 gives more in-depth coverage of the eligibility requirements for loan applicants and explains the basic concepts used in processing loan applications, SBA's guarantee liability, and the interest rates allowed on these SBA loans. It is hoped that the information in this and the next section will give the reader a better understanding of what the lending agency must provide the SBA throughout the loan period. Forms are referenced and some are presented as examples to ensure that the reader is familiar with them.

Section 4 describes the general processes involved in the loan application and approval processes.

Section 5 thoroughly explains the current special loan programs now available through the SBA, as well as some of the other support programs and resources available from the SBA to the small-business community.

Section 6 gives a list of SBA regional, district, and field offices where additional information can be obtained.

2 What Is the SBA?

The estimated 20 million small businesses in America today account for 39 percent of the gross national product (GNP), half of America's workforce, and 53.5 percent of all sales. Small Business Administration (SBA) programs stimulate capital formation, economic growth, and job creation. They address finance, marketing, production, and human resource management. The SBA's finance, investment, and procurement programs provide economic development tools to the nation's small businesses. Key programs rely on guarantees of loans made by private lenders, so the cost to the taxpayer is minimal. Credit programs boost the availability of capital and build the confidence of both lenders and borrowers.

The SBA is the largest source of long-term small-business financing in the nation. In fiscal year 1990, the San Francisco District by itself made 1,119 loans for over $349.2 million, the highest volume reached by any SBA district in the nation. Between 1980 and 1990, SBA provided guarantees for 180,000 loans worth more than $31 billion.

In fact, a four-year study revealed that businesses receiving a 7(a) loan (the largest guaranteed loan program) registered an average sales growth of 123 percent from 1985 to 1989 (the latest figures available), compared to 101 percent for a comparison group. And employment grew an average of 101 percent compared to only 36 percent for the comparison group.

Recipients of 7(a) loans also tend to have a greater survival rate. Approximately three-fourths of the 1,430 SBA-backed firms were still in business after the four-year study, compared to only 64 percent of those in the comparison group. The study also revealed that businesses with the money they need to continue growing have a greater chance of survival.

The vast majority of new and existing small businesses are eligible for SBA financial assistance if they do not dominate their field, are independently owned, and can prove that they have been unable to obtain a bank loan or other private financing without the SBA's assistance. In fact, the SBA's definition of a small business includes 80 to 90 percent of all businesses in the United States. So, you most likely have already met that requirement.

Although the SBA does make a very limited number of direct loans (primarily under the Vietnam veteran and handicapped programs), it normally provides a guarantee to a private lender, who in turn makes the loan directly to the borrower. With the exception of a few joint programs with state agencies and some specialty loan programs, the maximum amount the SBA can loan to any one business is currently $750,000. This includes working capital funds and long-term loans. The SBA can guarantee up to 90 percent of a loan, depending on the loan amount. Maturity may be up to 25 years. The average size of a guaranteed business loan is $175,000, with an average maturity of about eight years.

Guarantees require a commercial bank to actually supply the funds. The bank must participate 10 percent for loans up to $155,000, and 15 percent for loans between $155,000 and $750,000. Interest rates cannot be more than 2.25 to 2.75 percentage points above prime. The material to be purchased may serve as collateral, although personal guarantees might be required.

But things are changing rapidly in the world of the SBA. For example, the U.S. House and Senate small-business committees, which are working to reduce the cost and thus the programs of the SBA, reached consensus on a plan that would revamp the Small Business Administration's biggest loan program. The plan, which combines elements of legislation approved earlier by the House and Senate, would lower the taxpayer cost of the so-called 7(a) program by increasing fees to borrowers and lenders. It also would enable the agency to guarantee more loans for the fiscal year starting October 1, 1995.

The consensus version of the bill calls for the SBA to back 75 percent of the value of loans exceeding $100,000 under its 7(a) loan program. Loans below that amount would be eligible for an 80 percent guarantee. The SBA now guarantees between 70 and 90 percent of a loan's value, depending on the loan's size and repayment schedule.

Lenders would be required to pay a new 0.5 percent fee on the entire guaranteed portion of the loan. Currently, lenders pay an extra fee if they sell a loan on the secondary market. The plan would reduce the taxpayer expense for the program to $104.5 million a year, the committees said. The program now costs about $200 million annually.

Earlier in 1995, the Clinton Administration proposed to entirely eliminate the taxpayer cost of the loan program through a combination of increased fees to borrowers and lenders. Lenders have favored the congressional plan because it would require them to pay slightly lower fees. Under the combined committees' proposal, the agency will be able to support $9.86 billion in 7(a) lending. Loan volume under the program will total about $8 billion in fiscal year 1995.

Separately, the Senate is considering a proposal that would reduce the SBA's appropriation to $558 million for fiscal 1996. The agency's budget for fiscal year 1995 is $813 million. The measure would eliminate several SBA programs, including a new women's business council and small-business information centers partially funded by the private sector.

The Senate is also seeking to cut the agency's operating expenses to $232 million, leaving the SBA with $50 million less than had been requested. It has been estimated by the SBA administrator that the reduced funding would require the agency to cut 844 full-time jobs, reducing the staff size to 2,334, which might stretch SBA's resources too far.

The SBA offers assistance under several programs, some designated by the numbered section of the Small Business Act to which they apply.

The SBA's basic program includes:

I. **Regular business loans**

II. **Special loan programs that offer the following:**
   A. Contract loans
   B. Small general contractor loans
   C. Seasonal line of credit guarantees
   D. Minority enterprise development
      1. 8(a)
      2. 7(j)
   E. Handicapped loans
      1. HAL(1)
      2. HAL(2)
   F. Pollution control financing
   G. International trade loans
      1. Export working capital (EWCP)
   H. Disaster assistance
      1. Physical disaster loans
      2. Economic injury disaster loans
   I. Assistance to women and minorities
   J. Office of Veterans Affairs
      1. Assistance to veterans
   K. Business development programs
   L. Small Business Innovation Research Program (SBIR)

III. **Certified Lenders Program**

IV. **Development Company Loans (504)**

V. **Surety bond guarantees**

VI. **Small Business Investment Companies (SBICs)**

VII. **Minority Enterprise Small Business Investment Companies (MES-BICs), also known as Special Small Business Investment Companies (SSBICs)**

As you can see, there are a number of SBA programs and services. They will be briefly explained in the following paragraphs. Again, this book will concentrate on the special loan programs rather than the regular 7(a) loan program, which is covered in detail in the book *SBA Loans: A Step-by-Step Guide.*

SBA BASIC ELIGIBILITY REQUIREMENTS

Depending on the type of business seeking SBA financing, certain standards will determine eligibility. These standards are as follows:

- *Manufacturing.* The total number of employees may range up to 1,500, but the actual number is based on the industry in which the business is engaged.
- *Wholesale.* Up to 100 employees are permitted.
- *Service companies.* Maximum annual sales can range from $3.5 million to $14.5 million, depending on the industry.
- *Retail companies.* Maximum annual sales can range from $3.5 million to $13.5 million, depending on the industry.
- *General construction.* Maximum annual sales can range from $9.5 million to $17.0 million, depending on the industry.
- *Special trade construction.* Average annual receipts cannot exceed $7 million.
- *Agriculture.* Annual sales receipts cannot exceed $500,000 to $3.5 million, depending on the industry.

The SBA has issued what is called an alternate standard ruling, under which a company can qualify as a small business if its net worth is up to $6 million and it's had an annual after-tax net income of up to $2 million in each of the past two years. This alternate standard ruling opens the program to a much larger group of businesses while making no mention of providing additional funds to compensate for the influx of these larger businesses.

Ineligible Businesses

The Small Business Act excludes some forms of businesses from receiving loans, including the following:

- Not-for-profit organizations except sheltered workshops
- Newspapers
- Magazines
- Movie theaters
- Radio and television stations
- Theatrical productions
- Dinner theaters
- Book publishers
- Film, record, or tape distributors
- Businesses involved in the creation, origination, expression, or distribution of ideas, values, thoughts, or opinions
- Manufacturers, importers, exporters, retailers, or distributors of communications such as greeting cards, books, sheet music, pictures, posters, films, tapes, broadcasts, or other performances and recordings of musical programs (check with your local SBA office regarding March 1996 changes in this category)

Eligible firms include those engaged as commercial printers; those producing advertising and promotional materials for others or who provide motion pictures, video tapes, sound recording facilities, or technical services *without* editorial or artistic contribution; and general merchandisers that sell magazines, books, and so on.

Other businesses that are excluded are those engaged in floor planning, gambling, speculation of any kind, and illegal activities. Applications from incarcerated persons or persons on probation or parole for serious offenses will not be accepted.

To determine if your business or proposed enterprise is currently eligible, contact the nearest SBA office or your bank.

OTHER SBA LOAN REQUIREMENTS

Before the SBA will guarantee a loan through a lender, the applicant must demonstrate that the following conditions apply:

- The business will be able to repay its current debts in addition to the new loan requested.
- There is a reasonable amount of equity invested in the business, or collateral that the borrower can pledge for the loan. Generally, a new business applicant should have between 20 and 30 percent of the required equity investment to start a new business. The actual percentage is determined by the lender and the SBA. For existing businesses, the SBA considers a number of credit factors and the company's history before reaching a decision, which is essentially the same policy of any other lender.
- The company's past track record has been good and/or its financial projections are realistic and supportable.
- The company's management has the expertise to adequately conduct the operations of the business.

The fastest way to determine whether an SBA-guaranteed loan is a viable option for your financing needs is to call your banker for an appointment. After all, you have to be turned down by a bank before you can qualify for SBA assistance anyway. Maybe your bank won't give you a loan directly, but if it won't, ask if it would be interested in participating in an SBA-guaranteed loan. If the answer is yes, give the bank all of the information it requests. It will help you complete the loan application and forward it to the SBA for approval. The entire process can take just a few weeks, depending on how well your business plan and the application have been prepared.

GUARANTEED LOANS

Guaranteed loans are made by private lenders, with a percentage of the loan amount up to $750,000 guaranteed by the SBA. A loan application is submitted to a lender that participates in the SBA loan guarantee program. The application must meet the SBA eligibility and credit requirements as well as all requirements of the lender. If the application is approved by the lender, it is then submitted to the SBA for approval. The SBA usually makes a credit decision on loans within ten working days.

BASIC TERMS AND CONDITIONS OF SBA-GUARANTEED LOANS

Loan Limits

There is no maximum loan limit that can be obtained through the guarantee program. The standard maximum amount that SBA can guarantee is $750,000. SBA guarantees a percentage of the loan amount to the lender. There is a 2 percent fee on the guaranteed amount. The average loan made under the guarantee program is approximately $175,000. Although the SBA does not set minimum loan amounts, many lenders will not make loans below $50,000; very few lenders will consider loans below $25,000. (For very small loans see the Microloan program mentioned later.)

Use of Proceeds

The loan proceeds may be used for a variety of business purposes including working capital, inventory, machinery and equipment, leasehold improvements, and the acquisition or construction of commercial business property.

Loan Term

The maturity of the loan is dependent on the use of the loan proceeds and may vary from five to seven years for working capital, ten years for fixed assets, or 25 years for real estate acquisitions.

HOW TO APPLY FOR A LOAN

Applications may be obtained from participating lenders. Generally, the following documentation is required:

- A current profit and loss statement and balance sheet for existing businesses, or a pro forma statement for new businesses; provide a realistic projected cash flow and profit and loss statement for one year (monthly breakdown)
- A current personal financial statement of the owner/manager, or each partner or stockholder owning 20 percent or more of the corporate stock
- Itemized use of loan proceeds
- Collateral with an estimate of current market value and liens against the collateral
- A business plan, including resumes of the principals
- A schedule of business debt, aging of accounts receivable, and accounts payable
- Personal and business tax returns for the past three years

- Copy of lease (if property is to be leased)
- Any contracts or agreements pertinent to the applicant

SUMMARY OF SBA GUARANTEED LOANS

The following general information should provide you with a basic understanding of the SBA 7(a) guaranteed loan program. This program's rules and guidelines apply to all SBA loans unless specifically excepted. Each loan application is reviewed individually by an SBA lender and an SBA loan officer to determine eligibility.

I.   *The SBA generally* does not *make loans;* the SBA *guarantees* loans submitted and made by financial institutions, generally banks. The SBA *does not* have a "grant" program for starting small businesses (see the SBIR program mentioned later).
  A. The SBA guarantees loans up to $750,000. There is no theoretical minimum; however, most lenders are reluctant to process commercial loans of less than $25,000. The microloan and LowDoc programs have been created to cover these lower lending limits.
  B. The prospective borrower *will be required* to provide a capital contribution. This contribution will normally be 30 to 50 percent of the total capitalization of the business. Often, real estate acquisitions can be financed for up to 90 percent with only the support of the first deed of trust and the owner's personal guarantee.
  C. An existing business will be required to provide financial statements showing the business is a profit-making concern, does not have delinquent tax, and will have a debt to net worth ratio of approximately 3:1 after the loan is made.
  D. Many borrowers confuse collateral and equity. *Equity* is the owner's investment or net worth in the business. *Collateral* is anything of value, business or personal, that may be pledged to secure the loan.
  E. The SBA charges the lender a 2 percent guarantee fee on the guaranteed portion of the loan. SBA policy allows the lender to charge this guarantee fee to the borrower.

II. *The SBA-guaranteed loan program's "interest rates"* are based on the prime rate as advertised in the *Wall Street Journal* according to the following schedule:
  A. Loans of less than seven years: prime rate plus 2.25 percentage points.
  B. Loans of seven years or more: prime rate plus 2.75 percentage points.

III. *The SBA guaranteed loan maturity* (length of loan) is based upon the following schedule:
  A. Working capital loans: 5 to 7 years (no prepayment penalty)
  B. Fixed asset loans: 7 to 10 years (no prepayment penalty)
  C. Real estate and building loans: up to a maximum of 25 years (no prepayment penalty)

IV. *The average size standards* for SBA-guaranteed business loans are based on the average number of employees for the preceding 12 months or on the sales volume averaged over a three-year period according to the following schedule:
   A. *Manufacturing.* Maximum number of employees may range from 500 to 1,500, depending on the type of product manufactured.
   B. *Wholesaling.* Maximum number of employees may not exceed 100.
   C. *Services.* Annual receipts may not exceed $3.5 million to $14.5 million, depending on the industry.
   D. *Retailing.* Annual receipts may not exceed $3.5 million to $13.5 million, depending on the industry.
   E. *Construction.* General construction annual receipts may not exceed $9.5 million to $17 million, depending on the industry.
   F. *Special trade construction.* Annual receipts may not exceed $7 million.
   G. *Agriculture.* Annual receipts may not exceed $500,000 to $3.5 million, depending on the industry.

V. *Most importantly,* during your discussion with the lender, be prepared with data to answer the lender's questions. A business plan that includes the following items will help you in presenting your proposal:
   A. Projected profit and loss statement
   B. Cash flow projections
   C. Market analysis
   D. Marketing strategy
   E. Description of the business
   F. Product's or service's advantage
   G. Management ability—résumés of the key staff should be included
   H. Financial information (personal and business)
   I. Cash requirements

VI. *Business proposals* that are ineligible for the SBA-guaranteed loan program are as follows:
   A. Partial purchase of a business
   B. Lending institutions
   C. Real estate held for speculation, investment, or rental
   D. Opinion molders—magazines, newspapers, trade journals, radio, television, live entertainment, schools, and so forth
   E. Religious organizations and their affiliates

Please note that the SBA has issued the statement that they are not encouraging applications from businesses that are less than one year old.

3 Specialty SBA 7(A) Guaranteed Loan Programs

In the general area of financial assistance, the SBA offers several specialty loan programs. These are the subject of this book and will be discussed in detail throughout the remainder of this book.

504/503 DEVELOPMENT COMPANY LOAN PROGRAM

The 504/503 Development Company Loan Program uses public/private partnerships to finance fixed assets and has produced more than $5 billion in investments and more than 301,000 jobs since its beginning in 1980.

THE SMALL BUSINESS INVESTMENT COMPANY (SBIC) PROGRAM

Private capital combined with SBA-guaranteed funds provides venture capital for start-up and growth. SBICs have invested nearly $11 billion in more than 70,000 small businesses.

THE MICROLOAN PROGRAM

Small loans help entrepreneurs in inner-city and rural areas form small, often home-based enterprises.

EXPORT FINANCE

Normal and specialized loan guarantee programs offer working capital and longer-term financing to promote exporting.

DISASTER LOANS

Low-interest loans help individuals, homeowners, and businesses rebuild after a disaster.

THE 8(a) BUSINESS DEVELOPMENT PROGRAM

The 8(a) Business Development Program helps socially and economically disadvantaged individuals enter the economic mainstream, partly through access to federal contracts. It helps small, disadvantaged businesses obtain federal government contracts. Under the program, the SBA acts as a prime contractor and enters into all types of federal government contracts (including but not limited to supplies, services, construction, and research and development) with other government departments and agencies. The SBA then subcontracts the performance of that contract to small businesses in the 8(a) program.

To be eligible for the 8(a) program, firms must demonstrate that they are at least 51 percent owned and managed by one or more individuals who are U.S. citizens and who are determined to be socially and economically disadvantaged. The firm must also have been in business for at least two full years. Please note that 8(a) is not a certification program; it's a business development program.

Since 1977 the SBA has had an ongoing women's business ownership program. In 1983, under the 8(a) program, the SBA began organizing a series of business training seminars and workshops for women already running a firm, as well as those wanting to do so. The focus is on business planning and development. According to the SBA a woman-owned business is defined as a "business that is at least 51 percent owned by a woman, or women, who also control and operate it."

PROCUREMENT ASSISTANCE PROGRAM

The Procurement Assistance Program ensures maximum competition by encouraging contracts for small businesses. It saved taxpayers $230 million in 1991.

SURETY BOND GUARANTEE PROGRAM

The Surety Bond Guarantee Program has issued more than 236,000 surety guarantees for $19 billion in contracts since 1976, helping businesses win government construction contracts.

LOWDOC

The Low Documentation Loan Program (LowDoc) reduces the paperwork involved in loan requests of $100,000 or less. It uses a one-page application and relies on the strength of the individual applicant's character and credit history. The lender may require additional information. Those who hate paperwork will love LowDoc.

LowDoc meets short-term, cyclical, working capital needs of small businesses. Loan advances can be made against a borrower's certified level of inventory and accounts receivable. Generally, SBA regulations governing the 7(a) loan guarantee program also govern this program.

VIETNAM-ERA AND DISABLED VETERANS LOAN PROGRAM

The Vietnam-Era and Disabled Veterans Loan Program assists disabled veterans of any era and Vietnam veterans who cannot secure business financing on reasonable terms from private sector or other guaranteed loan sources. Veterans can apply for direct loans to establish a small business or expand an existing small business. The ceiling for these direct loans is $150,000.

HANDICAPPED ASSISTANCE LOANS

Handicapped Assistance Loans encourage the employment of the disabled and the ventures of "handi-capable" entrepreneurs. This loan program is earmarked for physically handicapped small-business owners and private nonprofit organizations that employ handicapped persons and operate in their interest—for example, sheltered workshops. Two loan programs, HAL-1 and HAL-2, assist public or private nonprofit organizations involved in the employment of the disabled, and active business owners who have disabilities.

WOMEN'S PREQUALIFICATION LOAN PROGRAM

The Women's Prequalificaiton Loan Program provides women business owners a preauthorized loan guarantee commitment, a streamlined application process, and a quick response to loan requests of $250,000 or less.

SMALL GENERAL CONTRACTOR LOANS

Small General Contractor Loans are designed to assist small construction firms with short-term financing. Loan proceeds can be used to finance residential or commercial construction or rehabilitation of property for sale. Proceeds cannot be used for owning or operating real estate for investment purposes.

SEASONAL LINE OF CREDIT GUARANTEE

Seasonal Line of Credit Guarantees are designed to provide short-term financing for small firms having a seasonal loan requirement due to a seasonal increase in business activity.

EXPORT REVOLVING LINES OF CREDIT

The Export Revolving Lines of Credit (ERLC) program offers guarantees to provide short-term financing for exporting firms that have been in existence for one year or more. Loans must be for the purpose of developing or penetrating foreign markets.

INTERNATIONAL TRADE LOANS

One of the SBA's most important missions is to encourage small businesses to export their products or services overseas. It has several programs to achieve this goal, including guaranteed loans to exporters of up to $1.25 million ($250,000 for working capital, $1 million for facilities or equipment to be used in the United States in the production of goods and services involved in international trade) and the ERLC. Through the ERLC, the SBA can guarantee up to 90 percent of a credit line extended by a bank to an exporter. The SBA also offers referrals to other agencies involved in exporting, sponsors regular export seminars and workshops, and has free counseling available through the Service Corps of Retired Executives (SCORE).

DISASTER ASSISTANCE

When the president of the United States or the administrator of the SBA declares a specific area to be a disaster area, two types of loans are offered:

- *Physical Disaster Loans* are made available to homeowners, renters, businesses (large and small), and nonprofit organizations within the disaster area. Loan proceeds can be used to repair or replace damaged or destroyed homes, personal property, and businesses.
- *Economic Injury Disaster Loans* are made available to small businesses that suffer substantial economic injury because of the disaster. Loan proceeds may be used for working capital and for paying financial obligations that the small business could have met had the disaster not occurred.

When a disaster is declared, the SBA establishes on-site offices staffed with experienced personnel to help with loan information, processing, and disbursement.

POLLUTION CONTROL LOANS

The SBA assists those small businesses needing long-term financing for planning, design, and installation of pollution control facilities or equipment. This financing is available through the loan guarantee program, which offers a maximum of $1 million per small business with a guarantee of up to 100 percent by the SBA.

ASSISTANCE TO VETERANS

The SBA makes special efforts to help veterans get into business or expand existing veteran-owned small firms. The agency, acting on its own or with the help of veterans' organizations, sponsors special business training workshops for veterans. In some areas of the country, the SBA sponsors special computer-based training and long-term entrepreneurial programs for veterans. Each SBA office has a veterans affairs specialist, or veterans advocate, to provide veterans with special consideration for loans, training, and/or procurement.

SECONDARY MARKET PROGRAM

The Secondary Market Program improves profitability and liquidity for lenders who already hold business loans guaranteed by the SBA, by selling the guaranteed portions of loans in the secondary market. Banks, savings and loan associations, credit unions, pension funds, and insurance companies are frequent buyers.

BUSINESS DEVELOPMENT PROGRAMS

Business development programs serve as the catalyst for today's small-business development and growth by providing marketing and training information. Programs focus on management training, international trade, veterans affairs, women's initiatives, and resource partnerships.

- *Business initiatives, education, and training.* This program produces a broad range of management and technical assistance publications and audio-visual materials. In 1991, the SBA distributed more than three million SBA publications and videotapes.

- *International trade.* This program provides information, advice, and export financing help that prepares businesses to take advantage of the new world markets, particularly Mexico, the Pacific Rim, Canada, and Europe.

- *Veterans affairs.* These programs provide business management and technical training and counseling. About 1,200 training conferences were held for prospective and established veteran business owners in fiscal year 1991.

In addition to loan guarantees, the SBA offers a number of other programs and activities to assist small businesses. Here are a few of them:

- *Women's business ownership.* Mentoring programs and training and counseling centers for women are provided nationwide. More than 119,000 women were counseled and more than 184,000 were trained in 1990. The program sponsors "Women Going International." Catalyst, a women's research group, reports that the number of women-owned businesses in the United States has jumped by 43 percent in the past three years to 7.7 million.

- *Small Business Innovation and Research (SBIR)*. This program provides competitive opportunities to win federal research and development contracts (grants).

- *Resource partners*. The Office of Advocacy works to reduce the burdens that federal policies impose on small firms and maximize the benefits small businesses receive from the government. Headed by the Chief Counsel for Advocacy, this program also conducts research on small-business issues.

- *Service Corps of Retired Executives (SCORE)* involves retired business executives whose collective experience spans the full range of American enterprise to assist small businesses in solving their operating problems through one-on-one counseling, prebusiness workshops, and formal training sessions.

- *Small Business Institutes (SBIs)* operate at universities and college campuses. Small-business owners receive management counseling from graduate and undergraduate business students working under faculty guidance. Students study the business and its problems, research potential solutions, and develop a comprehensive plan of attack to meet the needs of their client.

- *Small Business Development Centers (SBDCs)* extend a cooperative effort to the private sector, the education community, and federal, state, and local governments. Each state has a lead organization, coordinating services through a network of subcenters and satellite locations, that makes management assistance and counseling more widely available to existing and prospective small-business owners. These organizations handled more than 116,000 counseling cases during the first quarter of fiscal year 1992. Over 800,000 business owners were counseled or trained in fiscal year 1991.

As you can see, the SBA is a very far-reaching agency that attempts to help stimulate business in many different ways and through many different channels. From its original concept of merely guaranteeing loans to small businesses, the agency has grown to serve as the distribution channel for disaster assistance to both business and nonbusiness victims. The SBA has extended its services to include business training and education, as well as encouraging the direction of business development through export assistance. But since the SBA is an agency of a political organization, it has its politics to consider, as we will see in the following pages.

Section Two

4 The Dynamics of the SBA

As the first SBA administrator appointed by President Clinton, Erskine Bowles had the task of overcoming what the Reagan administration called "a billion-dollar rathole." While the SBA guaranteed $6.4 billion in bank loans to small businesses in 1994, it overspent its budget and had to go back to Congress for an emergency appropriation of $175 million. Mr. Bowles took over a shop that was ridiculed and insignificant in government circles and shored up its credibility and effectiveness. Besides performing the traditional duties of SBA chief, he provided the White House with expert advice on small-business financial issues.

However, the agency continues to be criticized for certain oversights that have occured and continue to occur even though companies such as Federal Express and Apple Computer have gotten their start through SBA loans. Take for example a report in 1994 by the General Accounting Office (GAO), Congress's investigative arm, on the SBA's minority business development program. It noted the agency neither tracked the kinds of assistance provided nor their effect. Without this type of information the effectiveness of this and other programs cannot be determined.

The General Accounting Office's report illustrates how successful companies remain eligible for certain contracts by "cooking" their books. These contracts are sheltered from open competition by the SBA program. In 1994 the Section 8(a) program directed U.S. government contracts valued at $4.4 billion to minority-owned firms.

The GAO report also describes lax oversight by SBA officials. The report includes a case in which the GAO determined that a Bethesda, Md., computer services firm improperly received at least $62 million in set-aside contracts, when SBA officials had previously concluded that the company had become financially too large to be eligible for special treatment under the 8(a) program.

In another case, congressional investigators found Coast Guard officials had manipulated a multimillion-dollar contract so as to award it without competitive bidding to a minority-owned, high-tech firm in Calverton, Md. The GAO discovered a telling exchange of E-mail messages between Coast Guard officials. One official defended the set-aside for the company as more convenient and efficient; the other official answered that, while he agreed, discovery of their exchange by auditors would be "absolute suicide. Erase it. Destroy the disk." Officials of these companies, of course, denied any wrongdoing and criticized the GAO report as misleading and unfair.

A senior SBA official said, "The GAO report points out a number of abuses in the 8(a) program during the 1980s and early 1990s. It focuses on two former 8(a) firms that were awarded large numbers of contracts. We have been working aggressively since 1993 to correct these types of abuses and have made substantial progress." Because of the abuses it cites, the GAO report will probably give reason for congressional proposals to reduce or kill the 8(a) program. Senator Sam Nunn (D. Ga.), who commissioned the GAO report, said that it "reveals how participating companies and government agencies exploit vulnerabilities in the 8(a) program."

One criticism of 8(a) is that because of the presumption that under 8(a) the SBA serves as intermediary for small "socially and economically disadvantaged" companies, a relatively small group of highly successful firms gets the majority of the contracts. The GAO said the two Maryland firms it investigated were among this select group. While in the program in the 1980s and 1990s, one of these firms, owned by an immigrant from India, received set-aside federal contracts worth at least $508 million, and the other, owned by a Hispanic, got U.S. government contracts worth at least $356 million.

The proclivity of federal agencies to manipulate the 8(a) contracting process to favor certain contractors has also attracted disapproval. According to the GAO, the Coast Guard sidestepped 8(a) rules by adjusting specifications such as estimated labor and other costs of a computer contract worth up to $14 million so it could be directed to a particular company. The E-mail exchange cited by the GAO pertained to this contract, which was awarded exactly one day prior to the date the company left the 8(a) program. GAO investigators also referred to a Coast Guard official's handwritten notes referring to the contract as a "graduation present" to the firm.

The company's general counsel described the contract as an extension of earlier work performed by the company and said that there wasn't anything improper about the Coast Guard making adjustments in the contract. He added that the contract was awarded at the last moment because the process was delayed by anonymous and unproven fraud allegations. "Because we understood all their requirements, and had such a good track record with the Coast Guard, we were the logical, and I would say a preferred, contractor," the general counsel said.

Investigators note in another section of the GAO report that "[The first company] submitted financial statements to SBA that misrepresented its size by excluding certain revenue from the total sales, which allowed it to meet size standards for contracts in 1991 and 1992." The GAO further said that the exclusion of millions of dollars of revenue was explained in footnotes to earlier financial statements, but the SBA didn't react until 1992. The first company's general counsel responded that the excluded amounts were associated with equipment sales to the government in which the company served as the middleman, but from which the company derived no profit. He went on to say the controversy with SBA is over "a technical accounting issue," and emphasized that the company had "fully disclosed its accounting methods to SBA in both the text and footnotes of financial statements and other reports."

The GAO further noted that by September 1992, SBA officials responsible for monitoring the company realized the firm had grown beyond the qualification size necessary to continue in the 8(a) program. However, the company was permitted to continue to participate until June 1994. During that time it was awarded set-aside contracts totaling at least $62 million. The GAO noted that GAO investigators were told by SBA officials that the SBA officials didn't believe they had authority to end the company's participation any earlier.

As you can see by the above story, there is much confusion regarding the administration of the 8(a) program both from within the SBA and from those particpating in the program. This gives Congress cause to question the advisability of the continuance of the program as well as other SBA programs that present similar histories. But the SBA's mission is politically positive, and it has a history of successfully helping small businesses to generate more than enough tax revenue to offset the government's costs of running the SBA. Because of this, Congress cannot easily justify closing down the SBA and, instead, attempts to fix the problems by continuing to change the available programs. In light of this, it is not strange that a spokesperson for the SBA stated the agency wanted to at least double the number of loans to 8(a) target groups by September 30, 1995.

In 1993, the SBA guaranteed 26,812 loans that totaled about $6.4 billion. (The total loan amount was expected to be $7 billion in 1994 and $9 billion in 1995.) Each of the SBA's 68 district directors was asked to sign an agreement committing the district to meet higher lending targets for minorities and women. This expansionary move came after agency research showed that black entrepreneurs received only 3 percent of the SBA's guaranteed loans during 1993; Hispanic business owners were granted 5 percent of those funds, and women, 14 percent. In each district, these groups' share of loans was very low in proportion to the number of minority- and women-owned businesses. The SBA Administrator, Erskine Bowles, declared that the lending pattern revealed by the statistics was wrong and expressed an intent to correct it. He went so far as to say "If we were a bank, we could be accused of redlining." Houston, Texas, for example, made a significant difference by actively marketing the SBA program. The district office there made 70 loans to black business owners during 1993. This was compared with only 14 such loans in Richmond, Va., which has a slightly higher percentage of black-owned companies in its area.

The SBA's loan program has grown rapidly in the past several years. This is due in part because banks generally consider small-business loans as too high risk to approve without the government guaranteeing 75 to 90 percent of the borrowed amount. At the latter part of 1994 Mr. Philip Lader took over for Mr. Bowles as Administrator for the SBA and is expected to keep the SBA on the course set by Mr. Bowles. He has stated that he plans to continue Mr. Bowles's role as an overall advocate for small business interests on issues ranging from easing government regulation to national economic policy.

Mr. Lader, has had close ties to Mr. Clinton. Additionally, his past experience as deputy director of management at the Office of Management and Budget (OMB) should serve the SBA well. The OMB has frequently proposed deeply reducing the agency's budget. This process, insist small-business advocates, must be stopped if the agency is going to be able to handle the proposed expanding loan programs.

Small-business authorities have mentioned that Mr. Lader's business background in his home state of South Carolina should benefit the SBA. He was president of Sea Pines Co., a developer of recreational communities, and a former director of the South Carolina Chamber of Commerce.

In past years, both the Republican and Democratic administrations have made a practice of appointing politicians who had just lost their bid for office to head the SBA. Mr. Lader's appointment, on the contrary, provides professional leadership for the agency, an agency where morale soared since Mr. Bowles took it over.

Nonetheless, Mr. Lader faces several problems, including:

- How to manage efficiently the agency's expanded loan programs, which include guaranteed loans for small businesses and real estate development, as well as a microloan program for start-up businesses with a staff that has been cut by one-third over the past decade. He is also faced with the problems of how to contain demand for government guarantees and convince banks to provide more loans independently.

- How to renovate the agency's 8(a) program, which is designed to help minority-owned companies become government contractors.

- How to regulate the SBA's venture capital program, the Small Business Investment Companies, to ensure that appropriate companies continue to participate.

- And the largest problem: Republicans don't like the SBA very much. In order to survive the attacks from the new Congress, the agency is being forced to increase certain functions and reduce others. All through its 41 years of existence the SBA has helped thousands of small businesses get loans and government contracts, but the agency may soon be required to cut back this role. Instead, the SBA will focus on helping small businesses to battle regulation.

To assist or hinder Mr. Lader in his efforts is Rep. Jan Meyers from Kansas. She is the new chairperson of the House Small Business Committee and is leading the charge for small business in Congress. This committee has no fiscal authority; its most visible role is overseeing the SBA. But the committee is a fact-finding body that can be influential in shaping legislative opinions. That's why all the major issues facing small business today will come across Ms. Meyers' desk—health care, government regulation and paperwork, taxation, and the SBA itself.

Meyers maintains that without the SBA to help maintain a focus on pertinent issues, the federal bureaucracy would likely lose that focus. As a result, programs to promote small business would become weak and ineffective. She also has noted that there are weaknesses in the agency. Once the committee conducts its review to determine which SBA programs are of value to small business—and the economy in general—and which have outlived their usefulness, the committee will bring forward proposals to ensure that the SBA and its programs are in step with the present and future needs of small business.

This committee has taken steps at the federal level to help small businesses tap modern technology, such as the information superhighway, to help them to succeed. That process has begun in the area of procurement, where the Defense Department is in the final stages of creating an on-line, computerized system for contract bidding. It is anticipated that this system, known as Factnet, will eventually be available to all small businesses via systems such as CompuServe or America Online. The intent is to make it easy for small businesses to obtain critical information on government procurement programs and to file bids.

While Mr. Lader will increase concentration on regulatory reform efforts, Jan Meyers sees business advocacy as exactly the direction that SBA reform should take. The agency has also announced that it would limit the size of most loans it guarantees to $500,000, blaming dwindling resources as a reason for the change. Loans of more than $500,000 accounted for 38 percent of the loans the SBA backed in fiscal year 1994.

Many government bureaucracies worry about their fate under a Republican Congress, but the SBA is under especially heavy pressure. Some GOP leaders have called for the organization's abolition because they believe the agency spends too much for what it accomplishes. Since its founding, the SBA has grown to have an annual budget of $813 million, excluding disaster relief. But according to Edward Hudgins, Director of Regulatory Studies at the libertarian Cato Institute in Washington, well under 1 percent of all small businesses have ever received any direct help from the SBA. Even the country's largest small-business trade group, the National Federation of Independent Business, doesn't defend the agency.

The SBA, however, has announced no plans to diminish its role in guaranteeing loans. The SBA's new Low Documentation Program, which simplifies application for SBA-guaranteed loans of less than $100,000, has generated nearly 12,000 loans totaling about $652 million since it began in June 1994. Its planned Small Loan Express Program frees small firms borrowing $100,000 or less from filing any documents with the SBA to get a guarantee.

The proposed changes at the agency don't sit well with some small-business owners. Numerous minority entrepreneurs believe set-aside programs would suffer without the direct involvement of the SBA. Moreover, the new emphasis on advocacy may itself sow the seed of a future conservative assault. Several private think tanks and trade groups already monitor regulation and lobby on behalf of small businesses. This begs the question, —Why do we need the SBA doing this? Along with attacks of this nature, the new Congress goes further and is contemplating sweeping revisions to the federal affirmative action policies, including changes in the way agencies hire minority contractors.

At issue are federal statutes and regulations that set contracting goals for firms owned by socially and economically disadvantaged individuals. Among these are the SBA's 8(a) program for minority-owned businesses, and a law requiring prime contractors to subcontract work to minority-owned firms. In the program, a company applies and convinces the SBA that it meets the program's criteria for a "socially and economically disadvantaged" small business. With the SBA's help, the concern seeks suitable government work. The concern reports its findings to the SBA. The SBA approaches the federal agency that needs the work done and arranges for a contract to be granted to the SBA. The agency then subcontracts the work to the 8(a) company. The other agencies cooperate because they are under mandate to set aside a portion of their contracting work for minority-owned firms.

Both the 8(a) program and subcontracting requirements have been the target of frequent criticism. The 8(a) program, in particular, has been faulted for, among other problems, providing contracts to relatively few firms and being poorly run. Some backers of the program have argued, however, that these structured contracting programs provide the only incentive that agencies have to seek out minority-owned firms. If such mandates were removed, they argue, the efforts of many prime contractors to hire minority-owned companies would likely diminish. Opponents of the programs state that large companies find complying with subcontracting requirements burdensome. They say, it takes special effort on a company's part to identify qualified (minority) suppliers. If their marketplace no longer demands compliance, these companies will read the signals.

Regardless of what the proponents and opponents of the 8(a) and related programs say, the concern grows that earlier reforms of these programs haven't worked. The agency is seeking advice on this front. Though the 8(a) program has helped produce some notable business successes, it has also been dogged by controversy and criticism concerning problems ranging from contractor fraud to bureaucratic ineptitude. The program dispenses more than $4 billion annually. In its lifetime, the 8(a) program has gone through a number of major reforms. The most recent occurred about five years ago in the wake of the Wedtech Corp. contracting scandal. Wedtech, a New York defense contractor that benefitted from the 8(a) program and had links to prominent national figures, was brought down by allegations of fraud and criminal activity in 1986.

The subsequent overhaul introduced competitive bidding into the program, streamlined the application and review process, modified eligibility requirements, increased penalties for companies misrepresenting their qualifications, and encouraged participants to expand their non-8(a) business. However, agreement is growing that those changes didn't work and that yet another effort is necessary to make the program more viable.

Fraud concerns are also growing about the SBA's disaster loan program. Federal criminal investigators began sifting through several dozen suspicious disaster-loan applications arising out of a string of disasters, ranging from riots to earthquakes, that hit the Los Angeles area. Some of the suspect loan packages had already been approved and several million dollars had been disbursed. Though the probe has focused on the Los Angeles area, the potential vulnerabilities, of the disaster loan to fraud are national. That is because the agency has traditionally conducted only limited review of disaster loan applications. One major area of inquiry in the present investigation is the possible use of phony tax returns. The agency normally didn't cross-check with the Internal Revenue Service concerning the accuracy of the tax returns filed with disaster-loan applications.

The disaster loan program is open to the same kind of fraud problem that has hit the SBA's huge small-business loan program. The business loan program has experienced a wave of phony applications in recent years that has initiated continuing criminal probes. These phony tax returns were contained in many business-loan applications and greatly overstated the applicant's income. "Packagers" often prepared these suspect applications. These are independent consultants who specialize in putting together SBA loan applications. The suspected fraud was aided by computer software that can easily prepare different versions of a firm's tax returns. Packagers are also involved in some of the suspect disaster loan applications.

Both a loan preparer and false tax returns were allegedly involved in the recent disaster loan criminal complaint. A criminal complaint filed in federal court by the U.S. Attorney's office charged one applicant with attempting to defraud the SBA out of $1.5 million on an application for two disaster loans. The complaint charged that the suspect filed financial documents with the SBA that showed the income of his gas station and market was $7 million a year when it actually was less than $50,000 a year. An affidavit filed by an SBA special agent connected with the criminal complaint states the SBA received an anonymous telephone tip from someone who claimed to have overheard the suspect "bragging" about using false tax returns to apply for SBA disaster assistance. The suspect also allegedly told of having a loan application preparer who, for a fee, would help prepare phony documentation for other business owners.

According to investigators, because the area has had so many disasters, Los Angeles has become a focal point of concerns over possible disaster loan fraud. The 1992 riots left hundreds of businesses damaged or destroyed. More recently, brush fires swept through large parts of Los Angeles, followed by rain-induced mudslides. These events generated thousands of applications for disaster relief. The Los Angeles earthquake which came in January, 1993, may be the costliest natural disaster in U.S. history. SBA officials said they received over 100,000 applications for disaster assistance in the eight weeks following the quake. Roughly 20,000 were from businesses.

Concern about potential fraud after the quake was so great that several government agencies—including the SBA, the Federal Bureau of Investigation, and the U.S. Attorney's office—formed a fraud task force. One of the task force's first cases was the aforementioned suspect's alleged fraud. However, SBA investigators have barely begun investigating possible quake-related fraud. The estimated potential government loss from 11 different disaster fraud investigations under way in the Los Angeles area alone is over $5 million.

In the disaster loan program, the SBA is giving earthquake victims the option of allowing the agency to obtain copies of tax returns directly from the IRS. So far, more than 90 percent of applicants are taking that option. If the process of getting returns directly from the IRS works well, the SBA will consider making that the standard method of obtaining tax information.

Not only are the programs being investigated but the financial institutions implementing these disaster programs are also being probed.

The government is going after many of the loan fraud suspects through a "fast track" civil fraud program at the U.S. Attorney's office. This program is aimed at getting quick monetary settlements in certain fraud cases that might not qualify for much more time-consuming-criminal prosecutions. The federal government is seeking financial penalties equal to 20 percent of the loan amount sought—even if the fraud is uncovered before the loan is approved. The concept here is that the penalties have to be sufficiently big to serve as a deterrent.

What is the point of this long discussion of fraud and abuse within the SBA system? The point is that the SBA is changing its ways—if not from within, it is being forced from without—especially by Congress and the budgetary process.

The SBA is one of the federal agencies under sharpest attack by Republican cost cutters. They proposed cutting its budget by 35 percent in the fiscal year starting October 1, 1995. The agency would be required to reduce staff, consolidate regional offices, and raise fees on the agency's biggest loan program. But the plan, which is subject to congressional approval, is drawing criticism from some conservative lawmakers who say it doesn't go far enough in shrinking the agency.

The plan, an element in the "reinventing government" proposals announced by President Clinton, called for the SBA to cut its budget for the fiscal year ending September 30, 1996, to $529 million from 1995's $813 million. The agency also proposed eliminating 500 full-time positions by the end of the 1995–1996 fiscal year, cutting its staff to about 3,100 employees nationwide. The plan also called for the agency to reduce its total spending by $1.2 billion, or 32 percent, over five years. A major portion of the savings would come from a change in the fee structure for loans the agency backs in its 7(a) program. By raising the fees it charges to borrowers and lenders, the SBA would eliminate costs associated with administering the program. The fee increase would also allow the agency to extend the program to an estimated 65,000 businesses, about 20 percent more than it currently serves.

Some entrepreneurs and lawmakers say the agency can do more cutting. Rep. Jan Meyers mentioned that Congress will want to look harder at some of the programs in the SBA that it may be possible to eliminate entirely. Ms. Meyers said she will target the SBA's 8(a) program. Ms. Meyers said a bill enacted in 1995, which requires all government agencies to set goals for minority subcontracting, makes the 8(a) program "duplicative and unnecessary." Her committee, which recently released a set of recommendations—similar to the SBA's plan—to revamp the SBA loan guarantee program, will release its own proposal to overhaul the entire agency. The loan overhaul program, while the centerpiece of the White House plan, will be only a component of the House panel's plan, according to Ms. Meyers. Most of the proposed changes to the SBA, including those contained in the Clinton overhaul, must be introduced as legislation and passed by Congress before they can be implemented.

The budgeting process under a GOP Congress has increased the prospects that the SBA will find it necessary to curtail its Business Development Centers program and raise fees on loans that it guarantees. The House Budget Committee approved balanced-budget legislation that specifically called for these measures. Similar legislation approved by the Senate Budget Committee didn't spell out specific SBA cuts. But SBA officials indicated that the thrust of the proposed cuts, at least, is in line with its own efforts to downsize the agency. The House Budget Committee has called for $340 million in SBA funding cuts for the fiscal year starting October 1, 1995. This compares with only $284 million in cuts called for by the administration the preceding spring.

Both the House committee and the administration called for the agency to "zero-out" the government's cost of making loans to small-business owners by raising the fees paid by borrowers and lenders. The SBA said this action would save taxpayers about $200 million. The House Budget Committee estimated savings of $247 million.

The House panel also asked for the agency to cease funding Small Business Development Centers, which would result in an annual savings of about $78 million. People directly involved in the program have stated that when one thinks about the ways in which government funds can be used to support economic development, the SBDC program is an incredibly efficient way to accomplish that purpose. The SBA earlier proposed reducing federal funding for the program by 50 percent over several years. The House committee proposal would eliminate all funding in the next fiscal year.

The idea of imposing fees at SBDCs isn't new however. The SBA has wanted the centers to eventually begin charging for their services, but some SBA directors have stated that SBDC clients often are too cash poor to do so. The House committee also called for the elimination of SBA's $15 million per year tree-planting program, which was suspended in fiscal year 1995. However, the House panel didn't recommend cuts in the disputed 8(a) program.

The SBA may cut the portion of a small business loan that it guarantees and increase the fee it charges lenders for the pledge. That would be the effect of similar proposals that the SBA and its lenders offered to bridge a projected budget gap in the government's flagship small-business loan guarantee program. The proposals were presented at a hearing of the House Small Business Committee. While the suggested changes are intended to help the government meet soaring demand for guaranteed loans, they also could invite greater lender scrutiny of potential borrowers as well as increase the cost of the loans. Lenders, of course, would have to assume more of a loan's risk than they do at present. Rep. Meyers said she is concerned the proposals might increase costs to borrowers or tighten lending standards that banks apply to them. But, she noted that she and her committee did not want to do anything that makes loans less available to smaller borrowers.

Lenders currently pay the SBA an annual fee equal to 0.4 percent of the guaranteed portion of the loan that the lender sells on the secondary market. One proposal would apply that fee to all loans the agency backs, regardless of whether they are sold to investors. Lenders also currently pay a "guarantee fee," normally equal to 2 percent of the guaranteed portion of their loan. This fee typically is passed on to borrowers. Though these changes would increase the costs to the lenders, they would help assure the continued growth of a program that has proven highly profitable for lenders, especially if they sell their loans in the secondary market.

Besides fee increases, the SBA has proposed several other measures to reduce its net costs. It will offer employee buyouts to cut staff size, shift functions such as loan processing out of district offices, and into a few loan-processing centers, absorb 10 regional offices into nearby district offices, and relocate its accounting functions out of Washington to a financial operations office in Denver.

The SBA and Congress have also been contemplating the establishment of an agency similar to the Federal Home Loan Mortgage Association's "Freddie Mac" program that provides for a secondary market for real estate loans. But a report issued by the Comptroller of the Currency said a "Freddie Mac" for small business loans won't work. This report had the effect of throwing cold water on the effort to encourage more small business loans by creating a secondary market for them. But some bankers have predicted that a secondary market will develop anyway. Even without a formal secondary market for such securities, lenders have already begun to sell off small business loans. Money Store Inc., for example, has securitized its portion of loans backed by the SBA. But institutions that have started to sell small-business loans have discovered that they must provide investors with a high level of loss protection to make up for the riskier environment. Unlike mortgages, which are a homogeneous group and don't really vary very much in their risks and returns, small-business loans vary considerably in their characteristics.

Despite continued interest in securitization, some banks say a secondary market wouldn't prompt them to make more loans to small businesses. One argument is that securitization serves as a lending prod only when banks want to make more loans but lack the liquidity to do so. If banks do not want to extend credit to small businesses, the presence of an active secondary market is not likely to prompt more lending.

As can be seen by the preceding, the SBA is changing in many ways. Some changes are the result of mere political machinations, but others are the result of the natural evolutionary process as the agency meets the changing needs of the population it is intended to serve and the needs of the institutions implementing those services, and doing so in a regulated manner that has proper checks and balances to keep the administrators of the programs "honest."

It is also evident that the voice of small business is growing stronger in Washington. Since the "downsizing" of big business, it has been noted that small business is the largest contributor to the economic stability and growth of this country. Big business has become stagnant and is shrinking while the economic base of small businesses has continued to grow through recessions and economic expansion.

For nearly six years, the owner of an accounting firm in Provo, Utah, tried to visit his congressman and senators whenever he traveled to Washington. His efforts resulted in a string of quick handshakes with lawmakers, or canceled appointments. But a recent visit was different. He reports that his congressman took time out of his schedule to take him to lunch. More and more small-business owners say they have seen their standing in Washington surge as lawmakers pursue a more conservative agenda. And, since Congress convened in 1995, groups representing small employers say they have been flooded with requests for research and expert testimony.

Members of the National Federation of Independent Business (NFIB), a 600,000-member advocacy group, have participated in at least four congressional hearings recently, most notably before the powerful House Ways and Means Committee. The NFIB says its members appeared before this committee only infrequently under the previous committee head, and wasn't invited to testify at all from mid-1989 to mid-1991. The NFIB adds that, with the new Congress, lawmakers and committees privately have increasingly solicited its comments in drafting legislation that will affect small companies. Other small-business organizations report heightened interest in their members' opinions as well.

Small-business groups credit their new-found popularity partly to enthusiastic courting by the new Republican majority in Congress. Rep. Jan Meyers has mentioned that she thinks that small business is an extremely important constituency for the Republican party. Now that the GOP is able to set the agenda, small business is being heard on many issues.

Traditionally, conservative lawmakers have tended to be more sympathetic than others to the concerns of small-business owners, business lobbyists say. But the new majority is also looking for testimony that supports its agenda. For example, when Democrats controlled Congress, left-leaning groups were often invited to present testimony supporting safety regulation. The new emphasis on reducing regulations means lawmakers will hear more testimony from business owners who favor a "small government" business environment.

Though some in Washington have always paid attention to small business, observers report unmistakable signs that this interest is growing. Even the House Small Business Committee, the only House organization devoted exclusively to small-business issues, is flexing new muscle. Republican leaders voted for expansion of the committee's reach, giving it the right to review other committees' legislation on two key, small-business issues—paperwork reduction and regulatory flexibility—before the bills were formally introduced in the House. The move added an extra layer of review by small companies and government staffers concerned specifically with small-business issues.

The small business lobby has actively campaigned for an enhanced role, too. The NFIB generated a great deal of publicity during 1994 in its effort to defeat certain elements of proposed health care reforms. In its campaign, the NFIB encouraged its membership of 600,000 to write to lawmakers expressing their opposition.

Big business has noticed small business's improved treatment. But many feel there is enough room at hearings and fund-raisers for both small- and big-business interests. Big- and small-business groups are pushing for many of the same items, such as reduction in regulation and capital gains taxes.

You can probably see which way the wind is blowing. The wind is known as the New Economy, and as mentioned above, it is sweeping aside the deadwood of old, industrial corporate America and leaving fertile soil for new small businesses. Especially in areas hard hit by the last recession, economic revival is being sparked by new entrepreneurial ventures. Even the President has felt the breeze on Pennsylvania Avenue.

President Clinton has said, "New forces, such as globalization, the rise of new technologies, and the development of new markets, are shaping a new American economy." Many experts believe that smaller firms, with their nimbleness and creativity, will play an increasingly important role in that economy. New businesses have helped to create five million jobs over the past 22 months, many of them high-wage jobs. In fact, there were more high-wage jobs created in 1994 than in the previous five years combined.

For years politicians and researchers have been stating that small business is the "engine of the economy," but much of the talk has been sheer rhetoric unsupported by any concrete action. In part, that's because the government, in the form of the SBA, has always defined (and still does) small business as companies with 500 or fewer employees. This accounts for 99 percent of all firms. Thus, unless you're a General Motors or Microsoft, chances are the government perceives you as a small business. And it's hard to make policy decisions that will meet the needs of 1-person, 10-person, and 499-employee businesses.

Despite many big businesses being defined as small, according to the government's definition, people imagine a monolithic small-business community as a bunch of mom-and-pop operations on Main Street. Mom and Pop may be pillars of the community, coach Little League, and pay their taxes every year, but they're not likely to turn into the next Federal Express. That means they won't create a lot of jobs—or wield real political clout. Even if Mom and Pop own a McDonald's franchise, they're only creating part-time hamburger-flipping jobs, not high-wage jobs.

But that thinking is old. The government has begun to collect statistics on a new segment of the small-business market, those companies with zero to four employees, and has started new thinking processes in Washington. Millions of corporate employees who were laid off during the late 1980s and early 1990s and who are running their own businesses have now come into focus. The picture that emerges shows that the supersmall businesses are creating high-wage jobs. According to the Commerce Department, 3.5 million jobs were created in 1994, the biggest yearly increase since 1984. The vast majority of these new jobs are being created by small businesses with fewer than four employees.

These newly formed and forming microbusinesses reflect the move from an industrial to an information economy, from a manufacturing to a service economy. These are relatively young, technology-dependent, and service-oriented firms with national or international reach. The ratio of revenues to employees is extremely high by historical standards, which accounts for the unexpectedly high wages. These companies live the model that big, downsizing corporations are striving for: a small central core of highly skilled managers, surrounded by remote teams of knowledge workers whose combined skills are greater than the sum of their parts. It's amazing how many of these companies were started by senior corporate officers—ex-IBM and ex-Citibank employees.

It's as if everyone were trying to put together a puzzle, with the biggest piece hidden under the rug. The new picture shows that Mom and Pop are still here, but they've been joined and superseded by a new breed of small-business owners who truly can revitalize the economy. Thus, such small-business entrepreneurs are beginning to enjoy newfound political clout. Jerry Glover, chief counsel of the Office of Advocacy at the U.S. Small Business Administration, has stated, "It's a phenomenon that has broad ramifications for government policy. We've basically been ignoring the most productive segment of the economy that's been creating almost all the new jobs."

Hearing this message at various levels of government, the Republican-led Congress has held hearings and voted on health reform, tax relief, and restoration of an improved home-office tax deduction. At the time of this writing Congress is deciding a bill that restores the ability of the self-employed to deduct a portion of their health insurance expenditures, retroactive to 1994. Speaker of the House Newt Gingrich says what's good for entrepreneurs is good for America.

Unlike a big-business executive, who is nonemotional and more concerned with stock options and personal liability, the small-business owner is more personally involved. How small-business owners feel about the government affects how they act, since they act emotionally. Businesses that have been reluctant to grow will now have confidence.

According to Mark Schultz, executive director of the White House Conference on Small Business, "We'll see changes in taxes, in regulatory reform, and in the ways we deal with the credit crunch. And we'll see more help for young entrepreneurs—with job training, stipends, and ways to get people interested in business." However, some people's optimism has been dulled by income-tax hikes and the push for employer-mandated health care coverage.

In truth, the Clinton Administration has made other efforts to aid small business, but these efforts were frustrated by Congress. Clinton favored increasing the write-off for equipment expenditures from $10,000 to $25,000; Congress finally approved a hike to $17,500. Clinton wanted to allow the self-employed to write off 100 percent of their health insurance premiums, but that provision was overshadowed by the hue and cry of the debate over health care reform. And Clinton favored reducing the capital gains tax from 28 to 14 percent on investments in small businesses that were held for five years. The Senate crushed that proposal as well.

During 1994, more than 1,800 delegates, elected at state conferences, convened to vote on policy recommendations and to ultimately submit a report to President Clinton and Congress (both of which will also appoint delegates). The main problem areas covered were capital formation, obtuse regulation, and lack of information. Here are some of the problems and solutions already discussed at 59 state conferences.

1. *Access to capital—particularly start-up and follow-up capital.* Small-business people are frustrated with the complexity of applying for loans and funding, the scarcity of capital, and the outdated standards by which loan applications are considered. And they feel current tax policies do little to encourage initial investment or reinvestment in their businesses. Solutions include the following:

   - Encouraging the SBA to expand the definitions of microloans and ease lending restrictions
   - Broadening and relaxing the credit standards used by both banks and

the SBA to include businesses with nontraditional histories and little or no collateral (for example, home businesses)
- Reducing the capital gains tax and replacing corporate tax rates with a flat tax

2. *Make government more user-friendly and less adversarial.* Cumbersome and costly regulations, unfair tax policies, and a punitive rather than incentive-based system of compliance are all obstacles to doing business. Solutions include the following:

- Clarifying and broadening the scope of the home-office tax deduction, especially the "principal place of business" test
- Allowing the self-employed to deduct 100 percent of health insurance expenditures
- Ensuring that individuals with preexisting medical conditions are covered by affordable health insurance
- Encouraging first-time exporters with tax credits or trade finance programs
- Consulting with small-business organizations before formulating regulations; in addition, allowing judicial review of all existing regulations
- Standardizing federal paperwork and making it available electronically
- Adopting clear and uniform definitions of employee and independent consultant
- Providing businesses with an amnesty period to comply with regulations

3. *Information to help small businesses.* Despite widespread consensus that government should be less involved, many businesspeople want the government to provide more and better information. Solutions include the following:

- Providing user-friendly, electronic access to federal information
- Ensuring low-cost access to the information superhighway, even in rural areas
- Improving communication about federal procurement and export opportunities
- Having the SBA publicize and educate financial institutions about SBA loans
- Establishing public and private clearinghouses for education programs that explain how small businesses can gain access to capital

It is yet to be seen whether Congress performs to its potential and enacts laws favoring small business, and whether it can do so without dismantling effective regulations affecting the environment and worker safety. But given the probusiness record of Congressional power brokers, there's little doubt they'll try. For example, the new chairs of the congressional committees on business affairs have strong probusiness voting records, according to the U.S. Chamber of Commerce. For the first time in decades, there are more businesspeople in Congress (191) than lawyers (170), according to *Business Week.* Republican National Committee Chairman Haley Barbour has mentioned: "It's great that we have so many people here who have signed the front side of a paycheck."

The SBA administrator, Bowles, had made comment that:

> People give the SBA a hard time, but its budget is less than the amount of taxes paid last year (1994) by three companies it helped start: Apple, Intel, and FedEx. Most of the criticism dates back 15 years ago, when the SBA did direct lending. Now, there's virtually no direct lending and no handouts. There's also an SBA nobody knows—it's the government's bank for disaster assistance. All disaster-related residential and commercial property loans come from the SBA. We were the major lender behind L.A.'s quick recovery from a devastating earthquake.
>
> The SBA has engineered a splendid public-private partnership that leverages $15 billion of private capital for entrepreneurs. Our LowDoc program has sparked a huge increase in demand and incredibly quick turnaround for loans of less than $100,000. And we've made internal reforms. We've started a small-loan express plan, letting banks use our paperwork and system, in exchange for which we guarantee 50 percent of the loan instead of 80 or 90 percent. There's no better way to use taxpayer's dollars than by leveraging information technology.
>
> Finally, since many banks find lending to women a risk, we've started the Women's Pre-qualification Pilot Loan Program. Women entrepreneurs submit a business plan to the SBA, which is approved (or not) within 48 hours. With that SBA guarantee in hand, we think banks will be more likely to lend money to women.
>
> We've increased our attention to the job-formation engine of microbusinesses, but we can't forget the gazelles that will turn into the next Apple Computer, the mom-and-pops, or the home-office workers. We cover a broad spectrum.
>
> We have instituted SBA Online. It's a fast and easy way for businesspeople to access information on government programs. We get about 1,000 calls per day [(800) 697-4636 limited access; (900) 463-4636 full access; (202) 401-9600 in Washington, D.C.]. And we've added an SBA home page on the Internet's World Wide Web (http://www.sbaonline.sba.gov), which provides an interactive guide to SBA programs. It's just one example of this Administration's commitment to 'reinventing government.'

The SBA has mentioned that federal agencies have awarded significantly more government contracts to small businesses during 1994–1995. More than 25 percent of their prime contracts went to small companies in the year ended September 30, 1994, up from 23.5 percent in the previous fiscal year. The dollar amount of those contracts was $42.3 billion, up slightly from the previous year's $42.2 billion. Total federal procurement in fiscal 1994 fell almost 7 percent to about $167 billion, from $179 billion in fiscal year 1993.

In addition to winning more direct business from the government, small businesses received more subcontracting work. In fiscal year 1994, small-business subcontracting dollars totaled about $22 billion, or 38 percent of all subcontracts, compared with $20.8 billion a year earlier. Participants in the SBA's 8(a) program garnered $5.5 billion in contracts, unchanged from the prior year. In the past fiscal year (1994–1995), small minority-owned and other disadvantaged businesses also won $5.1 billion in prime contracts without going through 8(a), up 2 percent from the previous period.

Until recently, the ExIm Bank was said to totally lack interest in small business. But since mid-1994, the agency has aggressively sought to aid small exporters through working-capital guarantee programs, including the SBA's EWCP and so-called tied-aid loans. Through the tied-aid program, the agency matches credits offered by many foreign countries to sweeten bids made by their companies.

The ExIm Bank's programs to help smaller companies remain tiny, but they are growing rapidly. According to a spokesperson, the agency expects its working-capital guarantees to small exporters to reach $300 million in the fiscal year ending September 30, 1995, up from $180.6 million the previous year. The guarantees, in which the agency backs 90 percent of a loan to small exporters, totaled $111 million in the six months ended March 31, 1995. Small companies now account for about 95 percent of U.S. exporters, but account for only about 30 percent of the export volume.

The paperwork reduction measure unanimously passed by Congress reauthorizes the Paperwork Reduction Act of 1980. Under the new legislation, all federal agencies would have to set goals to reduce paperwork demands on the public by 10 percent per year in 1996 and 1997 and by 5 percent annually from 1998 through 2001. Business owners expect these cuts to markedly ease the paperwork burden.

Republican congressional leaders recognized paperwork as a key small-business issue when it granted the House Small Business Committee the right to review the paperwork reduction bill before it went to the House floor for a vote. Though the legislation only requires agencies to set paperwork reduction goals—it does not mandate such efforts—advocates of the measure are confident that it will translate into real time and money savings for small companies.

If federal agencies can reduce even 10 percent of required paperwork, that will have a significant impact on most small companies. By some estimates, government paperwork is extremely burdensome. At Lancaster Laboratories Inc., in Lancaster, Pa., a recent affirmative action audit forced the 515-employee shop to put several projects on hold. Human resources staffers spent nearly four months preparing the paperwork for the federal audit, costing the company $50,000 in staff time. Rep. Jan Meyers said that paperwork for the federal government probably costs the public $510 billion a year.

Now that you have the flavor of the changes occurring in the legislative offices of our government regarding their attitudes toward small business and the SBA programs, let's look at a real-life experience of small-business financing and the SBA. A story going around about the SBA's specialty loans is one about a very persistent woman entrepreneur.

Ms. Jones' (assumed name) was raised in a broken home. Her father deserted the family at an early age leaving the family destitute. She grew up with three older sisters and her mother. Having had to wear hand-me-downs and recut thrift store clothes, she learned to recut these clothes herself. She especially learned to recut and alter jackets. She obtained jobs as a runway model because of this attention to clothes and her 5-foot 10-inch frame.

Having majored in mathematics throughout college, she got a marketing job at a major high-tech company earning $100,000 per year. She continued to make and wear feminine clothes of her own design—1940s-style work suits. Colleagues began asking where they could buy suits like hers. Her answer was that they couldn't. Similar suits were on the market in the $200–$250 price range. But none had her distinctive look.

Recognizing a business opportunity, Ms. Jones pursued it. Using $60,000 she received from cashing in company stock, she sought and received help in writing a business plan from the Wharton Small Business Development Center and started her business. She received $50,000 in orders from various women professionals. She went to a major retail chain and got their acceptance of her line of clothing but on condition she install an expensive on-line ordering system. Other New York clothing manufacturers expressed some interest. But she needed working capital to make her business grow.

Her local banker refused her because she had no collateral and no track record. A manufacturer voiced willingness to handle her first season of production on credit, but the catch was that it would cost her entire profit margin to pay the interest on that credit advance. She agreed to it and was overjoyed to see her 1992 suit line become a sales success at a major Boston clothing discounter.

Regardless of how hard she continued to work at her business, without sufficient working capital Ms. Jones remained in debt to financiers for an amount equal to most of the profits of her sales. She tried to attract venture capital but those deals fell through. She was behind on utility bills as well as a $2,000 IRS bill. Regardless of these setbacks she persisted. Knowing she was right, she kept on.

In desperation, she returned to her local bank which had merged with a larger banking organization. The original lending officer that had refused her before decided to finance her 1995 line. This change of mind was due to a new SBA program for women borrowers.

The fact of the $2,000 owed to the IRS came up during the process of making the loan. This killed the loan because of the rule that the SBA cannot guarantee the credit of anyone in arrears to the federal government.

Two days after that loan refusal, extremely depressed, and angry, Ms. Jones returned to the bank and stormed across the lobby to the lending officer. "This is my whole life!" she yelled at the lending officer. "I can't take no for an answer. You've got to do something to turn this around!" Knowing it would be difficult to get the SBA to reconsider but, because she had never seen such a determined survivor, the lending officer took the challenge. The SBA did reconsider. Ms. Jones raised the money and paid the IRS.

Ms. Jones and her company have now very successfully held their Seventh Avenue show. The rest is "history." Ms. Jones is looking forward to a successful year and years to come because of the SBA specialty loan program for women entrepreneurs.

So, as you can see, the SBA is a very dynamic government agency intent on assisting the budding entrepreneur in reaching his/her business goals. It now applies strict rules of conduct but, if you are focused, knowledgeable about your business, and persistent, you can obtain that assistance for yourself. You must realize, and this section has tried to present, that the SBA is a political agency, and the management's primary concern is for the political impact of its programs and action. The consumer of its programs is of secondary concern and must follow the rules.

5 Frequently Asked Questions and Some Answers

Q I've heard it takes forever to get a loan through the SBA. How long does it really take?

A SBA's goal is to respond to every guarantee loan request within 20 calendar days, although many offices have achieved a much faster turnaround. Requests submitted under the Certified Lender Program are processed within three working days. The single most significant element in slowing down SBA's response time is the submittal of incomplete loan packages.

Q Doesn't the SBA make loans only to minority-owned businesses?

A SBA loans are granted to eligible small businesses without regard to the ethnic composition of the ownership. In the fiscal year ended September 30, 1990, 13.6 percent of the loans guaranteed by SBA were made to minority-owned businesses.

Q We don't make marginal loans at the bank. Why should we make them now just because of an SBA guarantee?

A If a marginal loan is one where credit factors are weaker than prudent standards would dictate, SBA doesn't make marginal loans either. However, as a guarantor of long-term loans, SBA does envision taking on those elements of risk not found in short-term credits.

Q If the SBA's credit criteria are as strong as the bank's, why should I use the guarantee?

A In general, the guarantee is used when funding those businesses needing terms outside the scope of the bank's lending policies.

Q Why should we make SBA loans?

A In short, it's good business. Small-business borrowers can often benefit from maturities longer than those typically issued by lenders. A lender can develop new business by actively offering SBA loan terms. Higher yields can be achieved through the use of the secondary market. Also, active SBA involvement can help meet Community Reinvestment Act initiatives.

Q If the SBA's credit standards are so high, why have I heard your loss rate is so bad?

A Long-term lending tends to represent a higher degree of risk than does short-term lending. Many factors outside the control of the lender, and sometimes the borrower, can develop over a ten year period, for example, that might not develop within a year or two. Actually, SBA's loss rate in fiscal year 1989 was 3.7 percent and has been declining in recent years.

Q Do you have to be turned down by two banks before you can get an SBA loan?

A No. Turndown letters are required only for direct loan applicants. Lenders requesting SBA's guarantee simply state the opinion on the guarantee application form that the subject financing is not otherwise available. No other letters or statements are required.

Q Are SBA loans made at lower interest rates?

A No. SBA-guaranteed loans are made at competitive market rates of interest, but within ceilings established by the SBA. On loans with maturities less than seven years, the maximum rate is 2.25 percent over the New York prime rate, while on loans of seven years or longer, the maximum is 2.75 percent over the prime. There is no minimum.

Q Isn't the paperwork on an SBA loan overwhelming?

A No. The information required to be submitted by the applicant in support of the loan application is consistent with the practices of other prudent commercial lenders. The lender requesting the SBA's guarantee completes one form and, in lieu of completing the entire document, can attach a copy of its internal credit analysis, assuming it addresses the credit issues required on the lender's application for guarantee form.

Q Why does the SBA always tie up everything the borrower owns as collateral?

A Like most lenders, the SBA is interested in identifying a secondary means of repayment in the event that cash flow becomes inadequate to repay the debt. It is not the SBA's policy to overcollateralize its loans, but rather to make prudent evaluations of collateral in worst-case situations.

Q The SBA's image as a lender of last resort carries with it a perception of weak creditworthiness that bank customers don't want associated with their businesses. How can I overcome this problem in getting my customer to accept SBA financing?

A This problem originated in the 1960s and 1970s, when the credit standards in use today were not as consistently used throughout the country. However, the principal benefits to the borrower of financing the business's long-term needs with long-term debt remain the same. The reduced level of monthly payments results in cash flow improvement and increased availability of working capital. We are basically offering reasonably priced long-term financing.

Section Three

6 General Loan Eligibility

Most businesses are eligible for SBA loans. Eligibility of a particular case is determined by three factors:

- Type of business
- Size of business
- Purpose of loan

An eligible business must be organized for profit and must be engaged in or propose to do business in the United States or its possessions. The great majority of the types of businesses that exist are eligible for financial assistance from the SBA.

Those types of businesses that are not eligible include those with:

- Opinion-molding activities
- Lending activities
- Real estate investment activities
- Pyramid sales plans
- Other speculative activities
  - Illegal activities
  - Academic schools
  - Gambling activities

Opinion-molding activities are engaged in by newspaper publishers, radio and television broadcasters, and other businesses involved in originating or distributing ideas, values, or thoughts. While this restriction would extend to film and record producers, importers and exporters of sheet music, specialty book stores, and the like, exceptions can sometimes be justified. Exceptions to this ''media policy'' rule can be made when the matter being published is technical or when it is not capable of influencing public opinion. Check with your local SBA office regarding March 1996 changes.

Examples of exceptions include a cable broadcaster passively transmitting and receiving signals without being involved in programming, and a retailer selling a wide variety of published material as opposed to a retailer running a specialty bookstore. Commercial printers not sharing in the success of the printed material are eligible. Similarly, film production enterprises are not eligible; however, firms renting out production facilities without sharing in the commercial success of the production can be eligible, provided there is no common ownership between the two. Dinner theaters are eligible, since the principal activity is that of a restaurant. Movie theaters are not eligible.

Real estate investment firms are not eligible where the real property will be held for investment purposes, as opposed to loans to otherwise eligible small business concerns for the purpose of occupying the real estate being acquired. This issue is discussed further later in this chapter. Other businesses engaging in speculative activities include those firms developing profits from fluctuations in price rather than through the normal course of trade, such as wildcatting for oil and dealing in commodities futures, when not part of the regular activities of the business. Dealers of rare coins and stamps are not eligible.

Academic schools are those teaching academic subjects. The restriction does not cover technical, secretarial, vocational or trade schools, or nursery and prekindergarten schools.

Businesses engaging in lending activities include banks, finance companies, factors, leasing companies, insurance companies (not agents), and any other firm whose stock-in-trade is money.

Pyramid sales plans are characterized by endless chains of distributors and subdistributors where a participant's primary incentive is based on the sales made by an ever increasing number of participants. Such products as cosmetics, household goods, and other soft goods lend themselves to this type of ineligible business.

Illegal activities are by definition those that are against the law in the jurisdiction where the business is located. Included in these activities are the production, servicing, or distribution of otherwise legal products that are to be used in connection with an illegal activity, such as selling drug paraphernalia or operating a motel that permits illegal prostitution. Prudent discretion must be exercised in determining whether taxpayer funds should be used to finance questionable enterprises.

Gambling activities include any business whose principal activity is gambling. While this precludes loans to race tracks, casinos, and similar enterprises, the rule does not restrict loans to otherwise eligible businesses that obtain less than one-third of their annual gross income from either (a) the sale of official state lottery tickets under a state license, or (b) legal gambling activities licensed and supervised by a state authority. The one-third limitation applies both as a point of eligibility as well as a condition to be required during the term of the loan.

SIZE

Since the SBA can lend only to small business, it has defined "small," establishing standards by type of industry. Individual types of businesses within these broad industry categories may have different standards. Most businesses are considered small by the SBA's size standards.

The standard for an industry is based on either number of employees (calculated by averaging the total number of employees for each pay period during the most recently completed twelve calendar months) or average annual receipts for the most recently completed three fiscal years.

INDUSTRY	SIZE RANGE
Retail and Service	$3.5 to $13.5 million
Construction	$7.0 to $17.0 million
Agriculture	$500,000 to $3.5 million
Wholesale	No more than 100 employees
Manufacture	500 to 1,500 employees

If a potential borrower is close to these standards, discuss the size eligibility issue with the local SBA office. The specific standard for a particular business may change from time to time and some exceptions may apply.

When affiliations exist with other companies (for example, through common ownership, directorships, or by contractual arrangements), the primary business activity must be determined both for the applicant business as well as for the entire affiliated group. In order to be eligible for financial consideration, the applicant must meet the size standard for its primary business activity, and the affiliated group must meet the standard for its primary business activity.

PURPOSE

The proceeds of SBA loans can be used for most legitimate business needs. Purposes often include the purchase of real estate to house the small business's operations, construction of renovations or leasehold improvements, acquisition of furniture, fixtures, machinery, and equipment, purchase of inventory, and provision of cash to support operating costs.

Proceeds of an SBA loan cannot be used to:

- Finance floor plan needs.
- Purchase real estate, where the participant has issued a forward commitment to the builder/developer or where the real estate will be held primarily for investment purposes. Purchase of an existing building where more than 50 percent of the square footage will be occupied by the applicant small business is acceptable. The construction of a new building is acceptable where the applicant small business will occupy at least 66⅔ percent of its space and projections indicate a need in the near future for additional space that would not feasibly be constructed at that time.
- Make payments to owners or pay delinquent withholding taxes.
- Pay existing debt, unless it can be shown that the refinancing will benefit the small business and that the need to refinance is not indicative of imprudent management. Proceeds can never be used to reduce the exposure of the participant in the loans being refinanced. Interim advances made by a participant in anticipation of receiving an SBA guarantee are permitted, provided the advance is made for the same purposes as that of the

SBA loan and the SBA is notified at the time of the advance. It must be understood that the participant is at risk if the SBA loan is declined or does not disburse due to adverse changes occurring after approval.

SPECIAL CIRCUMSTANCES

Certain other considerations apply to a number of the SBA's specialized loan programs. These issues are addressed in Section 5, which describes these programs. Other special circumstances may develop that have an impact on eligibility.

Alter Ego

While investment in real estate occupied by anyone other than the small-business concern is not eligible, a holding company owned by the same parties and in the same proportion as the small business (alter ego) may be eligible if the following conditions are met:

1. The applicant holding company must be a small-business concern organized and operated for profit and in the business of owning and leasing real or personal property to the operating company. (When the property is to be titled in the name of individuals, it is presumed that the individuals are organized and operating for profit as a sole proprietorship or partnership, and so meet this requirement for the holding company.)
2. The operating concern must be eligible as to size, type, use of proceeds, and special circumstances.
3. Loan proceeds must be used only for acquisition, improvement, and eligible refinancing of real or personal business property.
4. Principals' ownership interest in the applicant holding company must be identical with and in the same proportion as the ownership interest in the operating company. An exception may be granted where this is not the case solely because one or more immediate members of the same family have variant interests. The identity of interests, generally, must remain throughout the life of the loan. (Consult with the local office when family members hold different interests in the holding and operating companies).
5. An assignment of the lease, between the holding company and the operating company, with a term (including options to renew) at least as long as the term of the loan is required in addition to the normal collateral.
6. The operating company must either co-sign or guarantee the loan.

Note: Alter ego financing applies only to fixed asset purposes; any working capital needs must be financed separately.

Franchises

Franchises are eligible except in situations where a franchisor retains power to control operations to such an extent that the franchise contract is tantamount to an employment contract. The franchisee must have the right to profit from efforts commensurate with ownership. A copy of the franchisor's FTC-required disclosure statement must be submitted with the application and consideration should be given to requiring the franchisor to guarantee the loan and/or standby on royalty payments when the SBA-guaranteed loan becomes delinquent. These considerations would generally be given when the franchisor is not well known or when credit factors warrant.

Recreational Facilities and Clubs

Recreational facilities and clubs are eligible provided:

a. the facilities are open to the general public, or
b. in "membership only" situations, membership is not selectively denied any particular group of individuals, and the number of memberships is not restricted either as a whole or by establishing maximum limits for particular groups.

Change of Ownership

Loans for the purpose of changing ownership are eligible provided the business benefits from the change. In most cases this benefit should be seen in promoting the sound development of the business or, perhaps, in preserving its existence. Loans cannot be made when proceeds would enable a borrower to purchase (a) part of a business in which it has no present interest, or (b) part of an interest, of a present and continuing owner. Loans to effect a change of ownership among members of the same family are discouraged, both because it can be difficult to assure an "arm's-length" transaction and because this type of transaction should generally be financeable within the family.

Farms and Agricultural Businesses

Farmers are eligible. However, these applicants should first be referred to Farmers Home Administration programs (FmHA), particularly if they have a prior or existing relationship with FmHA.

Fishing Vessels

Fishing vessels are eligible. However, those seeking funds for the construction or reconditioning of vessels with a cargo capacity of five tons or more must first request financing from the National Marine Fisheries Service (NMFS), a part of the Department of Commerce. Loans for another purpose may be considered without the applicant's having first applied to NMFS.

Medical Facilities

Hospitals, clinics, emergency outpatient facilities, and medical and dental laboratories are eligible. Convalescent and nursing homes are eligible provided they are licensed by the appropriate government agency, and services rendered go beyond those of room and board.

Aliens

Aliens are eligible. However, consideration should be given to the type of status possessed, for example, residents or lawful temporary residents, in determining the degree of risk relating to the continuity of the applicant's business. Excessive risk may be offset by full collateralization. The various types of visas is an issue that may be discussed in more detail with the local SBA office.

Probation or Parole

Applications will not be accepted from firms in which a principal (any one of those required to submit a personal history statement, SBA form 912)

a. is currently incarcerated, on parole, or on probation;
b. is a defendant in a criminal proceeding; or
c. whose probation or parole is lifted expressly because it prohibits an SBA loan.

This restriction would not necessarily preclude a loan to a business in which a principal had responded in the affirmative to any one of the questions on the Statement of Personal History. These judgments are made on a case by case evaluation of the nature, frequency, and timing of the offenses. Fingerprint cards (available from the local SBA office) are required any time a question on the form is answered in the affirmative.

LOAN PROCESSING

The purpose of the SBA's lending program is to help small businesses obtain credit, where that financing is not otherwise available on reasonable terms. Most SBA loans are long term in nature, since longer maturities are generally less available in the private sector. It is not the SBA's intent to finance those businesses that cannot meet prudent lending criteria involving management, owner capitalization, and repayment ability.

LOAN PURPOSE

Purchase inventory and materials

Purchase furniture, fixtures, machinery, and equipment

Purchase or construct business premises

Construct leasehold improvements

Purchase a business

Repay existing trade payables and/or other debt

Provide working capital

LOAN AMOUNT

An SBA-guaranteed loan can be in any amount; however, the guarantee is limited to $750,000 with the following three exceptions:

- *International trade loans.* Maximum of $1,250,000
- *Pollution control loans.* Maximum of $1,000,000
- *504 loans (exceptions).* Maximum of $1,000,000, if project involves public policy goals

MAXIMUM GUARANTEE PERCENTAGE

In no case will the SBA guarantee more than 90 percent of the amount of a loan. While the lender may request a smaller guarantee, the maximum is determined by three issues:

- Amount of loan
- Amount of any debt being refinanced by the loan
- Source of the debt being refinanced

TYPE	MAXIMUM % GUARANTEE
Loans $155,000 and less	90
Loans over $155,000	85
Portion of loan to pay debt	80
Portion of loan to pay debt due participant lender	0

Amount of Loan

Generally, SBA can guarantee a maximum of 90 percent on loans of $155,000 and less (including the balance of any existing SBA loans). The maximum guarantee on loans in excess of $155,000 is 85 percent (generally, to a maximum of $750,000).

Example 1a: Proposed $120,000 loan, no existing SBA loans, loan proceeds include no debt payment.

$120,000 $\times$ .90 = 108,000 (90%)
Answer: 90% guarantee

Example 1b: Proposed $120,000 loan, $40,000 balance on existing SBA guaranteed loan, loan proceeds include no debt payment.

$120,000 + $40,000 = $160,000 (exceeds $155,000)
$120,000 $\times$ .85 = $102,000 (85%)
Answer: 85% guarantee

Example 1c: Proposed $800,000 loan, loan proceeds include no debt payment.

$800,000 \times .85 = \$680,000\ (85\%)$
Answer: 85% guarantee

Example 1d: Proposed $950,000 loan, loan proceeds include no debt payment.

$950,000 \times .85 = \$807,500$ (exceeds $750,000 maximum
   dollar amount)
$750,000 \div \$950,000 = 78.947\%$
Answer: 78.947% guarantee

Note: The SBA's computer rounds decimals down to the third decimal place. The lender can round down to the nearest whole number, if it chooses.

Debt Refinancing

The maximum percentage guarantee of that portion of the loan being used to refinance existing debt (does not include trade payables) is 80 percent. Field offices have the authority to reduce this percentage, if the circumstances warrant. Refunding loans are ineligible where the creditor is in a position to sustain a loss and the SBA is likely to sustain all or part of the same loss by refinancing the debt.

Example 2a: Proposed $120,000 loan, $40,000 balance on existing SBA guaranteed loan, loan proceeds include $30,000 to repay note due another lender.

$120,000 + \$40,000 = \$160,000$ (exceeds $155,000)
(See Example 1b)
$90,000 \times .85 = \$76,500$
$30,000 \times .80 = \ \ 24,000$
$100,500\ (83.75\%)$
Answer: 83.75% guarantee

Example 2b: Proposed $400,000 loan, $150,000 to be used to repay notes due another lender.

$150,000 \times .80 = \$120,000$
$250,000 \times .85 = \ \ 212,500$
$332,500\ (83.125\%)$
Answer: 83.125% guarantee

Participant Debt Refinancing

Generally, existing SBA-guaranteed loans made by the same lender are not to be refinanced, but rather should have their terms renegotiated, if necessary. When the debt being refinanced is held by the lender requesting the guarantee (not guaranteed by SBA), the lender must retain its existing dollar amount of exposure. In these situations, the maximum guarantee percentage is the lesser of two calculations, as seen in these examples:

Example 3a: Assume a $400,000 loan, $150,000 to pay a note due the participant lender.

(1) $150,000 × .80 = $120,000
     $250,000 × .85 = 212,500
     $332,500 (83.125%)

or

(2) $400,000 − $150,000 = $250,000
     $250,000 ÷ $400,000 = 62.5%
SBA's maximum guarantee is the lesser of 83.125% and 62.5%.
Answer: 62.5% guarantee

Example 3b: Assume a $400,000 loan, $50,000 to pay a note due the participant lender.

(1) $ 50,000 × .80 = $ 40,000
     $350,000 × .85 = 297,500
     $337,500 (84.375%)

or

(2) $400,000 − $ 50,000 = $350,000
     $350,000 ÷ $400,000 = 87.5%
SBA's maximum guarantee is the lesser of 84.375% and 87.5%.
Answer: 84.375% guarantee

LOAN MATURITY

Most SBA loans are used to finance the long-term needs of small business. Maturities are expected to be commensurate with the business's ability to repay and the remaining useful life of the assets being financed.

The specific maturity of a loan is determined by:

• Use of the proceeds
• Useful life of the assets being financed
• Ability to repay

Loans for working capital purposes will not exceed seven years, except in cases where a longer maturity (up to ten years) may be needed to assure repayment. The maximum maturity of loans used to finance fixed assets other than real estate will be limited to the economic life of those assets—but not to exceed 25 years. The 25-year maximum will generally apply to the acquisition of land and buildings or the refinancing of debt incurred in its acquisition. Where business premises are to be constructed or significantly renovated, the 25-year maximum would be in addition to the time needed to complete construction. "Significant renovation" means construction costs of at least one-third of the current value of the property.

Where the loan proceeds are to be used for varied purposes, the maximum maturity and appropriate amortization will be either a weighted average or the sum of monthly installments for each purpose.

In the following examples, assume a 12 percent per annum rate of interest and that the equipment has a remaining useful life of 15 years.

Weighted average method:

PURPOSE	MAXIMUM AMOUNT ($)	% OF TOTAL	MATURITY MAX.
Purchase Land & Bldg.	200.0	50 × 25 =	12.50
Purchase M & E	100.0	25 × 15 =	3.75
Purchase Inventory	40.0	10 × 7 =	.70
Working Capital	60.0	15 × 7 =	1.05
Total	400.0	100	18.00

a. Maturity: 18 years
b. Amortization: $400,000 × .011320 (18 years at 12%) = $4,528 per month

Sum of monthly installments method:

PURPOSE	MAXIMUM AMOUNT ($)	AMORT. MATURITY (YRS.)	FACTOR	MONTHLY PAYMENT ($)
Purchase L & B	200.0	25	.010532	2,106.40
Purchase M & E	100.0	15	.012002	1,200.20
Purchase Inv	40.0	7	.017653	706.12
Working Cap	60.0	7	.017653	1,059.18
Total	400.0			

a. Maturity: 25 years
b. Amortization:

First 84 payments = $5,072 (rounded)
Payments 85–180 = 3,308 (rounded)
Payments 181–300 = 2,107 (rounded)

The sum of monthly installments method will require the payment of somewhat higher amounts during the early stages of the loan when repayment risk is generally higher. For this reason, the SBA ordinarily prefers the weighted average method in establishing maximum maturities.

Balloon notes written to amortize loans over periods longer than the maximum maturities already discussed are not permitted on guaranteed loans. Balloon notes written to mature within the maximum term permitted are discouraged, since this would be contrary to one of the principal purposes of the program—making long-term capital available to small businesses. This practice may also present the borrower with the potentially damaging burden of having to find new financing at the time of maturity, if the lender decides not to refinance.

INTEREST RATE

The interest rate on an SBA-guaranteed loan is negotiated by the lender and borrower and may be fixed or variable. Although rates cannot be higher than maximum levels set by SBA regulations. The maximum rates* are:

- 2.25 percentage points over "prime" on maturities less than seven years
- 2.75 percentage points over "prime" on maturities of seven years or more

For immediate participation loans, the maximum interest rate for the lenders share is one percentage point below the maximum guarantee rate for loans with comparable maturities.

Fixed Rate

The maximum fixed rate is based on the prime rate published in the *Wall Street Journal* on the day the guarantee request is received by the SBA. If the prime rate is expressed as a range, the lower rate is used as the base.

Variable Rate

The maximum variable rate is generally based on the *Wall Street Journal* reported lowest prime, but may be based on the "optional peg" rate calculated and published quarterly by the SBA in the Federal Register. This rate is an intermediate-term rate based on a weighted average of rates the federal government pays for loans with maturities similar to the average SBA loan and is generally lower than the *Wall Street Journal* prime.

Once the initial note rate has been established within the stated limits, an adjustment period is selected that will identify the frequency at which the note rate will change. It must change no more often than monthly and must change consistent, (e.g., monthly, quarterly, semiannually, annually, or any other defined, consistent period). While the base rate (e.g., prime) may change numerous times in one period, the note rate would be adjusted only once. The date of determination of the change must be the first business day of the period after the end of the last adjustment period. The effective date of adjustment is the first calendar day after the end of the last adjustment period.

The exception to the "no more often than monthly" policy is that the first adjustment can occur on the first calendar day of the month following disbursement based on the base rate in effect on the first business day of the month after disbursement.

On the day of the application, the participating lender must have de-

---

Note: The only exception to the stated maximum rates exists in the Small Loan Program, which permits a lender to charge one percentage point higher on loans between $25,000 and $50,000, and two percentage points higher on loans under $25,000 on loans approved through September 30, 1991.

termined (a) the base rate, (b) the spread, (c) the note rate, and (d) the adjustment period. The following is an example of this adjustment process.

A lender requests the SBA's guarantee on a loan with a ten-year maturity. Prime on the day the lender submits the application to the SBA is 9 percent. The lender and borrower agree that payments will be calculated at prime plus 2.50 percentage points and that the rate will fluctuate on a quarterly basis. The base rate is 9 percent, the spread is 2.50 percentage points, the note rate is 11.50 percent, and the adjustment period is quarterly. If the prime rate changes either up or down, the note rate will change by the same amount in effect on the first business day of the new calendar quarter, but will be effective as of the first calendar day of that calendar quarter. The spread stays constant throughout the term of the loan. Therefore, while the maximum note rate at the time this loan was made was 11.75 percent, if prime goes up to 12 percent during the life of the loan, the rate on the note at that time would go up to 14.50 percent.

AMORTIZATION

Fixed-rate guaranteed notes are generally amortized in equal periodic installments including principal and interest over the life of the loan. Principal plus interest and other methods of amortization may be permitted when circumstances warrant. It is noted that principal plus interest amortizations require substantially higher payments during the earlier stages of the repayment term.

Variable-rate notes are also typically amortized in equal periodic installments of principal and interest with payments calculated on the initial rate of interest. While fluctuation of the rate over the life of the loan will likely result in a prepayment or balloon payment, the constant level of payments will be of benefit to the borrower.

Other permissible methods of amortization include reamortization of loan payments at the time of each fluctuation, equal periodic payments of principal plus interest for the same period, splitting the rates charged on the guaranteed and unguaranteed portions, and calculation of loan payments using an interest rate up to two percentage points higher than the otherwise permitted rate when anticipating an increase in rates over the life of the loan.

CREDIT CONSIDERATIONS

The SBA, like any prudent lender, evaluates an applicant's loan proposal with the primary view of establishing repayment ability. Among the factors considered are depth and capabilities of management; financial health as presented by reliable historical financial statements; reasonableness of loan repayment through past and/or projected earnings of the business; and any secondary means of repayment, primarily collateral. While a working knowledge of the SBA's lending philosophy is best obtained through close interaction with the local office, some basic points concerning credit considerations follow.

Management is the single most important issue in evaluating the potential success of a business; yet it is the one issue that the SBA is least able to analyze. While we do look at personal resumes of members of management and their personal credit information, the individuals running a business are generally much better known to the lender. For this reason we rely heavily on the lender's analysis of management's capabilities and on the documentation of that analysis submitted with the guarantee request.

Repayment ability is evaluated through the examination of a company's past profit and loss statements and projections. Significant changes in the way the company does business, deviations from industry norms, and market and industry trends are studied. Ability to meet past obligations as agreed, particularly with the lender requesting the guarantee, is evaluated. The financial condition of the company is analyzed, with consideration given to weak and intangible asset values, and adjustments made, if necessary. Working capital adequacy is identified, a pro forma balance sheet is prepared reflecting the company's financial position once the loan has been granted, and ratio comparisons are made with the company's own past records as well as with industry standards. Loans being used to purchase or to start a business generally include comparisons with industry norms, evaluation of management's related experience, break-even analysis, and the reasonable valuation of the business being purchased.

Collateral and other secondary means of repayment are identified and evaluated. Personal guaranties of the principals owning 20 percent of the business are required, with lesser owners sometimes being required to provide limited guarantees. Assets acquired with the loan proceeds are generally expected to secure the loan, while other company owned and personally owned assets of the principals would be expected to offset any collateral deficiency, if they are available. Once all available assets have been pledged and a deficiency remains, approval of the guarantee request is still possible, if all other credit factors are positive.

TERMS AND CONDITIONS

The SBA's approval of a guarantee request is documented in its Authorization and Loan Agreement (SBA form 529 B). This document describes terms and conditions that must be met by both lender and borrower before the loan proceeds can be disbursed. Most SBA offices would be happy to provide its more active lender participants with a copy of the diskette.

Also referred to as the loan authorization, the document is first signed by the approving official at the SBA, then forwarded to the lender. A copy is to be given to the borrower for signature, with care given to explaining to the borrower any issues that might cause confusion. The conditions listed in the authorization are generally negotiated between the lender and the borrower before the request is submitted to the SBA. In those situations where the SBA feels additional conditions should be imposed, agreement of the lender is obtained before the guarantee is approved. The authorization must be signed by the borrower before any disbursement is made.

Section Four

7 Steps of an SBA Guarantee

The borrower must obtain the following forms from the lending institution, complete them accurately, and return them within a reasonable time if the loan is to be completed in minimum time. (The forms noted are fully illustrated and explained in *SBA LOANS: A Step-by-Step Guide*, second edition, published by John Wiley & Sons. Exceptions are included here for familiarization.)

1. *Application for Loan*, SBA form 4, or 4L
2. *Statement of Personal History*, SBA form 912
3. *Personal Financial Statement*, SBA form 413
4. *Detailed, signed balance sheet and profit and loss statements* that are current (within 90 days of application), and last three fiscal years' supplementary schedules required on current financial statements.
5. *Detailed one year projection of income and finances.* Attach written explanation as to how you expect to achieve these projections.
6. *A list of names and addresses of any subsidiaries and affiliates,* including concerns in which the applicant holds a controlling (but not necessarily a majority) interest, and other concerns that may be affiliated with the applicant by stock ownership, franchise, proposed merger, or otherwise.
7. *Certificate of Doing Business.* (If a corporation, stamp corporate seal on SBA form 4, section 12).
8. *By law, the agency may not guarantee a loan if a business can obtain funds independently* on reasonable terms from a bank or other private source. A borrower therefore must first seek private financing. A company must be independently owned and operated, not dominant in its field, and must meet certain standards of size in terms of employees or annual receipts. Loans cannot be made to speculative businesses, newspapers, or businesses engaged in gambling.

   Applicants for loans must also agree to comply with SBA regulations that state there will be no discrimination in employment or services to the public based on race, color, religion, national origin, gender, or marital status.
9. *Signed business federal income tax returns* for previous three years. A tax

release form may be required by the SBA to enable the SBA to request these tax documents directly from the IRS.

10. *Signed personal federal income tax returns* of principals for previous three years. A tax release form may be required by the SBA to enable the SBA to request these tax documents directly from the IRS.

11. *Personal resume* including business experience of each principal

12. *Brief history of the business and its problems.* Include an explanation of why the SBA loan is needed and how it will help the business.

13. *Copy of business lease,* or note from landlord giving terms of proposed lease

14. For purchase of an existing business the following are required:
    a. *Current balance sheet and profit and loss statement* of business to be purchased
    b. *Previous two years' federal income tax returns* of the business
    c. *Proposed bill of sale,* including terms of sale
    d. *Asking price* with schedule of the following items:
       1. Inventory
       2. Machinery and equipment
       3. Furniture and fixtures

The lending officer processing the loan must accomplish the following steps before the loan can be processed.

Step 1   Execute the Loan Guarantee Agreement (SBA form 750, see Figure 7.1) which specifies the rights and obligations of the lender and the SBA. This is a one-time document that serves as the basis for all future long-term guarantee loan requests submitted by the lender. (Form 750B covers all guarantee requests for short-term loans—maturities of 12 months or less, see Figure 7.2.)

Step 2   Analyze the specific loan request, weighing the factors and appropriate maturity and deciding whether an SBA guarantee will be requested.

Step 3   Determine eligibility as to size, type, and use of proceeds. Any doubt concerning eligibility should be resolved with the field office as early as possible in order to avoid processing delays.

Step 4   Give applicant an SBA loan package with instructions to return two complete packages to the lender.

Step 5   Finalize loan terms and conditions through lender's approval process.

Step 6   Complete Lender's Application for Guarantee (SBA form 4-1). A copy of any committee report may be used to supplement this form.

Step 7   Submit one complete package with original signatures and dates to the local SBA office.

While these are the standard procedures used by regular lender participants when requesting the SBA's guarantee on a loan, streamlined steps have been established for lenders who are more active in the program. These modified procedures are implemented through the Certified Lenders and Preferred Lenders Programs.

FEES

Guarantee Fee

The SBA charges a one-time guarantee fee to the lender obtaining its guarantee, which can be passed on to the borrower, once it has been paid by the lender. The amount of the fee is determined by the maturity and the amount of the loan.

For long-term loans (maturities in excess of 12 months), the lender is charged 2 percent of the guaranteed amount when the loan exceeds $50,000. For loans of $50,000 or less (Small Loan Program), the lender is charged 1 percent of the guaranteed amount. For these small loans, the Lender may elect to charge the standard 2 percent fee and retain the difference. The guarantee fee on long-term loans is required to be paid within 90 days of the loan authorization approval date.

For short-term loans (maturities of 12 months or less), the guarantee fee is 0.25 percent. This fee must be submitted at the time of application along with the request for guarantee.

Rebates of the guarantee fee can be issued on long-term loans when the loan remains completely undisbursed and the SBA receives a written request to cancel from the lender. Rebates on short-term loans must be requested by the lender within 30 days of the date the SBA approved the guarantee and will be honored only if the reason for cancellation is that the SBA approved the loan on terms that differed from those recommended by the lender.

Application Fees

Processing fees, origination fees, application fees, points, brokerage fees, bonus points, and other fees that might be charged an applicant are not permitted. The only time a commitment fee may be charged is for a loan made under the Export Revolving Line of Credit Program.

Packaging Fees

Reasonable packaging fees in line with those charged for similar services in the local geographic area may be charged an applicant small-business concern. If these services are being provided by the lender, it must give the applicant written notice that the applicant is not required to obtain or pay for services that are unwanted.

LOAN GUARANTY AGREEMENT (DEFERRED PARTICIPATION)

AGREEMENT, made the _____ day of _____ , 19 _____, by and between

_____

(Lender's name and full address)

and Small Business Administration (SBA), an agency of the United States Government.

WHEREAS, the parties intend for Lender to make and SBA to guarantee loans to small business concerns pursuant to the Small Business Act, as amended, and Title V of the Small Business Investment Act, as amended:

NOW, THEREFORE, the parties agree as follows:

1. Application for Guaranty. This agreement shall cover only loans duly approved hereafter for guaranty by Lender and SBA subject to SBA's Rules and Regulations as promulgated from time to time. Any loan approved by Lender contingent upon SBA's guaranty under this agreement shall be referred to SBA for authorization upon the separate application* of Lender and the loan applicant.

2. Approval of Guaranty. SBA shall either approve in a formal loan authorization or decline the guaranty by written notice to the Lender. Prior to full disbursement of the loan, any change in the terms or conditions stated in the loan authorization shall be subject to prior written agreement between SBA and Lender.

3. Closing and Disbursement of Loans. Lender shall close and disburse each loan in accordance with the terms and conditions of the approved loan authorization. Lender shall cause to be executed a note* and all additional instruments and take such other actions which shall, consistent with prudent closing practices, be required in order fully to protect or preserve the interests of Lender and SBA in the loan. Immediately after the first disbursement of each loan, Lender shall furnish SBA with a copy of the executed note, settlement sheet* and compensation agreement* and guaranty fee mentioned in paragraph 5 hereof. Immediately following any subsequent disbursements, Lender shall furnish SBA with an executed settlement sheet*. SBA shall be entitled at any time, after written notice to examine and obtain copies of all notes, security agreements, instruments of hypothecation, all other agreements and documents (herein collectively called "Loan Instruments"), and the loan repayment records held by Lender which relate to loans made pursuant to this agreement.

4. Report of Status. Lender shall complete and forward to SBA a written, quarterly status report.* This report shall be due within 20 days after the end of the reporting period specified in the report. SBA shall not be obligated to purchase the guaranteed percentage of the outstanding balance of the loan if SBA determines that Lender's failure to provide timely and accurate status information caused any substantial harm to the Government. This information collection requirement has been approved under OMB Number 3245-0095.

5. Guaranty Fee. Lender shall pay SBA a one-time guaranty fee amounting to one percent of the total amount guaranteed by SBA. The guaranty fee shall be paid within 90 days of the date of the loan approval stated in the loan authorization. If this fee is not paid within this time period, SBA will send the Lender a written notice which will state that the guaranty on this loan will be terminated if SBA does not receive the fee within the time specified in the written notice. The guaranty on this loan may be reinstated by SBA at its sole discretion pursuant to notice published by SBA in the Federal Register. There will be no rebate of the guaranty fee at any time unless the Lender has not made any disbursement of the guaranteed loan and requests a return of the fee together with cancellation of the loan authorization. Acceptance of the guaranty fee by SBA shall not constitute any waiver by SBA of any negligence or other misfeasance on the part of the Lender.

6. Administration of Loans. Lender shall hold the Loan Instruments, and shall receive all payments of principal and interest until transfer of the note to SBA. Holder of the note (Lender or SBA) shall not, without prior written consent of the other: (a) make or consent to any substantial alteration in the terms of any Loan Instrument ("Substantial" includes but is not limited to, increases in principal amount or interest rate or any action that benefits or confers a preference on the holder); (b) make or consent to releases of collateral having a cumulative value, as reasonably determined by the holder of the note, which is more than 20 percent of the original loan amount; (c) accelerate the maturity of any note; (d) sue upon any Loan Instrument; or (e) waive any claim against any borrower, guarantor, obligor or standby creditor arising out of any Loan Instrument. All servicing actions shall be the responsibility of the holder who shall follow accepted standards of loan servicing employed by prudent lenders generally, except that borrowers compliance with SBA's non-discrimination regulations (13 C.F.R., Part 113) shall be subject to action solely by SBA.

7. Purchase by SBA. Lender may demand in writing that SBA purchase the guaranteed percentage of the outstanding balance of the loan if default by a borrower continues uncured for more than 60 days (or less, if SBA agrees) in making payment, when due, of any installment of principal or interest on any note. By making written demand that SBA purchase the guaranteed portion of a loan, Lender shall be deemed thereby to certify that the loan has been disbursed and serviced in compliance with this agreement and that this agreement remains in full force and effect with respect to the loan. Within 30 days after receipt of Lender's demand, together with a certified transcript of the loan account, and the assignment of the Loan Instruments, without recourse, SBA will pay to Lender the guaranteed percentage of the balance of the loan plus accrued interest at the note rate, after adjustment for other charges, as appropriate; SBA will issue to Lender a certificate of interest* evidencing the percentage of loan retained by the Lender. If SBA consents that Lender may continue administration of the loan after SBA purchases the guaranteed percentage, Lender shall deliver to SBA at the time of purchase conformed copies of any of the Loan Instruments not previously furnished SBA and issue to SBA a certificate of interest* evidencing SBA's percentage of the loan. Purchase by SBA shall not waive any right of SBA arising from Lender's negligence, misconduct, or violation of any provision of this agreement.

_____

*Form to be furnished by SBA.

Figure 7.1a

8. **Fees or Commissions.** Lender shall not require certificates of deposit or compensating balances and shall not directly or indirectly charge or receive any bonus, fee, commission or other payment or benefit in connection with making or servicing any loan, except reimbursement for charges or expenses incurred or compensation for actual services rendered.

9. **Sharing of Repayment Proceeds and Collateral.** Lender shall not acquire any preferential security, surety or insurance to protect its unguaranteed interest in a loan. All repayments, security or guaranty of any nature, including without limitation rights of setoff and counterclaim, which Lender or SBA jointly or severally may at any time recover from any source whatsoever or have the right to recover on any guaranteed loan, shall repay and secure the interests of Lender and SBA in the same proportion as such interest bears respectively to the unpaid balance of the loan. Lender shall notify SBA of any loan or advance by Lender to a borrower subsequent to a guaranteed loan, and if, in SBA's opinion, circumstances require, and any borrower's consent required is first obtained, enter into a written agreement with SBA providing for the application of collateral (or proceeds realized therefrom) to the respective loans in a manner satisfactory to the parties hereto.

10. **Payment of Expenses.** All ordinary expense of making, servicing, and liquidating a guaranteed loan shall be paid by, or be recoverable from the borrower. All reasonable expenses incurred by Lender or SBA which are not recoverable from the borrower shall be shared ratably by Lender and SBA in accordance with their respective interests in any such loan.

11. **SBA Purchase Privilege.** Notwithstanding any provision of any agreement between SBA and Lender, SBA has the absolute right at any time to purchase its guaranteed percentage of any loan in the interest of the Government or the borrower. Within 15 days of the Lender's receipt of SBA's written demand to purchase the guaranteed percentage, Lender shall deliver to SBA a certified transcript of the loan account showing date and amount of each advance or disbursement and repayment and shall assign and deliver to SBA the Loan Instruments pursuant to paragraph 7 above. Upon receipt of these documents, SBA shall pay Lender the guaranteed portion of the amount then owing on the loan pursuant to paragraph 7 above.

12. **Assignment of Interest in Loan.** A. Either party may assign, in whole or part, its rights or obligations under this agreement on any guaranteed loan with the prior written consent of the other party including transfers pursuant to Secondary Participation Agreements (13 C.F.R. Part 120 §120.5(a)(3)). B. Nothing in this agreement prohibits, upon written notice to SBA, assignment by the Lender (or holder of the Note) to other banking institutions provided (1) the Lender retains an unguaranteed interest of not less than 10 percent of the outstanding principal amount of the loan, (2) SBA may continue to deal solely with the Lender as to the entire loan and (3) assignee shall have no greater rights than assignor. C. Nothing in this agreement prohibits Lender, without notice to SBA from using any guaranteed loan as security for (1) Treasury Tax and Loan Accounts (Treasury Department Circular 92), (2) the deposit of public funds, (3) uninvested trust funds, or (4) discount borrowings at the Federal Reserve Bank, provided (a) Lender has not sold or otherwise assigned any part of the guaranteed loan, and (b) Lender retains full authority to perform its responsibilities under this agreement.

13. **Termination.**

a. Either party may terminate this agreement upon not less than 10 days written notice by certified mail to the other party. Termination shall not affect the guaranty of any loan previously authorized by SBA. This subparagraph is not applicable where this agreement applies only to one designated borrower.

b. Lender may terminate the guaranty as to any unassigned loan guaranteed hereunder at any time prior to purchase by SBA upon notice to SBA. The guaranty of any loan shall be terminated if demand for SBA to purchase or a request to extend the maturity is not received by SBA within one year after the maturity of the note.

This agreement shall inure to the benefit of, and be binding upon the parties, their successors and assigns.

IN WITNESS WHEREOF, Lender and SBA have caused this agreement to be duly executed the date first above written.

(SEAL)

ATTEST:

_____
NAME OF LENDER

_____   BY _____
                                                                  TITLE

SMALL BUSINESS ADMINISTRATION

BY _____
                        TITLE

(Lender shall execute and submit two copies to SBA field office.)

☆U.S. GOVERNMENT PRINTING OFFICE: 1988 - 518-672-61847

SBA 750 (10-83)

Figure 7.1b

SMALL BUSINESS ADMINISTRATION

LOAN GUARANTY AGREEMENT (DEFERRED PARTICIPATION)
FOR SHORT-TERM LOANS

AGREEMENT, made the_____ day of _____ , 19__ , by and between

_____
(Lender's name and full address)

and Small Business Administration (SBA), an agency of the United States Government.

WHEREAS, the parties intend for Lender to make and SBA to guarantee "short-term loans" (loans with maturities of 12 months or less), to small business concerns pursuant to the Small Business Act, as amended, and Title V of the Small Business Investment Act, as amended:

NOW, THEREFORE, the parties agree as follows:

1. Application for Guaranty. This agreement shall cover only "short-term loans" duly approved hereafter by Lender contingent upon guaranty by SBA subject to SBA's Rules and Regulations as promulgated from time to time. Any loan approved by Lender contingent upon SBA's guaranty under this agreement shall be referred to SBA for authorization upon the separate application* of Lender and the loan applicant.

2. Approval of Guaranty. SBA shall either approve in a formal loan authorization or decline the guaranty by written notice to the Lender. Prior to full disbursement of the loan, any change in the terms or conditions stated in the loan authorization shall be subject to prior written agreement between SBA and Lender. After full disbursement paragraph 6 below shall govern.

3. Closing and Disbursement of Loans. Lender shall close and disburse each loan in accordance with the terms and conditions of the approved loan authorization. Lender shall cause to be executed a note* for the maximum amount authorized and all additional instruments and take such other actions which shall, consistent with prudent closing and disbursement practices, be required in order fully to protect or preserve the interests of Lender and SBA in the loan. Immediately after the first disbursement of each loan, Lender shall furnish SBA with a copy of the executed note, settlement sheet* and compensation agreement*. Immediately following any subsequent disbursements, Lender shall furnish SBA with an executed settlement sheet*. SBA shall be entitled at any time, after written notice, to examine and obtain copies of all notes, security agreements, instruments of hypothecation, letters of credit, all other agreements and documents (herein collectively called "Loan Instruments"), and the loan repayment records held by Lender which relate to loans made pursuant to this agreement.

4. Report of Status. Lender shall complete and forward to SBA a written, quarterly status report* (which may be combined with the quarterly report required by the SBA Form 750 Agreement). This report shall be due within 20 days after the end of the reporting period specified in the report received by the Lender from SBA. SBA shall not be obligated to purchase the guaranteed percentage of the outstanding balance of the loan if SBA determines that Lender's failure to provide timely and accurate status information caused any substantial harm to the Government. Lender shall also, upon receipt of information of any substantially adverse change in the financial or other condition of Borrower, provide SBA with written notice of such adverse change.

5. Guaranty Fee. Lender shall submit, with the loan application, a one-time guaranty fee amounting to one-fourth of one percent of the total amount to be guaranteed by SBA. SBA will return to Lender the guaranty fee if the loan application is declined or withdrawn prior to approval. There will be no rebate of the guaranty fee at any time after the date of loan approval stated in the loan authorization where the application for guaranty is approved as submitted by the Lender. If SBA approves the guaranty of the loan with any substantial modification or addition to the loan conditions submitted by the Lender, SBA will return to Lender the guaranty fee if SBA receives a written request from Lender, within 30 calendar days after SBA's approval date, to cancel the loan guaranty and to return the guaranty fee. Acceptance of the guaranty fee by SBA shall not constitute any waiver by SBA of any negligence or other misfeasance on the part of the Lender. If the loan or the guaranty portion is to be increased with SBA's written approval, the Lender will submit with its request for such increase an additional guaranty fee amounting to one-fourth of one percent of the increase in the guaranteed portion. No additional guaranty fee will be charged for loans extended beyond the original maturity date. No disbursements shall be made by the Lender after the original maturity date.

6. Administration of Loans. Lender shall hold the Loan Instruments, and shall receive all payments of principal and interest until transfer of the note to SBA. Holder of the note (Lender or SBA) shall not, without prior written consent of the other: (a) make or consent to any substantial alteration in the terms of any Loan Instrument ("Substantial" includes, but is not limited to, increases in principal amount or interest rate or any action that benefits or confers a preference on the Holder); (b) make or consent to releases of collateral having a cumulative value, as reasonably determined by the Holder of the note, which is more than 20 percent of the original loan amount; (c) accelerate the maturity of any note; (d) sue upon any Loan Instrument; or (e) waive any claim against any borrower, guarantor, obligor or standby creditor arising out of any Loan Instrument. All servicing actions shall be the responsibility of the Holder who shall follow accepted standards of loan servicing employed by prudent lenders generally, except that borrowers' compliance with SBA's non-discrimination regulations (13 C. F. R., Part 113) shall be subject to action solely by SBA.

7. Purchase by SBA. Lender may demand in writing that SBA purchase the guaranteed percentage of the outstanding balance of the loan if default by a borrower continues uncured for more than 60 days (or less, if SBA agrees) in making payment, when due, of any installment of principal or interest on any note. By making written demand that SBA purchase the guaranteed portion of a loan, Lender shall be deemed thereby to certify that the loan has been disbursed and serviced in compliance with this agreement and that this agreement remains in full force and effect with respect to the loan. Within 30 days after receipt of Lender's demand, together with a certified transcript of the loan account, SBA will pay to Lender the guaranteed percentage of the balance of the loan plus accrued interest at the note rate, after adjustment for other charges, as appropriate; SBA will issue to Lender a certificate of interest* evidencing the percentage of loan retained by the Lender. If SBA consents that Lender may continue administration of the loan after SBA purchases the guaranteed percentage, Lender shall deliver to SBA at the time of purchase conformed copies of any of the Loan Instruments not previously furnished SBA and issue to SBA a certificate of interest* evidencing SBA's percentage of the loan. Purchase by SBA shall not waive any right of SBA arising from Lender's negligence, misconduct, or violation of any provision of this agreement.

_____
*Form to be furnished by SBA.

Form 750B (3-80)

Figure 7.2a

64

8. Fees or Commissions. Lender shall not require certificates of deposit or compensating balances and shall not directly or indirectly charge or receive any bonus, fee, commission or other payment or benefit in connection with making or servicing any "short-term loan," except reimbursement for charges or expenses incurred or compensation for actual services rendered. However, after approval of the "short-term loan" by SBA, Lender may charge the borrower the guaranty fee paid by Lender pursuant to paragraph 5 and in addition may charge the borrower a "commitment fee" amounting to one-fourth of one percent of the unguaranteed amount of the "short-term loan."

9. Sharing of Repayment Proceeds and Collateral. Lender shall not acquire any preferential security, surety or insurance to protect its unguaranteed interest in a loan. All repayments, security or guaranty of any nature, including without limitation rights of setoff and counter-claim, which Lender or SBA jointly or severally may at any time recover from any source whatsoever or have the right to recover on any guaranteed loan, shall repay and secure the interests of Lender and SBA in the same proportion as such interest bears respectively to the unpaid balance of the loan. Lender shall notify SBA of any loan or advance by Lender to a borrower subsequent to a guaranteed loan, and if, in SBA's opinion, circumstances require, and any borrower's consent required is first obtained, enter into a written agreement with SBA providing for the application of collateral (or proceeds realized therefrom) to the respective loans in a manner satisfactory to the parties hereto.

10. Payment of Expenses. All ordinary expense of making, servicing, and liquidating a guaranteed loan shall be paid by, or be recoverable from the borrower. All reasonable expenses incurred by Lender or SBA which are not recoverable from the borrower shall be shared ratably by Lender and SBA in accordance with their respective interests in any such loan.

11. SBA Purchase Privilege. Notwithstanding any provision of any agreement between SBA and Lender, SBA has the absolute right at anytime to purchase its guaranteed percentage of any loan in the interest of the Government or the borrower. Within 15 days of the Lender's receipt of SBA's written demand to purchase the guaranteed percentage, Lender shall deliver to SBA a certified transcript of the loan account showing date and amount of each advance or disbursement and repayment and shall assign and deliver to SBA the Loan Instruments. Upon receipt of these documents, SBA shall pay Lender the guaranteed portion of the amount then owing on the loan pursuant to paragraph 7 above.

12. Assignment of Interest in Loan. A. Either party may assign, in whole or part, its rights or obligations under this agreement or in any guaranteed loan with the prior written consent of the other party, including transfers pursuant to secondary participation agreements (13 C. F. R., Part 120 § 120.5(a)(3)). B. Nothing in this agreement prohibits, upon written notice to SBA, assignment by the Lender (or Holder of the Note) to other banking institutions provided (1) the Lender retains an unguaranteed interest of not less than 10 percent of the outstanding principal amount of the loan; (2) SBA may continue to deal solely with the Lender as to the entire loan, and (3) assignee shall have no greater rights than assignor. C. Nothing in this agreement prohibits Lender, without notice to SBA, from using any guaranteed loan as security for (1) Treasury Tax and Loan Accounts (Treasury Department Circular 92), (2) the deposit of public funds, (3) uninvested trust funds, or (4) discount borrowings at the Federal Reserve Bank, provided (a) Lender has not sold or otherwise assigned any part of the guaranteed loan, and (b) Lender retains full authority to perform its responsibilities under this agreement.

13. Termination.

a. Either party may terminate this agreement upon not less than 10 days written notice by certified mail to the other party. Termination shall not affect the guaranty of any loan previously authorized by SBA. This subparagraph is not applicable where this agreement applies only to one designated borrower.

b. Lender may terminate the guaranty as to any unassigned loan guaranteed hereunder at any time prior to purchase by SBA upon notice to SBA. The guaranty of any loan shall be terminated if demand for SBA to purchase or a request to extend the maturity is not received by SBA within one year after the maturity of the note.

This agreement shall inure to the benefit of, and be binding upon the parties, their successors and assigns.

IN WITNESS WHEREOF, Lender and SBA have caused this agreement to be duly executed the date first above written.

(SEAL)

ATTEST:

NAME OF LENDER

BY _____
TITLE

SMALL BUSINESS ADMINISTRATION

BY _____
TITLE

(Lender shall execute and submit two copies to SBA field office.)

SBA Form 750B (3-80) REF SOP 70 50 Previous Editions are Obsolete

Figure 7.2b

Closing Fees

The following closing costs are typically borne by the borrower: surveys, title reports, appraisals, filing and recording fees, photocopy and delivery charges, and other direct charges related to the closing. The SBA does not require borrowers to obtain legal counsel, but most do.

Servicing Fees

On guaranteed loans purchased by the SBA, but being serviced by the original participant lender, a servicing fee can be charged, as follows:

- Up to 0.375 percent on the unpaid balance where the SBA's portion of the loan is 75 percent or less
- Up to 0.25 percent on the unpaid balance where the SBA's portion is more than 75 percent

Extraordinary servicing fees can be charged in those situations where the lender will have to expend added time to properly monitor the account. These would include the following:

- Construction loans requiring field inspections, monitoring of draw schedules, title reports, and so forth
- Loans secured by accounts receivable and/or inventory that require monitoring and inspections of that collateral

The extraordinary servicing fee permitted cannot exceed 2 percent of the portion of the loan being used for construction purposes or the portion of the loan secured by those assets requiring the added monitoring.

8 How the Lender Must Handle an SBA Loan

The following information is presented for the purpose of giving the borrower a full understanding and appreciation of how his or her loan application must be handled by the lending institution in order to successfully complete the lending process. Knowing this, the borrower may assist the lending process by providing complete, accurate, and prompt information to the lending officer so that the loan can be completed in minimum time. It also explains what can or will happen in the event of default.

The SBA-guaranteed loans are closed by the lender in accordance with prudent closing procedures and the terms and conditions specified in the loan authorization. Any change to the loan authorization must be approved by the SBA's local office in writing before any disbursements are made. Tight control of disbursements is encouraged through the use of joint payee checks. Costs of closing are generally paid by the borrower, including all recording and filing fees, title company reports, surveys, and attorney expenses.

Once the SBA has approved a guarantee request, the SBA's counsel sends the lender a closing letter specifying the documentation to be executed prior to loan disbursement. This documentation is derived from the terms and conditions found in the loan authorization.

While the lender can use many of its standard closing forms, the following SBA forms are required (see Figures 8.1–8.3):

FORM	SBA FORM NUMBER
Note	147
Guarantee	148
Compensation Agreement for Services	159
Settlement Sheet	1050

U.S. Small Business Administration

SBA LOAN NUMBER

NOTE

_____
(City and State)

$ _____   (Date) _____ , 19 _____

For value received, the undersigned promises to pay to the order of _____

_____
(Payee)

at its office in the city of _____ , State of _____

or at holder's option, at such other place as may be designated from time to time by the holder _____

_____ dollars,
(Write out amount)

with interest on unpaid principal computed from the date of each advance to the undersigned at the rate of _____ percent per

annum, payment to be made in installments as follows:

If this Note contains a fluctuating interest rate, the notice provision is not a pre-condition for fluctuation (which shall take place regardless of notice). Payment of any installment of principal or interest owing on this Note may be made prior to the maturity date thereof without penalty. Borrower shall provide lender with written notice of intent to prepay part or all of this loan at least three (3) weeks prior to the anticipated prepayment date. A prepayment is any payment made ahead of schedule that exceeds twenty (20) percent of the then outstanding principal balance. If borrower makes a prepayment and fails to give at least three weeks advance notice of intent to prepay, then, notwithstanding any other provision to the contrary in this note or other document, borrower shall be required to pay lender three weeks interest on the unpaid principal as of the date preceding such prepayment.

SBA Form 147 (5-87) Previous editions obsolete   Page 1

Figure 8.1a

68

The term "Indebtedness" as used herein shall mean the indebtedness evidenced by this Note, including principal, interest, and expenses, whether contingent, now due or hereafter to become due and whether heretofore or contemporaneously herewith or here-after contracted. The term "Collateral" as used in this Note shall mean any funds, guaranties, or other property or rights therein of any nature whatsoever or the proceeds thereof which may have been, are, or hereafter may be, hypothecated, directly or indirectly by the undersigned or others, in connection with, or as security for, the Indebtedness or any part thereof. The Collateral, and each part thereof, shall secure the Indebtedness and each part thereof. The covenants and conditions set forth or referred to in any and all in-struments of hypothecation constituting the Collateral are hereby incorporated in this Note as covenants and conditions of the under-signed with the same force and effect as though such covenants and conditions were fully set forth herein.

The Indebtedness shall immediately become due and payable, without notice or demand, upon the appointment of a receiver or liquidator, whether voluntary or involuntary, for the undersigned or for any of its property, or upon the filing of a petition by or against the undersigned under the provisions of any State insolvency law or under the provisions of the Bankruptcy Reform Act of 1978, as amended, or upon the making by the undersigned of an assignment for the benefit of its creditors. Holder is authorized to declare all or any part of the Indebtedness immediately due and payable upon the happening of any of the following events: (1) Failure to pay any part of the Indebtedness when due; (2) nonperformance by the undersigned of any agreement with, or any condition imposed by, Holder or Small Business Administration (hereinafter called "SBA"), with respect to the Indebtedness; (3) Holder's discovery of the undersigned's failure in any application of the undersigned to Holder or SBA to disclose any fact deemed by Holder to be material or of the making therein or in any of the said agreements, or in any affidavit or other documents submitted in connection with said appli-cation or the indebtedness, of any misrepresentation by, on behalf of, or for the benefit of the undersigned; (4) the reorganization (other than a reorganization pursuant to any of the provisions of the Bankruptcy Reform Act of 1978, as amended) or merger or con-solidation of the undersigned (or the making of any agreement therefor) without the prior written consent of Holder; (5) the under-signed's failure duly to account, to Holder's satisfaction, at such time or times as Holder may require, for any of the Collateral, or pro-ceeds thereof, coming into the control of the undersigned; or (6) the institution of any suit affecting the undersigned deemed by Holder to affect adversely its interest hereunder in the Collateral or otherwise. Holder's failure to exercise its rights under this paragraph shall not constitute a waiver thereof.

Upon the nonpayment of the Indebtedness, or any part thereof, when due, whether by acceleration or otherwise, Holder is em-powered to sell, assign, and deliver the whole or any part of the Collateral at public or private sale, without demand, advertisement or notice of the time or place of sale or of any adjournment thereof, which are hereby expressly waived. After deducting all expenses in-cidental to or arising from such sale or sales, Holder may apply the residue of the proceeds thereof to the payment of the Indebted-ness, as it shall deem proper, returning the excess, if any, to the undersigned. The undersigned hereby waives all right of redemption or appraisement whether before or after sale.

Holder is further empowered to collect or cause to be collected or otherwise to be converted into money all or any part of the Collateral, by suit or otherwise, and to surrender, compromise, release, renew, extend, exchange, or substitute any item of the Col-lateral in transactions with the undersigned or any third party, irrespective of any assignment thereof by the undersigned, and without prior notice to or consent of the undersigned or any assignee. Whenever any item of the Collateral shall not be paid when due, or otherwise shall be in default, whether or not the indebtedness, or any part thereof, has become due, Holder shall have the same rights and powers with respect to such item of the Collateral as are granted in this paragraph in case of nonpayment of the Indebtedness, or any part thereof, when due. None of the rights, remedies, privileges, or powers of Holder expressly provided for herein shall be ex-clusive, but each of them shall be cumulative with and in addition to every other right, remedy, privilege, and power now or hereafter existing in favor of Holder, whether at law or equity, by statute or otherwise.

The undersigned agrees to take all necessary steps to administer, supervise, preserve, and protect the Collateral; and regardless of any action taken by Holder, there shall be no duty upon Holder in this respect. The undersigned shall pay all expenses of any nature, whether incurred in or out of court, and whether incurred before or after this Note shall become due at its maturity date or otherwise, including but not limited to reasonable attorney's fees and costs, which Holder may deem necessary or proper in connection with the satisfaction of the Indebtedness or the administration, supervision, preservation, protection of (including, but not limited to, the maintenance of adequate insurance) or the realization upon the Collateral. Holder is authorized to pay at any time and from time to time any or all of such expenses, add the amount of such payment to the amount of the Indebtedness, and charge interest thereon at the rate specified herein with respect to the principal amount of this Note.

The security rights of Holder and its assigns hereunder shall not be impaired by Holder's sale, hypothecation or rehypothecation of any note of the undersigned or any item of the Collateral, or by any indulgence, including but not limited to (a) any renewal, exten-sion, or modification which Holder may grant with respect to the Indebtedness or any part thereof, or (b) any surrender, compromise, release, renewal, extension, exchange, or substitution which Holder may grant in respect of the Collateral, or (c) any indulgence granted in respect of any endorser, guarantor, or surety. The purchaser, assignee, transferee, or pledgee of this Note, the Collateral, and guaranty, and any other document (or any of them), sold, assigned, transferred, pledged, or repledged, shall forthwith become vested with and entitled to exercise all the powers and rights given by this Note and all applications of the undersigned to Holder or SBA, as if said purchaser, assignee, transferee, or pledgee were originally named as Payee in this Note and in said application or applications.

Figure 8.1b

This promissory note is given to secure a loan which SBA is making or in which it is participating and, pursuant to Part 101 of the Rules and Regulations of SBA (13 C.F.R. 101.1(d)), this instrument is to be construed and (when SBA is the Holder or a party in interest) enforced in accordance with applicable Federal law.

_____

_____

Note.—Corporate applicants must execute Note, in corporate name, by duly authorized officer, and seal must be affixed and duly attested; partnership applicants must execute Note in firm name, together with signature of a general partner.

SBA Form 147 (5-87)   Page 3

☆ U.S. GPO: 1994-379-770/19140

Figure 8.1c

STEPS TO CLOSING AN SBA-GUARANTEED LOAN

Step 1   Review terms and conditions of the loan authorization when received from the SBA.

Step 2   Discuss terms and conditions with borrower.

Step 3   Send to the SBA the 2 percent guarantee fee no later than 90 days from date the SBA signed loan authorization

Step 4   Obtain the SBA's approval in writing of any proposed change to the loan authorization

Step 5   Have borrower execute all required documentation in accordance with the loan authorization, including the Request for Copy of Transcript of Tax Form (SBA form 4506). An example copy is shown Figure 8.4.

Step 6   Disburse loan proceeds.

Step 7   Send copies of the following to the SBA field office:

Note
Settlement sheet
Compensation agreement
Guarantee (personal and corporate)

LOAN SERVICING

Once an SBA-guaranteed loan has been disbursed, loan servicing is the primary responsibility of the lender. It is expected that the lender use the same degree of prudence in servicing its SBA loans as it does its regular loans.

Paragraph 6 of the Loan Guarantee Agreement (SBA form 750) states in part, "All servicing actions shall be the responsibility of the holder who shall follow accepted standards of loan servicing employed by prudent lenders generally. . . ."

The same document at paragraph 7 specifies those servicing actions that require the SBA's written concurrence. These include the following:

• Increasing principal or interest rate
• Releasing collateral with a cumulative value exceeding 20 percent of the original loan amount
• Accelerating the maturity of the note
• Initiating a suit
• Waiving a claim against any borrower, guarantor, obligor, or standby creditor
• Taking any action that confers a preference upon the lender

Given the preceding actions that require SBA concurrence, the following are examples of servicing decisions that can be made unilaterally by the lender:

• Releasing collateral with cumulative value less than 20 percent of the original loan amount

OMB Approval No. 3245-0201
Expiration Date: 04-30-97

SBA LOAN NO.

U.S. SMALL BUSINESS ADMINISTRATION (SBA)
GUARANTY

_____ , 19_____

In order to induce _____ , (hereinafter called "Lender") to make a loan or loans, or
(SBA or other Lending Institution)

renewal or extension thereof, to _____
(hereinafter called "Debtor"), the Undersigned hereby unconditionally guarantees to Lender, its sucessors and assigns, the due and punctual payment when due, whether by acceleration or otherwise, in accordance with the terms thereof, of the principal of and interest on and all other sums payable, or stated to be payable, with respect to the note of the Debtor, made by

the Debtor to Lender, dated _____ in the principal amount of $ _____ .
with interest at the rate of _____ per cent per annum. Such note, and the interest thereon and all other sums payable with respect thereto are hereinafter collectively called "Liabilities." As security for the performance of this guaranty the Undersigned hereby mortgages, pledges, assigns, transfers and delivers to Lender certain collateral (if any), listed in the schedule on the reverse side hereof. The term "collateral" as used herein shall mean any funds, guaranties, agreements or other property or rights or interests of any nature whatsoever, or the proceeds thereof, which may have been, are, or hereafter may be, mortgaged, pledged, assigned, transferred or delivered directly or indirectly by or on behalf of the Debtor or the Undersigned or any other party to Lender or to the holder of the aforesaid note of the Debtor, or which may have been, are, or hereafter may be held by any party as trustee or otherwise, as security, whether immediate or underlying, for the performance of this guaranty or the payment of the Liabilities or any of them or any security therefor.

The Undersigned waives any notice of the incurring by the Debtor at any time of any of the Liabilities, and waives any and all presentment, demand, protest or notice of dishonor, nonpayment, or other default with repect to any of the Liabilities and any obligation of any party at any time comprised in the collateral. The Undersigned hereby grants to Lender full power, in its uncontrolled discretion and without notice to the undersigned, but subject to the provisions of any agreement between the Debtor or any other party and Lender at the time in force, to deal in any manner with the Liabilities and the collateral, including, but without limiting the generality of the foregoing, the following powers:

(a) To modify or otherwise change any terms of all or any part of the Liabilities or the rate of interest thereon (but not to increase the principal amount of the note of the Debtor to Lender), to grant any extension or renewal thereof and any other indulgence with respect thereto, and to effect any release, compromise or settlement with respect thereto;

(b) To enter into any agreement of forbearance with respect to all or any part of the Liabilities, or with respect to all or any part of the collateral, and to change the terms of any such agreement;

(c) To forbear from calling for additional collateral to secure any of the Liabilities or to secure any obligation comprised in the collateral;

(d) To consent to the substitution, exchange, or release of all or any part of the collateral, whether or not the collateral, if any, received by Lender upon any such substitution, exchange, or release shall be of the same or of a different character or value than the collateral surrendered by Lender;

(e) In the event of the nonpayment when due, whether by acceleration or otherwise, of any of the Liabilities, or in the event of default in the performance of any obligation comprised in the collateral, to realize on the collateral or any part thereof, as a whole or in such parcels or subdivided interests as Lender may elect, at any public or private sale or sales, for cash or on credit or for future delivery, without demand, advertisement, or notice of the time or place of sale or any adjournment thereof (the Undersigned hereby waiving any such demand, advertisement and notice to the extent permitted by law), or by foreclosure or otherwise, or to forbear from realizing thereon, all as Lender in its uncontrolled discretion may deem proper, and to purchase all or any part of the collateral for its own account at any such sale or foreclosure, such powers to be exercised only to the extent permitted by law.

SBA Form 148 (5-93) REF; SOP 70 50 USE 5-87 EDITION UNTIL EXHAUSTED

Federal Recycling Program ♻ Printed on Recycled Paper

Figure 8.2a

The obligations of the Undersigned hereunder shall not be released, discharged or in any way affected, nor shall the Undersigned have any rights or recourse against Lender, by reason of any action Lender may take or omit to take under the foregoing powers.

In case the Debtor shall fail to pay all or any part of the Liabilities when due, whether by acceleration or otherwise, according to the terms of said note, the Undersigned, immediately upon the written demand of Lender, will pay to Lender the amount due and unpaid by the Debtor as aforesaid, in like manner as if such amount constituted the direct and primary obligation of the Undersigned. Lender shall not be required, prior to any such demand on, or payment by, the Undersigned, to make any demand upon or pursue or exhaust any of its rights or remedies against the Debtor or others with respect to the payment of any of the Liabilities, or to pursue or exhaust any of its rights or remedies with respect to any part of the collateral. The Undersigned shall have no right of subrogation whatsoever with respect to the Liabilities or the collateral unless and until Lender shall have received full payment of all the Liabilities.

The obligations of the Undersigned hereunder, and the rights of Lender in the collateral, shall not be released, discharged or in any way affected, nor shall the Undersigned have any rights against Lender: by reason of the fact that any of the collateral may be in default at the time of acceptance thereof by Lender or later; nor by reason of the fact that a valid lien in any of the collateral may not be conveyed to, or created in favor or, Lender; nor by reason of the of the fact that any of the collateral may be subject to equities or defenses or claims in favor of others or may be invalid or defective in any way; nor by reason of the fact that any of the Liabilities may be invalid for any reason whatsoever; nor by reason of the fact that the value of any of the collateral, or the financial condition of the Debtor or any obligor under or guarantor of any of the collateral, may not have been correctly estimated or may have changed or may hereafter change; nor by reason of any deterioration, waste, or loss by fire, theft, or otherwise of any of the collateral, unless such deterioration, waste, or loss be caused by the willful act or willful failure to act of Lender.

The Undersigned agrees to furnish Lender, or the holder of the aforesaid note of the Debtor, upon demand, but not more often than semiannually, so long as any part of the indebtedness under such note remains unpaid, a financial statement setting forth, in reasonable detail, the assets, liabilities, and net worth of the Undersigned.

The Undersigned acknowledges and understands that if the Small Business Administration (SBA) enters into, has entered into, or will enter into, a Guaranty Agreement, with Lender or any other lending institution, guaranteeing a portion of Debtor's Liabilities, the Undersigned agrees that it is not a coguarantor whith SBA and shall have no right of contribution against SBA. The Undersigned further agrees that all liability hereunder shall continue notwithstanding payment by SBA under its Guaranty Agreement to the other lending institution.

The term "Undersigned" as used in this agreement shall mean the signer or signers of this agreeement, and such signers, if more than one, shall be jointly and severally liable hereunder. The Undersigned further agrees that all liability hereunder shall continue notwithstanding the incapacity, lack of authority, death, or disability of any one or more of the Undersigned, and that any failure by Lender or its assigns to file or enforce a claim against the estate of any of the Undersigned shall not operate to release any other of the Undersigned from liability hereunder. The failure of any other person to sign this guaranty shall not release or affect the liability of any signer hereof.

_____

_____

_____

_____

NOTE.—Corporate guarantors must execute guaranty in corporate name, by duly authorized officer, and seal must be affixed and duly attested; partnership guarantors must execute guaranty in firm name, together with signature of a general partner. Formally executed guaranty is to be delivered at the time of disbursement of loan.

☆ U.S. GPO: 1995-385-893/09106

(LIST COLLATERAL SECURING THE GUARANTY)

Figure 8.2b

U.S. Small Business Administration	OMB APPROVAL NO.: 3245-0200
Settlement Sheet	EXPIRATION DATE: 3/31/95

Lender (Name and Address - Include Zip Code)	Borrower (Name)
SBA Loan Number (10 digits)	Lender Computes Interest on a _____ day basis.

Sum of Prior disbursements $ _____ + This Disbursement $ _____ = Total $ _____

The provisions of 18 U.S.C. 1001 and 15 U.S.C. 645 provide certain criminal penalties for making false statements, willfully overvaluing collateral, or other prohibited acts. To induce SBA, directly or indirectly, to participate in this loan, the *Borrower*, subject to these provisions, acknowledges receipt of $ _____ on _____ and certifies (1) that the proceeds at this disbursement will be, and all previous disbursements have been, used in accordance with the Loan Authorization, (2) that there has been no substantial adverse change in financial condition, organization, operations, or fixed assets since application for this loan was filed or since the previous disbursement, and (3) that there are no liens or encumbrances against the real or personal property securing the loan except those disclosed in the application for this loan.

Lender certifies that disbursement of the loan proceeds was made and the loan proceeds were used as set forth below and in accordance with the Loan Authorization *by issuance of joint payee checks as detailed below, except checks for cash operating capital, cash to reimburse borrower for evidenced expenditures made after loan approval date for such authorized use of proceeds, or as otherwise directed by the Loan Authorization*, and that construction, paid with loan proceeds as listed below, has been completed. **(Any deviation from the Loan Authorization must be authorized in writing by SBA prior to expenditure of the loan funds.)**

See Paragraph _____ , of Authorization "Use of Proceeds"

Subparagraph	Name of Payee	Date and Amount of Payment	Purpose

To further induce SBA to participate in the loan, *Lender* certifies that neither the *Lender* nor its Associates, officers, agents, affiliates or attorneys have charged or will charge or receive, directly or indirectly, any bonus, fee, commission, or other payment or benefit, or require a compensating balance, Certificate of Deposit, or other security in connection with making or servicing of this loan (other than those reported on SBA Forms 4 or 159 "Compensation Agreement"). It is understood that all fees not approved by SBA are prohibited, except as may be specifically permitted by the Loan Authorization, SBA regulations or the SBA Form 750 "Guaranty Agreement".

Lender	Borrower
By _____	Signed _____
Date _____	Date _____

This Certification must be signed and returned to the SBA immediately after each disbursement. If there is a large number of checks, itemize on separate sheets, sign and attach hereto.

SBA Review By	Title	Date

The estimated burden for completion of this form is 1 hour per response. If you have any questions or comments concerning this estimate or any other aspects of this information collection, please contact Chief, Administrative Information Branch, U.S. Small Business Administration, Washington, D.C. 20416 and Clearance Officer, Paperwork Reduction Project (3245-0200), Office of Management and Budget, Washington, D.C. 20503.

SBA Form 1050 (8-93) REF SOP 70 50 Use 5-91 Edition Until Exhausted   Copy to: SBA, Lender, Borrower

*U.S. Government Printing Office: 1995 — 393-420/29013   Federal Recycling Program   Printed on Recycled Paper

Figure 8.3

- Waiving requirements for audited financial statements
- Approving payment of dividends and bonuses
- Deferring to maturity principal and interest payments totaling an amount less than 20 percent of the original loan amount
- Modifying insurance requirements

While notification to the SBA of any unilateral action taken is not required, it would be worthwhile to phone the SBA loan officer to advise of the action taken, or copy the SBA with the letter of advice sent to the borrower. This will serve to keep the SBA abreast of developments on the case as well as to maintain a healthy stream of communication between the lender and the local SBA office.

To obtain the fastest possible response from the SBA on requests requiring SBA concurrence, keep in mind that the decision will be based, in virtually all instances, on the same information that supported your decision to take the particular action. Generally, the kind of information that should be submitted with requests for concurrence would include the following:

- Reason for the proposed action along with benefits to borrower and ultimate collectibility
- Current financial data including a summation of the effects of the action on timely repayment
- Effect of the proposed action on our joint collateral position
- Summation of the account's servicing history
- Copies of relevant documents (e.g., appraisals, financial statements, buy and sale agreements)

LENDER'S DEMAND ON SBA GUARANTEE

The Loan Guarantee Agreement (SBA form 750) specifies the conditions under which SBA will purchase the guaranteed portion of the loan. The lender can request the SBA's purchase once an installment has remained unpaid for 61 days. Interest accrued for a reasonable period of time during which the lender has been attempting to collect will also be paid at the rate of interest in effect at the time the note goes into default.

The lender's written demand to purchase should be accompanied by a transcript of loan payments and all original loan documents assigned to the SBA. If the lender is to retain servicing of the account, copies of the loan documents should be forwarded; the originals should be held by the lender. A certificate of interest is prepared on SBA form 152, showing the percentage share of the loan, and is furnished the party not servicing the loan.

STEPS TO REQUEST SBA TO HONOR ITS GUARANTEE

1. Make written request of local SBA office.
2. Include Transcript of Account (SBA form 1149).

Form **4506**

(Rev. October 1994)

Department of the Treasury
Internal Revenue Service

Request for Copy or Transcript of Tax Form

▶ Please read instructions before completing this form.

▶ Please type or print clearly.

OMB No. 1545-0429

Note: *Do not use this form to get tax account information. Instead, see instructions below.*

1a Name shown on tax form	1b First social security number on tax form or employer identification number (See instructions.)
2a If a joint return, spouse's name shown on tax form	2b Second social security number on tax form

3　Current name, address (including apt., room, or suite no.), city, state, and ZIP code (See instructions.)

4　If copy of form or a tax return transcript is to be mailed to someone else, show the third party's name and address.

5　If we cannot find a record of your tax form and you want the payment refunded to the third party, check here . . . . ▶ ☐

6　If name in third party's records differs from line 1a above, show name here. (See instructions.) ▶

7　Check only one box to show what you want:

a ☐　Tax return transcript of Form 1040 series filed during the **current calendar year** and the **2 preceding calendar years.** (See instructions.) (The transcript gives most lines from the original return and schedule(s).) **There is no charge for a transcript request made before October 1, 1995.**

b ☐　Copy of tax form and all attachments (including Form(s) W-2, schedules, or other forms). **The charge is $14.00 for each period requested.**
　　Note: *If these copies must be certified for court or administrative proceedings, see instructions and check here* . . . . ▶ ☐

c ☐　Verification of nonfiling. **There is no charge for this.**

d ☐　Copy of Form(s) W-2 only. **There is no charge for this.** See instructions for when Form W-2 is available.
　　Note: *If the copy of Form W-2 is needed for its state information, check here* . . . . ▶ ☐

8　If this request is to meet a requirement of one of the following, check all boxes that apply.
　☐ Small Business Administration　☐ Department of Education　☐ Department of Veterans Affairs　☐ Financial Institution

9　**Tax form number** (Form 1040, 1040A, 941, etc.)

11	Amount due for copy of tax form:		
a	Cost for each period	$	14.00
b	Number of tax periods requested on line 10		
c	Total cost. Multiply line 11a by line 11b . .	$	0.00

10　**Tax period(s)** (year or period ended date). If more than four, see instructions.

Full payment must accompany your request. Make check or money order payable to "Internal Revenue Service."

Please Sign Here ▶

Signature. See instructions. If other than taxpayer, attach authorization document.　　　Date

Telephone number of requestor

Best time to call

Title (if line 1a above is a corporation, partnership, estate, or trust)

Instructions

A Change To Note.—Form 4506 may be used to request a tax return transcript of the Form 1040 series filed during the current calendar year and the 2 preceding calendar years. There is no charge for a tax return transcript requested before October 1, 1995 You should receive it within 10 workdays after we receive your request. For more details, see the instructions for line 7a.

Purpose of Form. — Use Form 4506 only to get a copy of a tax form, tax return transcript, verification of nonfiling, or a copy of Form W-2. But if you need a copy of your Form(s) W-2 for social security purposes only, do not use this form. Instead, contact your local Social Security Administration office.

Do not use this form to request Forms 1099 or tax account information. If you need a copy of a Form 1099, contact the payer. However, Form 1099 information is available by calling or visiting your local IRS office.

Note: *If you had your tax form filled in by a paid preparer, check first to see if you can get a copy from the preparer. This may save you both time and money.*

If you are requesting a copy of a tax form, please allow up to 60 days for delivery. However, if your request is for a tax return transcript, please allow 10 workdays after we receive your request. To avoid any delay, be sure to furnish all the information asked for on this form. You must allow 6 weeks after a tax form is filed before requesting a copy of it or a transcript.

Tax Account Information Only. —If you need a statement of your tax account showing any later changes that you or the IRS made to the original return, you will need to request tax account information. Tax account information will list certain items from your return including any later changes.

To request tax account information, do not complete this form. Instead, write or visit an IRS office or call the IRS toll-free number listed in your telephone directory.

If you want your tax account information sent to a third party, complete Form 8821, Tax Information Authorization. You may get this form by calling 1-800-TAX-FORM (1-800-829-3676).

Line 1b. — Enter your employer identification number only if you are requesting a copy of a business tax form. Otherwise, enter the first social security number shown on the tax form.

Line 2b. — If requesting a copy or transcript of a joint tax form, enter the second social security number shown on the tax form.

Note: If you do not complete line 1b and, if applicable, line 2b, there may be a delay in processing your request.

Line 3. — For a tax return transcript, a copy of Form W-2, or for verification of nonfiling, if your address on line 3 is different from the address shown on the last return you filed and you have not notified the IRS of a new address, either in writing or by filing Form 8822, Change of Address, you must attach either —

(Continued on back)

Figure 8.4a

76

• A copy of two pieces of identification that have your signature, or

• An original notarized statement affirming your identity.

Line 4. —If you have named someone else to receive the tax form or tax return transcript (such as a CPA, an enrolled agent, a scholarship board, or a mortgage lender), enter the name and address of the individual. If we cannot find a record of your tax form, we will notify the third party directly that we cannot fill the request.

Line 6. —Enter the name of the client, student, or applicant if it is different from the name shown on line 1a. For example, the name on line 1a may be the parent of a student applying for financial aid. In this case, you would enter the student's name on line 6 so the scholarship board can associate the tax form or tax return transcript with their file.

Line 7a. —If you are requesting a tax return transcript, check this box. Also, on line 9 enter the tax form number, on line 10 enter the tax period, and on line 11c enter "no charge." However, if you prefer, you may get a tax return transcript by calling or visiting your local IRS office.

A tax return transcript shows most lines from the original return (including accompanying forms and schedules). It does not reflect any changes you or the IRS made to the original return. If you have changes to your tax return and want a statement of your tax account with the changes, see **Tax Account Information Only** on the front. A tax return transcript is available for any returns of the 1040 series (such as Form 1040, 1040A, or 1040EZ) filed during the current calendar year and the 2 preceding calendar years.

In many cases, a tax return transcript will meet the requirement of any lending institution such as a financial institution, the Department of Education, or the Small Business Administration. It may also be used to verify that you did not claim any itemized deductions for a residence.

Line 7b. — If you are requesting a certified copy of a tax form for court or administrative proceedings, check the box to the right of line 7b. It will take at least 60 days to process your request.

Line 7c. —Check this box only if you want proof from the IRS that you did not file a return for the year. Also, on line 10 enter the tax period for which you requesting verification of nonfiling, and on line 11c, enter "no charge."

Line 7d. —If you need only a copy of your Form(s) W-2, check this box. Also, on line 9 enter "Form(s) W-2 only," and on line 11c enter "no charge."

Forms W-2 are available only from 1978 to the present. Form W-2 information is only available 18 months after it is submitted by your employer. But you can get this information earlier if you request a copy of your tax return and all attachments. See line 7b.

If you are requesting a copy of your spouse's Form W-2, you must have your spouse's signature on the request. If you lost your Form W-2 or have not received it by the time you are ready to prepare your tax return, contact your employer.

Line 10. —Enter the year(s) of the tax form or tax return transcript you are requesting. For fiscal-year filers or requests for quarterly tax forms, enter the date the period ended; for example, 3/31/93, 6/30/93, etc. If you need more than four different tax periods, use additional Forms 4506. Tax forms filed 6 or more years ago may not be available for making copies. However, tax account information is generally still available for these periods.

Line 11c. —Write your social security number or Federal employer identification number and "Form 4506 Request" on your check or money order. If we cannot fill your request, we will refund your payment.

Signature. —Requests for copies of tax forms or tax return transcripts to be sent to a third party must be signed by the person whose name is shown on line 1a or by a person authorized to receive the requested information.

Copies of tax forms or tax return transcripts for a jointly filed return may be furnished to either the husband or the wife. Only one signature is required. Sign form 4506 exactly as your name appeared on the original tax form. If you changed your name, also sign your current name.

For a corporation, the signature of the president of the corporation, or any principal officer and the secretary, or the principal officer and another officer are generally required. For more details on who may obtain tax information on corporations, partnerships, estates, and trusts, see Internal Revenue Code section 6103.

If you are **not** the taxpayer shown on line 1a, you must attach your authorization to receive a copy of the requested tax form or tax return transcript. You may **attach a copy of the authorization document** if the original has already been filed with the IRS. This will generally be a **power of attorney** (Form 2848), or **other authorization,** such as Form 8821, or evidence of entitlement (for Title 11 Bankruptcy or Receivership Proceedings). If the taxpayer is deceased, you must send Letters Testamentary or other evidence to establish that you are authorized to act for the taxpayer's estate.

Note: *Form 4506 must be received by the IRS within 60 days after the date you signed and dated the request.*

Where To File. — Mail Form 4506 with the correct total payment attached, if required, to the **Internal Revenue Service Center** for the place where you lived when the requested tax form was filed.

Note: *You must use a separate form for each service center from which you are requesting a copy of your tax form or tax return transcript.*

If you lived in:	Use this address:
New Jersey, New York (New York City and counties of Nassau, Rockland, Suffolk, and Westchester)	1040 Waverly Ave. Photocopy Unit Stop 532 Holtsville, NY 11742
New York (all other counties), Connecticut, Maine, Massachusetts, New Hampshire, Rhode Island, Vermont	310 Lowell St. Photocopy Unit Stop 679 Andover, MA 01810
Florida, Georgia, South Carolina	4800 Buford Hwy. Photocopy Unit Stop 91 Doraville, GA 30362

Indiana, Kentucky, Michigan, Ohio, West Virginia	P.O. Box 145500 Photocopy Unit Stop 524 Cincinnati, OH 45250
Kansas, New Mexico, Oklahoma, Texas	3651 South Interregional Hwy. Photocopy Unit Stop 6716 Austin, TX 73301
Alaska, Arizona, California (counties of Alpine, Amador, Butte, Calaveras, Colusa, Contra Costa, Del Norte, El Dorado, Glenn, Humboldt, Lake, Lassen, Marin, Mendocino, Modoc, Napa, Nevada, Placer, Plumas, Sacramento, San Joaquin, Shasta, Sierra, Siskiyou, Solano, Sonoma, Sutter, Tehama, Trinity, Yolo, and Yuba), Colorado, Idaho, Montana, Nebraska, Nevada, North Dakota, Oregon, South Dakota, Utah, Washington, Wyoming	P.O. Box 9953 Photocopy Unit Stop 6734 Ogden, UT 84409
California (all other counties), Hawaii	5045 E. Butler Avenue Photocopy Unit Stop 52180 Fresno, CA 93888
Illinois, Iowa, Minnesota, Missouri, Wisconsin	2306 E. Bannister Road Photocopy Unit Stop 57A Kansas City, MO 64999
Alabama, Arkansas, Louisiana, Mississippi, North Carolina, Tennessee	P.O. Box 30309 Photocopy Unit Stop 46 Memphis, TN 38130
Delaware, District of Columbia, Maryland, Pennsylvania, Virginia, a foreign country, or A.P.O. or F.P.O. address	11601 Roosevelt Blvd. Photocopy Unit DP 536 Philadelphia, PA 19255

Privacy Act and Paperwork Reduction Act Notice. — We ask for the information on this form to establish your right to gain access to your tax form or transcript under the Internal Revenue Code, including sections 6103 and 6109. We need it to gain access to your tax form or transcript in our files and properly respond to your request. If you do not furnish the information, we will not be able to fill your request. We may give the information to the Department of Justice or other appropriate law enforcement official, as provided by law.

The time needed to complete and file this form will vary depending on individual circumstances. The estimated average time is:

Record keeping	13 min.
Learning about the law or the form	7 min.
Preparing the form	25 min.
Copying, assembling, and sending the form to the IRS . .	17 min.

If you have comments concerning the accuracy of these time estimates or suggestions for making this form more simple, we would be happy to here from you. You can write to both the **Internal Revenue Service,** Attention: Reports Clearance Officer, PC:FP, Washington, DC 20224; and the **Office of Management and Budget,** Paperwork Reduction Project (1545-0429), Washington, DC 20503. **DO NOT** send this form to either of these offices. Instead, **see Where To File** on this page.

Figure 8.4b

3. Include copies of promissory note and all loan instruments properly assigned to the SBA without recourse, assuming the SBA will take over servicing. Originals must be received by the SBA before a check will be issued.

SBA attempts to complete the purchase within 30 days of receipt of this information.

Denial of Liability

Occasionally, the SBA has denied a lender's demand for payment under the guarantee. This is a very rare occurrence and should not cause undue fear that SBA will arbitrarily deny liability on any particular loan. The SBA makes every reasonable effort to avoid a denial of liability, often renegotiating the guarantee to reach an amicable settlement with the lender.

The reasons supporting a decision to deny liability almost invariably center on a lender's failure to close or service a loan in accordance with prudent, accepted standards. Most denials occur because loan proceeds were used for purposes not approved and cited in the loan authorization, or required liens were not taken or perfected.

Reporting Requirements

Once an SBA-guaranteed loan has been disbursed, required reports are minimal. While frequent communication between the lender and SBA loan officers is encouraged, the Quarterly Guaranteed Loan Status Report is the only routine report required. The format is prepared in the SBA's fiscal office in Denver and mailed directly to the lender ten days before the end of each three-month period. After completing the report, the lender should forward it to the local SBA office.

Where the SBA has purchased the guaranteed portion of the loan and has agreed to the lender's continued servicing of the loan, the SBA's share of any payments received will be forwarded to the SBA along with a Report on Transactions Loans Serviced by Banks (SBA form 172). If the lender is not to retain servicing, confirmed copies of all loan instruments along with an executed Participation Certificate (SBA form 152) should be forwarded to the local office. No other reports are required.

9 Other Contact Organizations

The following are organizations that can provide needed support for your business whether you're starting up or a more mature company.

National Association for the Self-Employed, Member Services
2121 Precinct Line Road
Hurst, TX 76054
(800) 232-NASE

This organization represents over 320,000 entrepreneurs, most of whom have five or fewer employees. The annual membership fee of $72 provides more than 100 benefits including SHOPTALK 800 (an advice hotline), legislative advocacy, and discount vehicle leases, office equipment, magazines, and travel services. It publishes *Self-Employed America, Capitol Connections Update,* and the *Small Business Resource Guide* in conjunction with the SBA.

National Federation of Independent Business
600 Maryland Ave. SW, Suite 700
Washington, DC 20024
(800) NFIB-NOW

This organization provides lobbying efforts based on member responses to bimonthly ballots on crucial issues. It publishes *Independent Business* magazine and *Capitol Coverage,* which are available to its 600,000 members. Membership fee ranges from $100 to $1,000.

The Council of Growing Companies
7910 Woodmont Ave., Suite 1206
Bethesda, MD 20814
(301) 951-1138

Its membership consists of 1,800 CEOs, or companies with $3 million to $100 million in revenue. It provides lobbying, education, and networking via seminars, national conferences, and international trade missions. Offers CEOlink on-line, corporate partnerships, a national directory and database, and exposure through a weekly segment on PBS's *Small Business Today.* It publishes *Agenda* magazine and *Progress* newsletter. Annual membership fee is $600.

> National Association of Women Business Owners (NAWBO)
> 1413 K Street NW, Suite 637
> Washington, DC 20005
> (301) 608-2590

> National Foundation for Women Business Owners (NFWBO)
> 1100 Wayne Ave., Suite 830
> Silver Spring, MD 20910-5603
> (301) 495-4975

NAWBO fosters leadership training, lobbying, international trade, and financial support for nearly 7,000 members. Member dues are $75 plus some additional chapter dues. It offers a forum on Women's Wire on-line, investment, credit, and mentor programs, and an economic summit, business expo, and annual meeting. It publishes *Enterprising Women* magazine. NFWBO—NAWBO's research and education arm—represents the Gillian Rudd Leadership Institute, a management retreat for established women business owners.

> National Minority Supplier Development Council
> 1412 Broadway, 11th Floor
> New York, NY 10018
> (212) 944-2430

This organization builds business relationships between corporate purchasers and minority-owned business members through referrals, business opportunity fairs, an annual conference, and inclusion of a database of 15,000 certified minority suppliers. It offers working capital loans, research, training, and technical assistance.

> Environmental Protection Agency Office of Asbestos and Small
>   Business Ombudsman
> 401 M Street SW
> Washington, DC 20460
> (800) 368-5888

This office provides an EPA Helpline for Small Business that offers information on regulation requirements and proposals, helps to resolve complaints, and provides publications to help small companies get through the maze of environmental compliance.

Section Five

10 Financial Assistance Programs

The SBA offers a variety of loans and financial assistance to eligible small businesses, to privately owned small business investment companies, and to area development companies.

- *Regular Business Loan.* The majority of SBA's business loans, both regular 7(a) and special loans, are made by private lenders with partial guarantees by the SBA.

- *Special Loan Programs* include: Small Loans, Contract Loans, Small General Contractor Loans, Seasonal Line of Credit Guarantees, International Trade Loan Guarantees, Export Working Capital, Minority Enterprise Development Programs, Handicapped Assistance Loans, Pollution Control Financing, Microloan Program, LowDoc Loans, and Disaster Loans.

- *Surety Bond Guarantees.* The SBA makes the bonding process accessible to small contractors who find bonding unavailable to them. The agency will guarantee to a qualified surety up to 80 percent of losses incurred under bid, payment, or performance bonds issued to contractors on contracts valued up to $1.25 million. The contracts may be used for construction, supplies, or services provided for government or nongovernment work.

- *Small Business Investment Companies (SBICs).* SBICs are privately organized and licensed by the SBA; a share of their financing is guaranteed by the SBA. The program makes equity capital and long-term debt financing available to small firms for their growth, expansion, and modernization. They primarily assist small firms with significant growth potential, or new small firms in new industries.

- *Certified Development Company Programs (504).* These programs are designed to enhance community economic development and to create or save jobs. The SBA offers state and local development companies special financing that enables them to extend long-term, fixed-asset financing to small businesses operating in their area.

- *SBA Direct Loan Program.* Direct loans from the SBA are available to eligible small businesses that are unable to obtain the needed credit through either conventional loans or the SBA's guarantee loan program. Direct loan funds are very limited and are presently available only to Vietnam-era veterans, handicapped and sheltered workshops, 8(a)-certified companies, and companies owned by low-income individuals or those located in low-income or labor surplus areas.

Eligible businesses are those that present a letter of declination from a lender in communities with a population of 200,000 or less. Letters of declination are necessary from two unaffiliated lenders if the population exceeds 200,000. These letters should include the name and telephone number of the persons contacted at the lending institution, the amount and terms of the loan requested, the reasons for decline, and a statement that the lender will not extend the requested credit with or without the SBA's guarantee. The SBA anticipates that lenders will issue decline letters based on their policies and analysis of the credit factors, not as an accommodation. Applicants must also meet, as a minimum, the same credit, size, and eligibility requirements that applicants for guarantee loans must meet.

Loan amounts are generally limited to $150,000 to any one borrower for any combination of direct loans. Loan proceeds and maturities of direct loans are generally the same as those available under the guarantee loan program. Note, however, that none of the special short-term loan guarantees are available as direct loans.

WOMEN'S BUSINESS OWNERSHIP

The SBA sponsors special programs for women business owners and those interested in starting their own businesses. Regional conferences focus on such topics as business expansion, while local training programs cover general business topics or specialized areas such as home-based businesses, franchising, or selling to the federal government.

OFFICE OF VETERANS AFFAIRS

The SBA created the Office of Veterans Affairs in response to a congressional mandate that requires special consideration to veterans and all their survivors or dependents in all the SBA's programs. This mandate requires the SBA to take positive steps to assure that veterans are aware of and participate in each of the agency's programs.

The SBA must do the following:

- Check the needs of the veteran community through outreach with veteran organizations and community associations.
- Assure that veterans are aware of all of the SBA's programs and develop applications to meet specific veteran needs.
- Start joint action with the SBA's program offices to assure veteran participation in programs where they are not represented.

- Check performance by the SBA field offices for veteran participation in SBA's programs.
- Report the agency's compliance with the congressional mandate to Congress.

SMALL BUSINESS DEVELOPMENT CENTER PROGRAM

The SBA organized the Small Business Development Center Program to make management assistance and counseling widely available to present and prospective small-business owners. SBDCs offer "one-stop" assistance to small businesses, providing a wide variety of information and guidance in central and easily accessible locations.

The program is a cooperative effort of the private sector, the educational community, and federal, state, and local governments. It enhances economic development by providing small businesses with management and technical assistance.

There are now 56 small-business development centers—one in every state (Texas has four), the District of Columbia, Puerto Rico, and the U.S. Virgin Islands—with a network of more than 950 service locations. In each state there is a lead organization that sponsors the SBDC and manages the program. The lead organization coordinates program services offered to small businesses through a network of subcenters and satellite locations in each state. Subcenters are located at colleges, universities, community colleges, vocational schools, chambers of commerce, and economic development corporations.

SBDC assistance is tailored to the local community and the needs of individual clients. Each center develops services in cooperation with local SBA district offices to ensure statewide coordination with other available resources.

Each center has a director, staff members, volunteers, and part-time personnel. Qualified individuals recruited from professional and trade associations, the legal and banking community, academia, chambers of commerce, and the Service Corps of Retired Executives (SCORE) are among those who donate their services. SBDCs also use paid consultants, consulting engineers, and testing laboratories from the private sector to help clients who need specialized expertise.

Funding

The SBA provides 50 percent or less of the operating funds for each state SBDC; one or more sponsors provide the rest. These matching fund contributions are provided by state legislatures, private sector foundations and grants, state and local chambers of commerce, state-chartered economic development corporations, public and private universities, vocational and technical schools, community colleges, and so forth. Increasingly, sponsors' contributions exceed the minimum 50 percent matching share.

What the Program Does

The SBDC Program is designed to deliver up-to-date counseling, training, and technical assistance in all aspects of small-business management. SBDC services include, but are not limited to, assisting small businesses with financial, marketing, production, organization, engineering and technical problems, and feasibility studies. Special SBDC programs and economic development activities include international trade assistance, technical assistance, procurement assistance, venture capital formation, and rural development.

The SBDCs also make special efforts to reach minority members of socially and economically disadvantaged groups, veterans, women, and the disabled. Assistance is provided to both current or potential small-business owners. They also provide assistance to small businesses applying for Small Business Innovation and Research (SBIR) grants from federal agencies.

Eligibility

Assistance from an SBDC is available to anyone interested in beginning a small business for the first time or improving or expanding an existing small business, who cannot afford the services of a private consultant.

SMALL BUSINESS DEVELOPMENT CENTERS

University of Alabama, Birmingham, AL   (205) 934-7260
University of Alaska/Anchorage, Anchorage, AK   (907) 274-7232
Maricopa County Community College, Tempe, AZ   (602) 731-8202
University of Arkansas, Little Rock, AR   (501) 324-9043
California Trade and Commerce Agency, Sacramento, CA
        (916) 324-5068
Office of Business Development, Denver, CO   (303) 892-3809
University of Connecticut, Storrs, CT   (203) 486-4135
University of Delaware, Newark, DE   (302) 831-2747
Howard University, Washington, DC   (202) 806-1550
University of West Florida, Pensacola, FL   (904) 444-2060
University of Georgia, Athens, GA   (706) 542-6762
University of Hawaii at Hilo, Hilo, HI   (808) 933-3515
Boise State University, Boise, ID   (208) 385-1640
Dept. of Commerce & Community Affairs, Springfield, IL   (207) 524-5856
Economic Dev. Council, Indianapolis, IN   (317) 264-6871
Iowa State University, Ames, IA   (515) 292-6351
Wichita State University, Wichita, KS   (316) 689-3193
University of Kentucky, Lexington, KY   (606) 257-7668
Northeast Louisiana University, Monroe, LA   (318) 342-5506
University of Southern Maine, Portland, ME   (207) 780-4420
Dept. of Economic and Employment Development, Baltimore, MD
        (301) 333-6995
University of Massachusetts, Amherst, MA   (413) 545-6301
Wayne State University, Detroit, MI   (313) 577-4848
Dept. of Trade and Economic Development, St. Paul, MN   (612) 297-5770
University of Mississippi, University, MS   (601) 232-5001
University of Missouri, Columbia, MO   (314) 882-0344

Department of Commerce, Helena, MT   (406) 444-4780
University of Nebraska at Omaha, Omaha, NE   (402) 554-2521
University of Nevada in Reno, Reno, NV   (702) 784-1717
University of New Hampshire, Durham, NH   (603) 862-2200
Rutgers University, Newark, NJ   (201) 648-5950
Santa Fe Community College, Santa Fe, NM   (505) 438-1362
State University of New York, Albany, NY   (518) 443-5398
University of North Carolina, Raleigh, NC   (919) 571-4154
University of North Dakota, Grand Forks, ND   (701) 777-3700
Dept. of Development, Columbus, OH   (614) 466-2711
S.E. Oklahoma State University, Durant, OK   (405) 924-0277
Lane Community College, Eugene, OR   (503) 726-2250
University of Pennsylvania, Philadelphia, PA   (215) 898-1219
University of Puerto Rico, Mayaguez, PR   (809) 834-3590
Bryant College, Springfield, RI   (401) 232-6111
University of South Carolina, Columbia, SC   (803) 777-4907
University of South Dakota, Vermillion, SD   (605) 677-5498
University of Memphis, Memphis, TN   (901) 678-2500
Dallas Community College, Dallas, TX   (214) 565-5833
University of Houston, Houston, TX   (713) 752-8444
Texas Tech University, Lubbock, TX   (806) 745-3973
University of Texas at San Antonio, San Antonio, TX   (210) 558-2450
University of Utah, Salt Lake City, UT   (801) 581-7905
Vermont Technical College, Randolph Center, VT   (802) 728-9101
University of the Virgin Islands, St. Thomas, US VI   (809) 776-3206
Dept. of Economic Development, Richmond, VA   (804) 371-8258
Washington State University, Pullman, WA   (509) 335-1576
Governor's Office of Community and Industrial Development, Charleston, WV
    (304) 558-2960
University of Wisconsin, Madison, WI   (608) 263-7794
University of Wyoming, Laramie, WY   (307) 766-3505

SMALL BUSINESS DEVELOPMENT CENTERS

Fiscal Year 1992 Funding

ALABAMA	$1,224,012	LOUISIANA	1,272,423
ALASKA	252,706	MAINE	441,100
ARIZONA	866,282	MARYLAND	1,225,043
ARKANSAS	753,436	MASSACHUSETTS	0[1]
CALIFORNIA	3,203,725	MICHIGAN	2,680,831
COLORADO	974,001	MINNESOTA	1,313,639
CONNECTICUT	969,465	MISSISSIPPI	805,138
DELAWARE	270,701	MISSOURI	1,521,406
D.C.	540,348	MONTANA	320,739
FLORIDA	3,203,725	NEBRASKA	538,481
GEORGIA	1,900,408	NEVADA	433,635
HAWAII	408,455	NEW HAMPSHIRE	408,182
IDAHO	379,966	NEW JERSEY	1,468,544
ILLINOIS	3,272,295	NEW MEXICO	521,050
INDIANA	1,551,518	NY (UPSTATE)	0[1]
IOWA	871,000	NY (DOWNSTATE)	1,801,871
KANSAS	765,300	NORTH CAROLINA	1,529,424
KENTUCKY	1,123,309	NORTH DAKOTA	277,324

OHIO	2,208,608	TEXAS (LUBBOCK)	575,020
OKLAHOMA	973,642	TEXAS (S. ANT.)	958,610
OREGON	889,545	UTAH	578,044
PENNSYLVANIA	3,399,002	VERMONT	256,300
PUERTO RICO	863,000	VIRGIN ISLANDS	200,000
RHODE ISLAND	378,300	VIRGINIA	855,040
SOUTH CAROLINA	1,068,922	WASHINGTON	1,452,239
SOUTH DAKOTA	293,649	WEST VIRGINIA	576,862
TENNESSEE	1,454,724	WISCONSIN	1,457,497
TEXAS (DALLAS)	336,953[2]	WYOMING	221,263
TEXAS (HOUSTON)	1,384,182		
		TOTAL	$58,929,525

[1] Agreement expiration date extended one day from 9/29/92 to 9/30/92. SBDC will be re-funded on 10/1/92 from fiscal year 1993 funds.
[2] Three-month agreement for the period 10/1/92 through 12/31/92.

SMALL BUSINESS INSTITUTE PROGRAM

The Small Business Institute (SBI) Program gives small-business owners an opportunity to receive intensive management counseling from qualified graduate and undergraduate business students working under expert faculty guidance. The SBI Program was established in 1972 by the SBA in cooperation with 36 colleges and universities. Today, more than 500 schools of business participate in the SBI Program.

The emphasis of the program is on practical, realistic, and affordable solutions to problems confronting individual small businesses. Students who best achieve these goals receive national awards each year.

Benefits and Services

Every year, about 18,500 SBI students provide assistance to approximately 7,500 businesses. SBI teams have counseled approximately 150,000 businesses to date, provided 370,000 students with real world experience in applying business skills, and involved 6,000 professors in local economic development efforts. Over the course of an academic term the SBI students meet frequently with the small-business owner to solve specific management problems. Business clients receive a detailed report and an oral presentation on the actions needed to improve their business operations.

SBI counseling studies focus on the full range of management problems and solutions, including market studies, accounting systems, personnel policies, production design, exporting, expansion feasibility, and strategic planning.

Also, SBI teams occasionally engage in community development projects that involve other SBA business development resources, such as Small Business Development Centers (SBDCs). The program also involves SCORE whose volunteers frequently advise SBI teams and offer follow-up counseling to clients.

Eligibility

All small-business owners/managers are eligible to participate. The business must be independently owned and operated, and not dominant in its field, and must conform to SBA business size standards. Interested business people should call their local SBA district office to learn how to contact the nearest SBI school.

Any accredited four-year college or university can contact the SBA about becoming an SBI school.

Administration of the Program

Student teams counsel their small-business clients under the supervision of a faculty adviser. Small-business institute directors work closely with the SBA, which, along with the Small Business Institute Directors Association (SBIDA), shares responsibility for direction and administration of the SBI Program. Both the SBA and the national SBIDA negotiate the statement-of-work document that defines the SBI contract performance. This activity is authorized under the Small Business Act of 1953, section 2, as amended, Public Law 95-510, U.S.C. 637, and appears in the Catalog of Federal Domestic Assistance in section 59.005, Business Development Assistance to Small Business.

Funding

Total annual funding for the SBI Program is allocated to ten SBA regional offices for distribution to local SBI schools at the rate of $500 (as of fiscal year 1992) per successfully completed case.

Additional Information

For additional information about the nearest SBI services, contact your local SBA office and ask for the business development officer.

11 Business Initiatives

Providing technical and managerial aids is the mission of the Office of Business Initiatives (BI). The BI cosponsors small-business management courses and conferences, prepares general business informational brochures and management and technical assistance booklets. BI encourages research into the operational/management problems of small-business concerns. Through the agency's field offices and major resource partners—Small Business Institutes (SBI), Service Corps of Retired Executives (SCORE), Small Business Development Centers (SBDC), and professional trade associations—the BI counsels and conducts management workshops, training, and courses for established as well as prospective small-business persons, and enlists the aid of volunteer executives to assist small-business persons in overcoming and solving their management problems. Also, BI contracts with college and university schools of business for counseling services and training by qualified students.

Working through the Office of Marketing (OM) and the Office of Business Education and Resource Management (BERM), BI manages a mix of programs to educate the small-business person and address business-related issues concerning the small-business community. The OM provides marketing support to field offices and other agency program areas, and manages BI's publication and videotape program and outreach efforts. The BERM directs the 13,000 SCORE and the 530 SBI colleges and universities, develops conferences for special initiatives, provides technical expertise for management assistance publications, and maintains the Business Development Management Information System (BDMIS) to track program delivery.

BUSINESS DEVELOPMENT ASSISTANCE

The SBA provides business development assistance to exporters, including trade counseling, training, legal assistance, and publications. (See the preceeding section for additional information.)

COUNSELING

Counseling is available through SBA's resource partners: the Service Corps of Retired Executives (SCORE), the Small Business Development Centers (SBDCs) and Small Business Institutes (SBIs). SCORE is an organization of nearly 13,000 retired and active executives who volunteer their time to provide management and technical assistance to small businesses. A SCORE counselor can also assist you in developing an international business plan. The local SBA office can match you with a SCORE volunteer experienced in exporting.

SBDCs, located on college and university campuses, provide a wide variety of information services at more than 900 locations nationwide. SBDC services include, but are not limited to, financial guidance, marketing, production, organizational development, engineering and feasibility studies, and technical assistance. Some SBDCs have designated international trade centers; all SBDCs provide export counseling, referral, and/or training.

In conjunction with colleges and universities across the United States, the SBA has established over 500 SBIs. Under the supervision of instructors, upper-level undergraduate and graduate business students provide intensive management assistance to small businesses that need special help.

12 Small and Short-Term Loan Programs

Section 7(a) of the Small Business Act authorizes the SBA to make and guarantee loans to small businesses, when the necessary financing is unavailable on reasonable terms through normal lending channels. The SBA's basic guarantee program is generally used to fund the varied long-term capital needs of small businesses, as seen by the fact that 96 percent of fiscal year 1989 guaranteed loans were approved with maturities of over three years.

In addition to its regular loan program, the SBA has designed a number of specialized programs to meet the particular needs of various segments of the small-business community. These programs are the particular subject of this book.

SMALL LOAN PROGRAM

The SBA started the Small Loan Program to meet the ever-growing need for loans of $50,000 or less. These loans will be particularly valuable to small firms in the service sector. A simplified application form (SBA form 4 Short Form, see Figure 12.1) has been designed by the SBA to make the program easier to use.

Under this program, the SBA changed the guarantee fee to participating lenders and simplified the application form to encourage lenders to consider SBA-guaranteed loans of $50,000 or less. The change in the program allows lenders making SBA-guaranteed loans of $50,000 or less with maturities greater than 12 months to retain half of the guarantee fee that is normally paid to the SBA. For example, a $50,000 loan with a 90 percent guarantee has an SBA-guaranteed portion of $45,000, and the 2 percent guarantee fee would be $900. Under the new changes, the lender may retain $450 and forward $450 to SBA or, at its option, the lender may choose not to charge the small business borrower the half of the guarantee that it could have retained.

U.S. Small Business Administration
Application for Small Business Loan
(Short Form)
(May be used for Participation Loans of $50,000 and under)

OMB Approval No: 3245-0016
Expiration Date: 6/30/94

Applicant	Address
Name of Business	**Tax I.D. No.**
Street Address	**Tel. No. (Include A/C)** ( ).
City **County** **State** **Zip**	**No. of Employees (including subsidiaries and affiliates)**
Type of Business **Date Business Established**	**At Time of Application** _____ **If Loan is Approved** _____
Bank of Business Account and Address	**Subsidiaries or Affiliates** _____ **(Separate from Above)**
Amount Requested	**Show how the proceeds are to be used (round to the nearest hundreds)**
Term Requested _____ yrs.	

The following schedules must be completed and submitted as a part of the loan application. (Applicant's name and address need only be provided once.) <u>ALL SCHEDULES MUST BE SIGNED AND DATED BY THE PERSON SIGNING THIS FORM:</u>

1. Include financial statements of the applicant as listed below: <u>ALL FINANCIAL STATEMENTS MUST BE SIGNED AND DATED.</u>

    a. For an <u>existing</u> business, include yearend financial statements composed of a balance sheet, income statement and reconciliation of net worth for each year in business up to three years. (Federal tax returns may be substituted for income statements.) In addition, submit a balance sheet and income statement for the current period (within 90 days of filing of the application) together with an aging of accounts receivable and payable. A projection of income and expenses for one year after the proposed loan is most helpful and may be requested by SBA.

    b. For a <u>new</u> business, prepare a balance sheet reflecting the assets, liabilities and net worth of the business assuming the loan is approved and disbursed. In addition, provide a projection of income and expenses for one year after the loan is disbursed.

2. List all assets to be pledged as collateral.

    a. For machinery and/or equipment, provide an itemized list that contains identification numbers for all items with an original value greater than $500.

    Collateral lists additionally should contain the year acquired, original cost, present market value, current balance owed, and name of lienholders. Mark this <u>Schedule A</u>. (SBA Form 4, Schedule A, or a computer-generated facsimile, <u>may</u> be used for this purpose.)

3. The following SBA forms must be submitted by each owner (20% or more ownership), partner, or officer:

    a. A current personal financial statement (SBA Form 413 may be used for this purpose),

    b. SBA Form 912, Personal History Statement. (This also may be required of hired managers with authority to commit the applicant.)

4. Please provide the following information (in the order shown below) for all members of management including owners, partners, officers and directors :

    <u>Name, Social Security Number</u>, <u>Position held</u>, <u>Home Address</u>, <u>Percentage Ownship (Total 100%)</u>, *<u>Date of Entry/Discharge from Military Service</u> ,*<u>Race</u>, *<u>Sex</u> (*This data is collected for statistical purposes and has no bearing on the credit decision.)

    In addition, provide a brief description of the educational, technical and business background for all people listed under management. Mark this <u>Schedule B.</u>

5. Please supply the following information (in the order shown below) on all the applicant's short-term and long-term debt. Indicate by an asterisk (*) items to be paid by loan proceeds and give reasons for payments.

    <u>Orig. Date</u>, <u>Orig. Amt ($)</u> , <u>Lender</u>, <u>Present Bal($)</u>, <u>Rate of Int.</u>, <u>Maturity Date</u>, <u>Monthly Pmt($)</u>, <u>Collateral</u>, <u>Current or Past Due</u>

    (Principal balance shown should agree with the amounts on the latest balance sheet submitted.) Mark this <u>Schedule C.</u>

6. Please sign and date SBA Form 1624 regarding certification of debarment and suspension.

PLEASE NOTE: The estimated burden hours for the completion of SBA Forms 4 (short form) and 4I is 19.5 hours per response. If you have any questions or comments concerning this estimate or any other aspect of this information collection please contact, Chief Administrative Information Branch, U.S. Small Business Administration, Washington, D.C. 20416 and Gary Waxman, Clearance Officer, Paperwork Reduction Project (3245-0016), Office of Management and Budget, Washington, D.C. 20503.

SBA Form (5-92) Short Form

Figure 12.1a

COMPLETE THE FOLLOWING INFORMATION ONLY IF IT APPLIES TO YOUR APPLICATION

7.   If you have any co-signers and/or guarantors for this loan, please submit their names, tax identification number, addresses and personal financial statements. Mark this <u>Schedule E.</u>

8.   If you are buying machinery and/or equipment with the loan, you must include a list of the equipment and cost (as quoted by the supplier) and the supplier's name, address and telephone number. Mark this <u>Schedule F.</u>

9.   If you, your business, or any of the officers of your business are, or have been, involved in pending lawsuits, bankruptcy or insolvency proceedings, please provide the details. Mark this <u>Schedule G.</u>

10. If you or your spouse or any member of your household, or anyone who owns, manages or directs your business or their spouses or members of their households, work for the Small Business Administration, Small Business Advisory Council, SCORE, ACE, any Federal agency, or the participating lender, please provide the name and address of the person and the office where employed. Mark this <u>Schedule H.</u>

11. If the applicant, its owners or majority stockholders own or have a controlling interest in other businesses, please provide their names and the relationship with your company along with the most recent yearend financial statements for each affiliate. Mark this <u>Schedule I.</u>

12. If the applicant buys from, sells to, or uses the services of any concern in which someone in your company has a significant financial interest, please provide details. Mark this <u>Schedule J.</u>

13. If the applicant or any principals or affiliates have ever requested previous SBA or other Government financing, or are delinquent on the repayment of any Federal debt, supply the following information: Identify the applicant, name the Government agency, date of request, whether approved or declined, original amount of the loan, present balance, monthly payments, whether current or past due, and purpose of the loan. Mark this <u>Schedule K.</u>

14. If anyone assisted in the preparation of this application other than the applicant, please list the name(s), occupation(s), their address(es), total fees paid and fees due. Mark this <u>Schedule L.</u>

FRANCHISE LOANS ONLY

15. If the applicant is a franchise, include a copy of the Franchise Agreement and a copy of the Federal Trade Commission disclosure statement available from the Franchisor (by law). Mark this <u>Schedule M.</u>

FOR CONSTRUCTION AND/OR RENOVATIONS OVER $10,000

16. Include as a separate schedule (schedule N) the estimated cost of the project as well as a statement of the source of any additional funds beyond the loan requested. Mark this <u>Schedule N.</u>

18. Provide copies of preliminary construction plans and specifications. Include them as <u>Schedule O.</u> Final plans will be required prior to disbursement.

EXPORT LOANS ONLY

19. If loan proceeds will be used for exporting, check here_____

TO BE COMPLETED BY ALL APPLICANTS AGREEMENTS AND CERTIFICATIONS

Agreements of Nonemployment of SBA Personnel: I agree that if SBA approves this loan application, I will not, for at least two years, hire as an employee or consultant anyone that was employed by SBA during the one year period prior to the disbursement of the loan.

Certification: I certify:

(a) I have not paid anyone connected with the Federal government for help in getting this loan. I also agree to report to the SBA Office of Inspector General, Washington, D.C. 20416, any Federal government employee who offers, in return for any type of compensation, to help get this loan approved.

(b) All information in this application and the schedules is true and complete to the best of my knowledge and is submitted to SBA so that SBA can decide whether to grant a loan or to participate with a lending institution in a loan to me. I agree to pay for or reimburse SBA for the cost of any surveys, title or mortgage examinations, appraisals, credit reports etc., performed by non-SBA personnel provided I have given my consent.

(c) I understand that I need not pay anybody to deal with SBA. I have read and understand Form 159 which explains SBA policy on representatives and their fees.

(d) If I make a statement that I know to be false or if I overvalue a security in order to help obtain a loan under the provisions of the Small Business Act, I can be fined up to $5,000 or be put in jail for up to two years or both.

(e) As consideration for any management, technical, and Business Development Assistance that may be provided, I waive all claims against SBA and its consultants.

(f) I have reade and received a copy of the "STATEMENTS REQUIRED BY LAWS AND EXECUTIVE ORDER" which was attached to this application.

If Applicant is a proprietor or general partner, sign below:

By: _____   Dated: _____

If Applicant is a corporation, sign below:

_____   Dated: _____
Corporate Name and Seal

By: _____
Signature of President

Attested by: _____
Signature of Corporate Official

The Proprietor, each General Partner (or Limited Partner owning 20% or more), each Guarantor, each Corporate officer, each Director, each Stockholder owning 20% or more, and, where appropriate, the spouses of each of these must sign. The person signing on behalf of the business must also sign individually.

_____   Date: _____
Signature

_____   Date: _____
Signature

Figure 12.1b

PLEASE READ DETACH AND RETAIN FOR YOUR RECORDS
STATEMENTS REQUIRED BY LAW AND EXECUTIVE ORDER

Federal executive agencies, including the Small Business Administration (SBA), are required to withhold or limit financial assistance, to impose special conditions on approved loans, to provide special notices to applicants or borrowers and to require special reports and data from borrowers in order to comply with legislation passed by the Congress and Executive Orders issued by the President and by the provisions of various inter-agency agreements. SBA has issued regulations and procedures that implement these laws and executive orders, and they are contained in Parts 112, 113, 116, and 117, Title 13, Code of Federal Regulations Chapter 1, or Standard Operating Procedures.

Freedom of Information Act (5 U.S.C. 552)
This law provides, with some exceptions, that SBA must supply information reflected in agency files and records to a person requesting it. Information about approved loans that will be automatically released includes, among other things, statistics on our loan programs (individual borrowers are not identified in the statistics) and other information such as the names of the borrowers (and their officers, directors, stockholders or partners), the collateral pledged to secure the loan, the amount of the loan, its purpose in general terms and the maturity. Proprietary data on a borrower would not routinely be made available to third parties. All requests under this Act are to be addressed to the nearest SBA office and be identified as a Freedom of Information request.

Right to Financial Privacy Act of 1978 (12 U.S.C. 3401)
This is notice to you as required by the Right to Financial Privacy Act of 1978, of SBA's access rights to financial records held by financial institutions that are or have been doing business with you or your business, including any financial institutions participating in a loan or loan guarantee. The law provides that SBA shall have a right of access to your financial records in connection with its consideration or administration of assistance to you in the form of a Government loan or loan guaranty agreement. SBA is required to provide a certificate of its compliance with the Act to a financial institution in connection with its first request for access to your financial records, after which no further certification is required for subsequent accesses. The law also provides that SBA's access rights continue for the term of any approved loan or loan guaranty agreement. No further notice to you of SBA's access rights is required during the term of any such agreement.

The law also authorizes SBA to transfer to another Government authority any financial records included in an application for a loan, or concerning an approved loan or loan guarantee, as necessary to process, service or foreclose on a loan or loan guarantee or to collect on a defaulted loan or loan guarantee. No other transfer of your financial records to another Government authority will be permitted by SBA except as required or permitted by law.

Flood Disaster Protection Act (42 U.S.C. 4011)
Regulations have been issued by the Federal Insurance Administration (FIA) and by SBA implementing this Act and its amendments. These regulations prohibit SBA from making certain loans in an FIA designated floodplain unless Federal flood insurance is purchased as a condition of the loan. Failure to maintain the required level of flood insurance makes the applicant ineligible for any future financial assistance from SBA under any program, including disaster assistance.

Executive Orders -- Floodplain Management and Wetland Protection (42 F.R. 26951 and 42 F.R. 26961)
The SBA discourages any settlement in or development of a floodplain or a wetland. This statement is to notify all SBA loan applicants that such actions are hazardous to both life and property and should be avoided. The additional cost of flood preventive construction must be considered in addition to the possible loss of all assets and investments in future floods.

Occupational Safety and Health Act (15 U.S.C. 651 et seq.)
This legislation authorizes the Occupational Safety and Health Administration in the Department of Labor to require businesses to modify facilities and procedures to protect employees or pay penalty fees. In some instances the business can be forced to cease operations or be prevented from starting operations in a new facility. Therefore, in some instances SBA may require additional information from an applicant to determine whether the business will be in compliance with OSHA regulations and allowed to operate its facility after the loan is approved and disbursed.

Signing this form as borrower is a certification that the OSA requirements that apply to the borrower's business have been determined and the borrower to the best of its knowledge is in compliance.

Civil Rights Legislation
All businesses receiving SBA financial assistance must agree not to discriminate in any business practice, including employment practices and services to the public, on the basis of categories cited in 13 C.F.R., Parts 112, 113 and 117 of SBA Regulations. This includes making their goods and services available to handicapped clients or customers. All business borrowers will be required to display the "Equal Employment Opportunity Poster" prescribed by SBA.

Figure 12.1c

Equal Credit Opportunity Act (15 U.S.C. 1691)
The Federal Equal Credit Opportunity Act prohibits creditors from discriminating against credit applicants on the basis of race, color, religion, national origin, sex, marital status or age (provided that the applicant has the capacity to enter into a binding contract); because all or part of the applicant's income derives from any public assistance program, or because the applicant has in good faith exercised any right under the Consumer Credit Protection Act. The Federal agency that administers compliance with this law concerning this creditor is the Federal Trade Commission, Equal Credit Opportunity, Washington, D.C. 20580.

Executive Order 11738 -- Environmental Protection (38 F.R. 25161)
The Executive Order charges SBA with administering its loan programs in a manner that will result in effective enforcement of the Clean Air Act, the Federal Water Pollution Act and other environmental protection legislation. SBA must, therefore, impose conditions on some loans. By acknowledging receipt of this form and presenting the application, the principals of all small businesses borrowing $100,000 or more in direct funds stipulate to the following:

1. That any facility used, or to be used, by the subject firm is not cited on the EPA list of Violating Facilities.

2. That subject firm will comply with all the requirements of Section 114 of the Clean Air Act (42 U.S.C. 7414) and Section 308 of the Water Act (33 U.S.C. 1318) relating to inspection, monitoring, entry, reports and information, as well as all other requirements specified in Section 114 and Section 308 of the respective Acts, and all regulations and guidelines issued thereunder.

3. That subject firm will notify SBA of the receipt of any communication from the Director of the Environmental Protection Agency indicating that a facility utilized, or to be utilized, by subject firm is under consideration to be listed on the EPA List of Violating Facilities.

Debt Collection Act of 1982 Deficit Reduction Act of 1984 (31 U.S.C. 3701 et seq. and other titles)
These laws require SBA to aggressively collect any loan payments which become delinquent. SBA must obtain your taxpayer identification number when you apply for a loan. If you receive a loan, and do not make payments as they come due, SBA may take one or more of the following actions:

-Report the status of your loan(s) to credit bureaus
-Hire a collection agency to collect your loan
-Offset your income tax refund or other amounts due to you from the Federal Government
-Suspend or debar you or your company from doing business with the Federal Government
-Refer your loan to the Department of Justice or other attorneys for litigation
-Foreclose on collateral or take other action permitted in the loan instruments.

Immigration Reform and Control Act of 1986 (Pub. L. 99-603)
If you are an alien who was in this country illegally since before January 1, 1982, you may have been granted lawful temporary resident status by the United States Immigration and Naturalization Service pursuant to the Immigration Reform and Control Act of 1986 (Pub. L 99-603). For five years from the date you are granted such status, you are not eligible for financial assistance from the SBA in the form of a loan or guaranty under section 7(a) of the Small Business Act unless you are disabled or a Cuban or Haitian entrant. When you sign this document, you are making the certification that the Immigration Reform and Control Act of 1986 does not apply to you, or if it does apply, more than five years have elapsed since you have been granted lawful temporary resident status pursuant to such 1986 legislation.

Lead-Based Paint Poisoning Prevention Act (42 U.S.C 4821 et seq.)
Borrowers using SBA funds for the construction or rehabilitation of a residential structure are prohibited from using lead-based paint (as defined in SBA regulations) on all interior surfaces, whether accessible or not, and exterior surfaces, such as stairs, decks, porches, railings, windows and doors, which are readily accessible to children under 7 years of age. A "residential structure" is any home, apartment, hotel, motel, orphanage, boarding school, dormitory, day care center, extended care facility, college or other school housing, hospital, group practice or community facility and all other residential or institutional structures where persons reside.

U.S. GPO : 1993 - 347-414

Figure 12.1d

The guarantee fee remains at 2 percent of the amount that the SBA guarantees on loans exceeding $50,000 with maturities greater than 12 months. The lender pays the guarantee fee to SBA. However, the lender may charge the fee to the small-business borrower.

Eligibility

To be eligible, a business must be for-profit and qualify as small under the SBAs size standard criteria. Businesses engaged in speculation or investment in rental real estate are not eligible.

Interest Rates

Maximum rates are based on the lowest prime rate on the date the SBA receives the application. For loans of $25,000 or less with original maturities of less than seven years, the maximum allowable rate cannot exceed 4.25 percentage points over the prime rate. For loans of $25,000 or less with original maturities of seven years or more, the maximum allowable rate cannot exceed 4.75 percentage points over the prime rate. For loans between $25,000 and $50,000, the maximum interest rate is at least 1 percentage point lower than those stated above (i.e., 3.25 percent and 3.75 percent).

CONTRACT LOAN PROGRAM

The Contract Loan Program is designed to assist small businesses in the short-term financing of the labor and material costs of a specific, assignable contract. Each contract loan finances one contract; the program does not have a revolving feature. These loans are available only under the SBA's guarantee program.

Eligibility

To be eligible, a business must be for-profit and qualify as small under the SBA's size standard criteria, with an exception for sheltered workshops under the Handicapped Assistance Loan Program. Businesses engaged in speculation or investment in rental real estate are not eligible.

Eligible businesses are small construction, manufacturing, and service contractors, and subcontractors who provide a specific product or service under an assignable contract. This program is designed to provide the funds necessary to perform on such contracts. Loan proceeds may be used only to finance the labor and materials necessary to comply with the terms of such contracts.

Eligible businesses may have more than one contract loan outstanding at any given time as long as the SBA's total exposure does not exceed

$750,000. Also, the business must have been in continuous operation for 12 months immediately preceding the application date.

Amounts, Terms, and Interest Rates

The SBA can guarantee as much as 85 percent of the loan up to $750,000. For loans of $155,000 or less, the maximum guarantee is 90 percent. Under the program, loan maturity cannot exceed 12 months from the date of first disbursement, except in cases of large contracts, which may be approved for up to 18 months. Any request for any maturity longer than 18 months requires special approval from the chief of the SBA Loan Policy and Procedures Branch. This is not a revolving fund but rather a loan to finance a specific contract.

Interest rates are negotiated with the lender but may not exceed the SBA's maximum interest rates under its regular guarantee loan program.

Collateral

Collateral will include an assignment of contract proceeds and may also include the pledge of other company assets and/or outside assets and secured personal guarantees.

Tax Requirements

All applicants must be current on payroll taxes and have in operation a depository plan for the payment of future withholding taxes. Such a plan protects the SBA and the participating lender from the Federal Tax Lien Act of 1966, which holds lenders liable for unpaid income taxes when loan proceeds are used for payroll purposes.

Special Program Requirements

Applicants must submit a projected cash flow for all business operations over the term of the contract and the loan. The cash flow must provide for anticipated needs plus fixed obligations.

The Process

The applicant can apply to the lender prior to or after a contract has been received; however, detailed information on the bid or contract must be available at the time of application.

SMALL GENERAL CONTRACTOR LOAN PROGRAM

The Small General Contractor Loan Program was created to finance the construction or renovation of residential and commercial buildings for sale. These loans are available only under the guarantee loan program.

Eligibility

Eligible businesses are construction contractors and homebuilders which meet SBA's size and policy standards. Eligibility rules require construction contractors and homebuilders to have already demonstrated the managerial and technical ability to build or renovate projects comparable in size to those for which they are seeking SBA financing. In addition, they must meet the agency's credit criteria.

Amount

The SBA can guarantee as much as 85 percent of the loan up to $750,000. The maximum guarantee for loans of $155,000 or less is 90 percent.

Repayment

Principal repayment may be required in a single payment when the project is sold. Interest payments, however, are required at least twice a year and must be paid from the applicant's own resources, not from loan proceeds.

Maturity

The loan maturity cannot be more than 36 months plus a reasonable estimate of the time it takes to complete the construction or renovation.

Interest Rates

Interest rates are negotiated with the lender but may not exceed the SBA's maximum interest rates under its regular guarantee loan program.

Use of Proceeds

Loan proceeds may be used solely for the direct expenses of acquisition, immediate construction, and/or significant rehabilitation of the residential or commercial structures. Loan proceeds can be used only for direct expenses of the project. Rehabilitation projects qualify if they are "significant" and if, at the time of loan application, the estimated costs are equal to or more than one-third of the purchase price or the fair market value of residential or commercial buildings at the time they are offered for sale.

Loans also can be used to purchase vacant land if the price is no more than 20 percent of the total loan. Not more than 5 percent of the loan can be used for streets, curbs, and other developmental costs that benefit properties other than the one being built or rehabilitated.

Special Application Requirements

In addition to the requirements of the SBA's regular business loan program, the applicant must submit three letters to the SBA (or to the participating lender) as follows:

- One letter must be from a mortgage lender doing business in the area, affirming that permanent mortgage financing for qualified purchasers of comparable real estate is normally available in the project's area.
- Another letter must come from an independently licensed real estate broker with three years of experience in the project area. The letter must state whether a market for the proposed structure exists and whether it is compatible with other buildings in the neighborhood.
- The third letter must be from an independent architect, appraiser, or engineer, confirming availability of construction inspection and certification at intervals during the project. The writer of this letter cannot be affiliated with the applicant in any way.

The cost of construction inspections must be paid by the applicant and can be paid from the loan proceeds.

Collateral

Collateral must at least include a second lien on the property to be constructed or renovated. Additional collateral will be required when necessary. The total amount of the first and second liens on a property cannot exceed 80 percent of the project's anticipated selling price. The first lien must include provisions for transferring clear title to the purchaser of each parcel. The SBA will not take a second position in a subdivision that is subordinate to a lien requiring the entire loan to be paid in full before any property is released.

SEASONAL LINE OF CREDIT PROGRAM

The Seasonal Line of Credit Program was created to finance the increased receivables and inventory of eligible small businesses arising from a seasonal upswing in business activity.

This program offers short-term loans to help small businesses get past cash crunches attributable to seasonal changes in business volume. The loans are guaranteed by the SBA and are used to finance increases in trading assets, such as receivables and inventory, required as a result of seasonal upswings in business. These loans are available only under the guarantee loan program.

Eligibility

Any small business is eligible which has a seasonal loan requirement, has been in business for the preceding 12 months, and meets the SBA's size and policy standards. This loan program does not have a revolving feature.

Eligible businesses must be for-profit operations. They also must qualify as small according to SBA's size standards, although an exception is provided for sheltered workshops qualifying under the Handicapped Assistance Loan Program. Loans cannot be made to businesses engaged in speculation or investment in rental real estate. In addition, businesses must have been in operation continuously for one year immediately preceding the application date. They also must have established a definite pattern of seasonal activity.

Applicants who are eligible under the Contract Loan Program are not eligible under this loan program.

Amount of Loan

The loan amount cannot exceed the amount necessary to overcome working capital deficiencies arising from the seasonal upswing in business activity. The SBA can guarantee as much as 85 percent of the loan up to $750,000. For loans of up to $155,000, the agency can guarantee up to 90 percent of the principal.

Maturity

The term of a seasonal line of credit loan cannot be more than 12 months from the date of the SBA's first disbursement. The loan must be structured to be repaid from the company's cash flow in the shortest time possible. Except for agricultural enterprises, only one seasonal line of credit may be outstanding at any time, and each loan must be followed by an out-of-debt period of at least 30 days.

Collateral

The collateral required for the loans is primarily liens on all inventory and accounts receivable. Additional collateral, including the pledge of outside assets and personal guaranties, may also be required.

The guarantee fee must be submitted with the loan application. An additional service fee of up to two percent may be charged by the lender when justified by extraordinary servicing requirements.

13 International Trade Assistance

The SBA assists businesses in obtaining the capital needed to explore, establish, or expand international markets. Export loans are available under SBA's guarantee program. If your lender is unable or unwilling to make a loan directly, you should request that the lender seek SBA participation. The financing staff of each SBA district and branch office administers the financial assistance programs. You can contact the finance division of your nearest SBA office for a list of participating lenders.

INTERNATIONAL TRADE LOAN PROGRAM

Under the International Trade Loan Program, the SBA provides long-term financial and business development assistance to help small businesses take advantage of export markets. It also assists small businesses engaged or preparing to engage in international trade, and small businesses adversely affected by competition from imports.

Eligible concerns will submit (a) a business plan to include both a profit and loss projection and narrative substantiating the development of new or expansion of existing export markets, or (b) a narrative explanation and financial statements demonstrating how directly competitive imported items have made an important contribution to a decline in the firm's competitive position.

The SBA's maximum guarantee on these loans is $1,250,000, less any outstanding SBA guarantee. No more than $1,000,000 of the SBA's guarantee can finance facilities and equipment, and no more then $250,000 can be used for working capital.

Maturities will be consistent with the borrower's ability to repay and will generally adhere to the limits of 7 years for working capital and 25 years for real estate.

It is required that a first position on those items financed be taken as collateral along with any other security considered appropriate.

EXPORT WORKING CAPITAL PROGRAM

The SBA has established a new program within the international trade program to help small businesses obtain working capital to complete their export sales. The program was a key feature of the President's National Export Strategy, which was submitted to the Congress on October 5, 1995. The Export Working Capital Program (EWCP), which replaces the SBA's Export Revolving Line of Credit (ERLC), encourages lenders to "bank" small-business exporter deals by significantly reducing the risk associated with the deals. Accordingly, the regulations for the ERLC program (13 CFR Sec. 122.54) will not apply to EWCP loans. The program was scheduled to end September 30, 1995, at which time it was to be evaluated to determine what, if any, aspects of the program should be made permanent.

The Export Working Capital Program (EWCP) provides short-term working capital to finance small-business export transactions. The EWCP can support single transactions or multiple export sales. Under this program, the SBA can guarantee up to 90 percent or $750,000, whichever is less, of a loan made by a participating lender. Loan maturities are generally for 12 months; revolving credit lines may be renewed twice, up to a total of 36 months.

Guarantees can be extended for preshipment working capital, postshipment exposure, or a combination of the two. A preshipment guarantee is used to finance the production or acquisition of goods and services for export. A postshipment guarantee is used to finance receivables resulting from export sales.

Under the EWCP, you can apply directly to the SBA for a preliminary commitment for a guarantee. With SBA's preliminary commitment in hand, you can then find a lender willing to extend the credit. The lender must apply to the SBA for the final commitment.

The International Trade Loan Program provides long-term financing to help small businesses compete more effectively and to expand or develop export markets. Under this program, the SBA's guarantee can extend up to $1.25 million. The SBA's maximum share for facilities and equipment is $1 million; the maximum share for working capital is $750,000. Loan maturities cannot exceed 25 years, excluding the working capital portion of the loan.

Proceeds may be used to purchase or upgrade facilities or equipment, and to make other improvements that will be used within the United States to produce goods or services. No debt payment is allowed. Proceeds can be used to buy land and buildings; build new facilities; renovate, improve, or expand existing facilities; and purchase or recondition machinery, equipment, and fixtures. The working capital portion of the amount borrowed could be in the form of either an EWCP loan or a portion of the term loan.

Applicants must establish either of the following to meet eligibility requirements:

- Loan proceeds will significantly expand existing export markets or develop new ones; or
- The applicant's business is adversely affected by import competition.

The SBA and the Export Import Bank of the United States (ExIm Bank) are working to harmonize their export financing programs. Accordingly, many features of the SBA's EWCP and ExIm Bank's Export Working Capital Program are similar. By design, the SBA's program will assist smaller businesses that need a guarantee of $750,000 or less and ExIm Bank's program will serve the larger businesses and small businesses that have larger credit needs.

Small business can use EWCP proceeds (a) to finance labor and materials for manufacturing goods for export, (b) to purchase goods or services for export, or (c) to finance accounts receivable generated from export sales. Proceeds may not be used to establish operations overseas, acquire fixed assets, or pay existing debt.

Interest rates are negotiable between the applicant and the lender. SBA charges a guarantee fee of 0.25 percent; other fees may apply.

EWCP loans are made under the authority of SBA's regular business loan program known as the 7(a) program. The policies and procedures governing the EWCP pilot are contained in operating guidelines developed for the program. These guidelines describe the eligibility, credit, and processing considerations for the program.

Eligibility

The SBA considers several factors in reviewing an EWCP application, including the following:

- Is the transaction viable?
- How reliable is the repayment source?
- Can the exporter perform under the terms of the deal?

To be eligible for a guarantee under the EWCP, a company must meet SBA's size standards. The standards vary by industry and are determined by either the number of employees or the volume of annual receipts. Check with your local SBA district office to determine if your company falls within the small business size standards. A company also must have been in business, but not necessarily exporting, for at least 12 continuous months before filing an application.

The applicant's business generally must be operated for profit. Export trading companies (ETCs) and export management companies (EMCs) also may qualify for the SBA's business loan guarantee program.

Ineligible borrowers include businesses engaged in speculation or investment in rental real estate.

Under EWCP, SBA guarantees short-term working capital loans made by participating lenders to exporters. Loan proceeds may only be used to finance the acquisition or production of goods and services being exported and accounts receivable of such export sales under EWCP.

- A preshipment guarantee is used to finance the acquisition or production cost of export goods and services. The term of these loans is usually no more than 12 months. Payment is secured by letter of credit, valid purchase orders or contracts, or other such arrangement.

- A postshipment guarantee is used to finance receivables resulting from export sales. The maximum term of these loans should not exceed six months.

- A combined guarantee is use to finance both the acquisition or production of export goods and services, and the account receivables resulting from such export sales. The maximum term of a combined guarantee is 18 months.

Although payment may be made through one of several arrangements, usually ExIm Bank insurance (or other comparable insurance) will be required in conjunction with an EWCP guarantee where postshipment or combined guarantees are being extended, unless payment is being made by a confirmed, irrevocable letter of credit.

A loan guarantee may be for a single transaction or for a revolving line of credit which is used to finance "bundles" of individual transactions. Credit lines may be for as long as three years, subject to annual renewals. Such renewals will be granted unless an adverse change has occurred in the exporter's financial condition or operations sufficient to jeopardize the company's ability to preform on export transactions. If a line of credit is terminated, no additional bundles will be financed, and a reasonable period will be provided to liquidate the outstanding balance on the line of credit.

Standby letters of credit are issued by a bank to cover a particular contingency. Frequently, they are used in place of a bid, performance, or financial bonds. EWCP loans can be used to facilitate a standby letter of credit.

Most products are eligible for EWCP financing. In some cases, however, federal restrictions cause the product to be ineligible. For example, if ExIm Bank export credit insurance is required, the product must contain at least 51 percent U.S. content. Also, certain defense products are not eligible for ExIm Bank insurance. Where the product is customized or designed for special use, care must be taken to assure that the exporter has sufficient capability of payment should the transaction not be consummated.

Although service exports are eligible for EWCP financing, they entail greater risk than product exports, especially those that are independent of product sales. EWCP financing of service exports will usually require progress payments and possibly additions collateral.

Applicants who produce, manufacture, or sell products or provide services that enter into the export channel but do not directly export their products or services, including suppliers to other domestic manufacturers, are eligible for EWCP financing. In such cases, the applicant shall provide evidence to SBA that the goods or services are in fact being exported.

The dollar amount of the SBA guarantee is of an EWCP loan limited to the lesser of two factors. First, EWCP loans are limited to the exporter's cost, if they are for preshipment financing, or the receivable associated with the product being exported, if they are for postshipment or combined financing. Second, with few exceptions, the maximum guarantee amount that may be outstanding or committed to any small business concern under the 7(a) and the 504 programs in the aggregate is $750,000. EWCP loans are considered 7(a) loans for this calculation.

As is the case for regular 7(a) loans, EWCP loans of $155,000 or less will be eligible for an SBA guarantee of 90 percent of the principal amount of the loan. For loans over $155,000, the SBA guarantee may not exceed 85 percent; however, loans made under the SBA's preferred lender authority may not exceed 70 percent. It is noted that legislation is pending before Congress that would increase the maximum guarantee coverage for all EWCP loans to 90 percent. This legislative change will cause the guarantee percentage to be the same as ExIm Bank's guarantee percentage.

The SBA will monitor, but not regulate, the interest charges and fees imposed by lenders for EWCP loans. This approach is consistent with the policies of ExIm Bank and most state export finance programs.

A $100 application fee will be assessed each applicant for an EWCP loan application or a Preliminary Commitment (PC) Application. However, an application fee will not be assessed to the lender on a loan application for an exporter who had previously received a preliminary commitment and paid a fee. The normal guarantee for 7(a) loans will be assessed: 0.25 percent for a loan under one year and 2 percent for loans over one year.

As previously stated, an SBA-guaranteed EWCP loan is obtained by an exporter from a lender participating in the SBA's EWCP loan program. The exporter and the lender prepare the loan application which the lender submits to the SBA for a loan guarantee. In cases where an exporter is unable to find a lender willing to make the loan, the exporter can submit an application to the SBA for a preliminary commitment. A PC is a 60-day conditional commitment issued by the SBA to an exporter specifying that the SBA will guarantee a loan to the exporter in accordance with the terms and conditions specified in the PC. It should be noted that PCs are not required as an interim step to obtaining the EWCP loan; rather, they help an exporter find a lender who will make the loan. Another benefit of PCs is that they allow an exporter to take advantage of SBA financial counseling and technical assistance without first having a participating lender.

In some areas, SBA-approved intermediaries will be available to assist exporters in loan packaging, deal structuring, and credit analysis. Pursuant to an agreement with the exporter, these intermediaries may charge an amount not to exceed 1 percent of the loan amount. SBA-approved resource partners will be available to assist exporters with management and technical assistance.

Applicants must be identifiable small businesses organized in the United States as for-profit entities with operations in the United States. The size standards applicable to regular business loans under the 7(a) program also apply to EWCP loans. While a business organized and/or located outside the United States is ineligible for EWCP financing, a U.S. subsidiary of a foreign corporation may be eligible. Finally, Export Trading Companies and Export Management Companies are eligible for EWCP financing if they take title to the goods being exported.

Applicants must have sufficient experience and capability to complete the export transaction. Generally, exporters should have been in operations, though not necessarily in exporting, for at least 12 continuous months prior to filing an application. Exceptions will be considered where the applicant is a new business but the principals have proven expertise in the exporter's line of business.

The exporter's ability to perform is one of the most important considerations in the EWCP loan-making process. This includes the exporter's ability to acquire or produce the export product or service, complete the export transaction, and present the proper documents for payment. Therefore, loan applications shall be approved only where such performance capability is determined to exist.

Collateral

Collateral may include export inventory, foreign receivables, assignments of contract and letter of credit proceeds and domestic receivables. Personal guarantees usually are required to support the credit.

Credit Considerations

All SBA-guaranteed loans, including EWCP loans, are statutorily required to demonstrate reasonable assurance of repayment. Usually, regular 7(a) loans are term loans, and collateral is not linked to loan payment. Assessment of the applicant's ability to repay the loan from operations over an extended period is a primary concern, and collateral is important as a secondary source of repayment. Strength of the balance sheet, including net worth and liquidity, are essential, as well as the reasonableness of projections.

Conversely, EWCP loans are short-term and transaction based. The primary repayment source is the collateral associated with the transaction in which the lender has taken an assignment. The primary concern is the borrower's ability to perform on the contract and the ability to realize on the collateral. The horizon is short on these transactions. Balance sheet strength, reasonableness of projections, and so forth are important only as they relate to the primary concern.

The SBA does not assess foreign commercial or political risk. Therefore, exporters are required to have an acceptable letter of credit, valid purchase orders and contracts, acceptable export receivables, and/or ExIm Bank export credit insurance or private insurance that is acceptable. Transactions financed by EWCP loans must be payable in U.S. dollars unless the SBA permits otherwise on an exceptions basis. This policy addresses both the foreign currency and foreign exchange risks.

It is essential that EWCP loans be secured with a first lien on all collateral associated with the transactions financed by the loan. Also, an assignment of proceeds from the borrower to the lender shall be required as a condition to the SBA's guarantee. The SBA has modified its policy on personal guarantees due to the short-term nature of these loans and their structure.

Subject to appropriate approvals, the SBA and ExIm Bank plan to utilize a joint loan application form. This will enable potential borrowers to better understand the program functions and uses. Also, it will facilitate the referral of applications to the appropriate agency. Other SBA forms required by law or policy will be used by the SBA.

How to Apply

The new EWCP offers several advantages for both the exporter and the lender, including a simplified application form (SBA form 4EX, see Figure 13.1) and a quicker turnaround time on the SBA's review and commitment.

Under the program, small businesses can apply directly to the SBA for a preliminary commitment for a guarantee. With the SBA's preliminary commitment in hand, an exporter can then find a lender willing to extend the credit. The lender must apply to the SBA for the final commitment.

To apply for a working capital guarantee, a lender—or the exporter if a preliminary commitment is sought—should submit to SBA a completed EWCP application, along with the following:

Background

- Brief resume of principals and key employees
- History of business and copy of business plan, if available

Transaction(s)

- Business financial statements (balance sheet and income statement) for the last three years, if applicable
- Current financial statement (interim) dated within 90 days of the date of application filing
- Aging of accounts receivable and accounts payable, as of list balance sheet date
- The most recent federal and state income tax returns for the business
- Schedule of all principals' (officers'/owners') compensation for the past three years and current year to date
- Personal financial statement(s) of the major shareholder(s)/partner(s) of the company (over 20 percent ownership) and their most recent federal income tax return
- Monthly cash flow projections for the term or the loan, highlighting the proposed export transaction

Processing Considerations

EWCP loan applications are processed on a three-track system. Track one is regular processing and all participating lenders in EWCP have the authority to submit EWCP loan applications on this track. Track two is the Certified Lenders Program (CLP), where greater reliance is placed on the lender's analysis and three day turnaround is the standard. Track three is the Preferred Lender's Program (PLP) where lenders are given delegated authority to make loans.

In addition to regular processing, EWCP participating lenders that meet the eligibility criteria for CLP and/or PLP will have the authority to submit loans for processing on track two and/or three as the case may be. It should be noted that all EWCP participating lenders must have successful experience in providing trade finance to exporters and an acceptable collateral management system. Also, it is noted that all applications for preliminary commitments will be processed on track one, regular processing.

SBA district offices that have affiliated U.S. export assistance centers will be processing centers for EWCP loan and preliminary commitment applications. Other district offices may be designated as EWCP processing centers based on activity and capability. District offices that are not so designated will forward loan applications for processing to the designated EWCP processing center. All SBA district offices, whether or not designated as processing centers, will promote the pilot program and will continue to offer business development assistance to exporters. During the term of the pilot, the SBA Office of International Trade will work closely with the SBA processing offices to provide technical support on loan structuring and foreign risk assessment.

Because EWCP loans are short-term and often require swift action by staff familiar with the loan, the SBA recommending loan officer will retain the responsibility for loan servicing. If the lender does not handle the loan liquidation, the SBA district office that approved the loan will liquidate it. During the pilot, EWCP loans will not be eligible for sale in the secondary market that exists for 7(a) loans.

In summary, the SBA's Export Working Capital Program is a loan guarantee program for exporters to provide transaction financing. There are three important considerations in this program: (a) the existence of a transaction(s), (b) the capability of the exporter to preform and satisfy the requirements of the transaction(s), and (c) loan payment (adequacy of documents, security interest in the collateral, and assignment of proceeds).

TRAINING

SBA district offices sponsor export training programs, often in conjunction with SCORE, SBDCs, and other public and private trade groups. Offering something for the beginner as well as the more advanced exporter, topics range from export financing to joint ventures. You can also learn how to do business outside our borders through the various market- and region-specific workshops offered.

PUBLICATIONS

The SBA publishes books and fact sheets on international trade, including *Breaking into the Trade Game: A Small Business Guide to Exporting*, which takes you step-by-step through the export process.

|---|---|---|
Date Received	**U.S. SMALL BUSINESS ADMINISTRATION**	Lender Transaction
	EXPORT-IMPORT BANK OF THE UNITED STATES	☐ PLP ☐ DA Level A ☐ PLP
C.I.D. No.	**JOINT APPLICATION FOR WORKING CAPITAL GUARANTEE**	☐ PEFCO ☐ DA Level B ☐ DA
		☐ Regular

PART A. PRINCIPAL PARTIES

1. Borrower/Exporter

Company Name	D&B No.	Telephone
Name and Title of Contact Person	Federal ID No.	FAX
Address	City	State	Zip
Gross Sales $	No. of Full-Time Employees	Primary SIC Code

Management (Proprietors, partners, officers, directors and all holders of outstanding stock - 100% of ownership must be shown). Use separate sheet if necessary.

Name and Social Security Number	Complete Address	% Owned	* Military Service From	To	*Race	*Sex

*This information is collected for statistical purposes only. It has no bearing on the credit decision to approve or decline this application.

2. Personal Guarantor(s)

Name	SSN	Telephone
Address	City	State	Zip	FAX

3. Lender

Name	Federal ID No.	Telephone
Address	City	State	Zip	FAX

PART B. INFORMATION ABOUT THE TRANSACTION

Loan Amount $	Type (check one)
Terms and Fees ☐ 6 months ☐ 1 year ☐ Other (specify)	☐ Revolving ☐ Transaction(s) Specific
Interest Rate to be Charged Other Fees or Charges (type & amount)	Renewal? ☐ Y ☐ N Conversion of Preliminary Commitment? ☐ Y ☐ N If Yes, # _____

SBA Temp Form 4EX (9-94)

Figure 13.1a

PART C. CERTIFICATIONS

1. Borrower/Exporter Certification

The Borrower/Exporter certifies that the representations made and the facts stated by it in the application for a Working Capital Guarantee by the Export-Import Bank of the United States *(Eximbank)* or the Small Business Administration *(SBA)* are true, and that it has not misrepresented or omitted any material facts relevant to said representations. The Borrower/Exporter agrees that the validity and completeness of such representations and facts shall be a condition precedent to any liability of Eximbank or SBA under any guarantee issued. The Borrower/Exporter certifies that it does not have any actual knowledge and further certifies that it did not withhold any actual knowledge which could reasonably be expected to cause or tend to cause a loss to Eximbank or SBA under its guarantee. If after the date of this Application, the Borrower/Exporter comes into possession of any such knowledge, the Borrower/Exporter agrees not to withhold it, and the undersigned agrees to immediately communicate such knowledge to Eximbank or SBA by facsimile or letter, as appropriate. Attach complete information for any box marked "yes".

1. Are there any pending or threatened liens, judgments or material litigation against the:

    Borrower   ☐ YES   ☐ NO   Guarantor   ☐ YES   ☐ NO

2. Has the Borrower/Exporter or its owner*(s)*, or the Guarantor ever filed for protection under U.S. bankruptcy laws? Has either had an involuntary bankruptcy petition filed against it?

    Borrower   ☐ YES   ☐ NO   Guarantor   ☐ YES   ☐ NO

3. Has the Borrower/Exporter or its owner*(s)* or affiliates ever previously requested U.S. Government financing?

    Borrower   ☐ YES   ☐ NO   Guarantor   ☐ YES   ☐ NO

4. Are any of the individuals listed in Part A (a) presently under indictment, on parole or probation, or have they ever been (b) charged for any criminal offense other than a minor vehicle violation, or (c) convicted, placed on pretrial diversion, or placed on any form of probation including adjudication withheld pending probation for any criminal offense other than a minor vehicle violation?

    ☐ YES   ☐ NO   If YES, SBA Form 912 must be submitted with this application *(SBA applicants only)*.

Name of Borrower/Exporter	
Signature	Date
Name and Title *(Print or Type)*	

2. Lender Certification

The Lender certifies that the representations made and the facts stated by it in the application for a Working Capital Guarantee by the Export-Import Bank of the United States *(Eximbank)* or the Small Business Administration *(SBA)* are true, to the best of its knowledge and belief, and that it has not misrepresented or omitted any material facts relevant to said representations. The Lender agrees that such representations and facts shall be a condition precedent to any liability of Eximbank or SBA thereunder. The Lender certifies that it does not have any actual knowledge and further certifies that it did not withhold any actual knowledge which could reasonably be expected to cause or tend to cause a loss to Eximbank or SBA under its guarantee. If after the date of this Application, the Lender comes into possession of any such knowledge, the Lender agrees not to withhold it, and the undersigned agrees to immediately communicate such knowledge to Eximbank or SBA by facsimile or letter as appropriate. By signing and submitting this application, the Lender certifies that it would not be willing to make this loan without the guarantee of Eximbank or SBA.

The Lender further certifies to the best of his or her knowledge and belief, that if any funds have been paid or will be paid to any person for influencing or attempting to influence an officer or employee of any agency, a member of Congress, an officer or employee of Congress, or an employee of a member of Congress in connection with this commitment providing for the United States to guarantee a loan, the undersigned shall complete and submit Standard Form-LLL, "Disclosure Form to Report Lobbying" in accordance with its instructions. Submission of this statement is a prerequisite for making or entering into this transaction imposed by Section 1352, Title 31, US Code. Any person who fails to file the required statement shall be subject to a civil penalty of not less than $10,000 and not more than $100,000 for each such failure. If Standard Form-LLL is necessary, it may be obtained from Eximbank or SBA.

Name of Lender	
Signature	Date
Name and Title *(Print or Type)*	

Figure 13.1b

APPLICATION INSTRUCTIONS

PART A. PRINCIPAL PARTIES

1. **Borrower/Exporter.** Complete this section with information on the individual or corporate borrower. Provide the primary SIC code of the borrower, rather than the product being exported.

   Management. Complete this section for each proprietor, partner, officer or director owning 20 or more of the company.

2. **Personal Guarantor(s).** The personal guarantee of the owner(s) is required in most cases.

3. **Lender.** Leave blank if you are applying for a Preliminary Commitment and a prospective lender has not been identified.

PART B. INFORMATION ABOUT THE TRANSACTION

Provide the loan amount, term and type of loan requested. (See also Checklist item 3 below.)

PART C. CERTIFICATIONS

This section must be signed by an authorized representative of the borrower and, if a request for a final commitment, an authorized representative of the lender.

CHECKLIST OF INFORMATION TO BE ATTACHED

	YES	N/A
BACKGROUND		
1. Brief resume of principals and key employees.	☐	☐
2. History of business; copy of business plan, if available; identify whether sole proprietorship, general partnership, corporation and/or subchapter-S corporation.	☐	☐
3. Explanation of use of proceeds and benefits of the loan guarantee, including details of the underlying transaction(s) for which loan is needed, including country(s) where the buyers are located.	☐	☐
4. Products to be exported are on the United States Munitions Control List (Part 121 of Title 22 of the Code of Federal Regulations), OR require a validated export license from the Bureau of Export Administration; If Yes, please attach explanation. If uncertain whether a validated export license is required, written verification from the appropriate licensing agency may be required before loan approval.	☐	☐
TRANSACTION		
5. Description of products/services to be exported, including SIC codes and literature. (Indicate the percentage foreign content.)	☐	☐
6. Copy of letter of credit and/or copy of buyer's order/contract, if available.	☐	☐
7. Export credit insurance-related material (policy, application, buyer credit limit), if applicable.	☐	☐
8. Copy of export license, if required.	☐	☐
FINANCIAL INFORMATION		
9. Business financial statements (Balance Sheet, Income Statement, Statement of Cash Flows) for the last three (3) years, if applicable.	☐	☐
10. Current financial statement (interim) dated within ninety (90) days of the date of application filing.	☐	☐
11. Aging of accounts receivable and accounts payable.	☐	☐
12. The most recent Federal income tax return for the business.	☐	☐
13. Schedule of all principal officer/owner's compensation for the past three (3) years and current year to date [if none, please indicate].	☐	☐
14. Signed personal financial statement(s) of the major shareholder(s)/partner(s) of the company (over 20%) and their most recent federal income tax return; (not required for venture capital partners).	☐	☐
15. Estimate of monthly cash flow for the term of the loan, highlighting the proposed export transaction.	☐	☐
16. Description of type and value of proposed collateral to support the loan (company assets/export product, i.e., inventory, accounts receivable, other).	☐	☐
17. Credit memorandum attached, if the Lender is the applicant.	☐	☐
18. Nonrefundable $100 check or money order made out to the Eximbank or the SBA, as appropriate.	☐	☐

Figure 13.1c

MAILING/FORWARDING INSTRUCTIONS

1. **If submitted by a Borrower/Exporter**
   a. Is Borrower/Exporter's requested loan amount in Part B,   YES ☐   NO ☐
   $833,333 or less?
   b. Is Borrower/Exporter a small business, as defined by Title 13 CFR Part 121.601,   YES ☐   NO ☐
   Standard Industrial Classification Codes and Size Standards?

**If answer to *both* of the above is YES, send entire set of materials to the
SBA District Office nearest you. Call (800) 827-5722 for the address.**

Send your application to Eximbank in all other situations:

Export-Import Bank of the U.S.
Quality Review Unit
811 Vermont Avenue, NW,
Washington, DC 20571

2. **If submitted by a Lender.**

Is Lender using its Eximbank Delegated Authority?   YES ☐   NO ☐

**If YES, send the application, the Loan Authorization Notice
and the $100 application fee to the Eximbank address above,
*irrespective of the guarantee amount.***

If you knowingly make a false statement or over value a security in order to obtain a guaranteed loan from SBA or Eximbank, you can be fined up to $10,000 or imprisoned for not more than five years (or both) under 18 USC 1001.

Public Burden Statements

Public burden reporting for this collection of information is estimated to average 2 hours per response, including time required for searching existing data sources, gathering the necessary data, providing the information required, and reviewing the final collection. Send comments on the accuracy of this estimate of the burden and recommendations for reducing it to: The Office of Management and Budget, Paperwork Reduction Project (3048-0003), Washington, DC 20503.

Figure 13.1d

LEGAL ASSISTANCE

Under the Export Legal Assistance Network (ELAN), your local SBA office can arrange a free initial consultation with an attorney to discuss international trade questions. This is possible through an agreement between the Federal Bar Association, the SBA, and the U.S. Department of Commerce. Questions may include contract negotiation, agent/distributor agreements, export licensing requirements, credit collection procedures, documentation, and so forth.

MARKET RESEARCH

The SBA's Automated Trade Locator Assistance System (SBAtlas) is a market research tool that can help you select the best markets for your particular product or service. Two types of free reports are available: product specific and country specific. The SBAtlas product report ranks the top 35 import and export markets for a particular good or service. The country report identifies the top 20 products most frequently traded in a target market.

JOINT VENTURES

The SBA offers an on-line system for matching U.S. small businesses with potential international joint venture partners. Reach Strategic Venture Partners (RSVP) contains profiles of companies from around the world interested in developing partnerships with U.S. companies. RSVP is available through SBA Online, the SBA's electronic bulletin board at 1-900-463-4636 (9600, n, 8, 1).

SBA EWCP LENDER'S GUIDE

I. **Introduction**

The SBA is an independent federal agency created by Congress to aid, counsel, and protect the interests of small businesses. Since its inception in 1953, the SBA has offered a variety of loan programs to eligible small-business concerns. Among the the SBA's special loan programs is the Export Working Capital Program (EWCP).

The EWCP was developed under authority of section 7(a) (14) of the Small Business Act to help small businesses finance the sales of their products and services to overseas markets. The program provides repayment guarantees to eligible lenders for secured loans that would not be made commercially without the SBA's guarantee. The SBA commits the full faith and credit of the government of the United States of America.

Many small U.S. firms with the potential to export are often not able to access adequate working capital financing. Pursuant to the Small Export Expansion Act of 1980, the SBA developed the EWCP to meet this need by providing loan guarantees to lenders to support their secured short-term working capital loans to small business exporters. In order to provide support for a loan, the SBA must determine that a reasonable assurance of repayment exists. Since inception of the EWCP, the SBA has approved over 400 loans, supporting over $120 million of working capital financing.

II. **Program Guidelines**

A. *Eligibility criteria.* Participants under the EWCP must meet certain eligibility criteria.

   1. *Participating lenders.* Any bank or financial institution that has a continuing capability to evaluate, process, close, disburse, and service export working capital loans. Capability includes expertise in export finance and the ability to manage asset-based loans. Participants also must have continuing good character and reputation; and be subject to continuing supervision and examination by state or federal chartering, licensing, or similar regulatory authority as the SBA may deem satisfactory. Eligible lenders may be approved by the SBA as EWCP Certified Lenders and/or EWCP Preferred Lenders. The eligibility requirements for Certified Lender or Preferred Lender status under the EWCP are outlined in Sections III and IV, respectively.

   2. *Exporters.* Any for-profit business that qualifies as a "small business" by SBA standards and currently exports or plans to export, may apply for financing under the EWCP. Exporters must be domiciled in the United States, although ownership by foreign nationals or foreign entities is acceptable. Applicants must have an operating history of at least one year, but not necessarily in exporting. Start-up and development-stage entities are ineligible under the EWCP.

B. *Term and type of loan.* A loan can support a single export transaction (transaction-specific loan) or multiple export transactions (revolving loan). A transaction-specific loan is a nonrevolving loan that supports a specifically identified export transaction. A revolving loan supports multiple export transactions on a continuous basis during the term of the loan. The term of a transaction-specific loan generally does not exceed one year. The term of a revolving line of credit can extend up to three years, but the term for specific transactions within the revolving line generally do not exceed one year.

C. *Guarantee coverage, risk retention, and interest rate.* The SBA's guarantee covers up to 90 percent of the principal and interest thereon. The lender must retain at least 10 percent risk in the loan. The lender is not permitted to separately collateralize its retained percent risk. In the event of a claim, the guaranteed portion of the principal balance of the loan is paid. Interest at the note rate is paid up to the date of claim payment (penalty interest and other fees are excluded from coverage). Under the EWCP, the SBA does not impose any interest rate ceiling or limitation on lender's fees.

D. *Use of loan proceeds.* Loan proceeds may be used for the following:

1. To acquire inventory and pay for direct and indirect costs (e.g., labor and overhead) used for the manufacture of goods (including work in progress), or the purchase of goods or services for export

2. To support standby letters of credit used as bid bonds, performance bonds, or payment guarantees to foreign buyers

E. *Collateral and other credit enhancements.*

1. *Collateral.* The SBA requires that the lender obtain valid and enforceable first priority security interests in sufficient collateral to cover at least 100 percent of any loan disbursement, with the exception of loan proceeds used to support bid and performance bonds to foreign buyers. At a minimum, collateral must consist of all export-related accounts receivable financed under the loan. If any export related inventory is taken as collateral, the lender must obtain a security interest in both the export-related inventory and the corresponding accounts receivable.

   a. *Inventory.* Inventory (raw materials, work in progress, and finished goods) taken as collateral must be located within the United States.

   b. *Accounts receivable due and collectable in the United States.* Receivables held as collateral must be payable to the exporter in the United States and be denominated in U.S. dollars (or in other currencies preapproved by the SBA).

   c. *Additional collateral.* While export-related inventory and export-related accounts receivable are standard collateral for most loans, the SBA may require that the lender take additional collateral, such as junior liens on other assets of the exporter. The SBA will consider requests to include other assets (e.g., domestic inventory, domestic receivables) as collateral.

2. *Personal and corporate guarantees.* Generally, principals who have over 20 percent ownership in a closely held company will be required to guarantee repayment of the loan. Parent corporate guarantees or other guarantees may also be required.

3. *Export credit insurance.* The SBA or the lender may determine that export credit insurance is required to enhance the quality of export-related accounts receivable. Export credit insurance is available through ExIm Bank as well as through several private companies. In order to use non–ExIm Bank export credit insurance, the lender must specifically request that the SBA approve the insurance coverage and submit a copy of the policy with the application.

F. *Disbursement rates.* A lender may make disbursements only against signed or otherwise verified export purchase orders, sales contracts, or letters of credit. Disbursements must be made in accordance with stipulated rates, set by the SBA (or by the lender in the case of EWCP Preferred Lender transactions). Disbursements must be tied to acceptable collateral (i.e., export-related inventory and export-related accounts receivable).

1. *Inventory.* Disbursement rates against eligible export-related inventory (raw materials, work in progress, and finished goods) vary depending on inventory quality, and will be set forth in the loan authorization. Disbursement rates of up to 75 percent are typically allowed. In certain exceptional cases, the SBA may allow a disbursement rate of up to 100 percent. Inventory must be located in the U.S. and must be valued at the lower of actual cost or market value, including cost of work-in-progress inventory valued in accordance with Generally Accepted Accounting Practices (GAAP).

2. *Accounts receivable due and collectible in the United States.* Disbursement rates of up to 90 percent are typically allowed against eligible export-related accounts receivable due and collectible in the United States; the rate, however, may be lower depending on the quality of the export-related receivables.

G. *Application process.* The SBA will accept applications for either a preliminary commitment from the exporter or a lenders application for guarantee from the lender. All applications must contain the information requested in the SBA/ExIm Bank joint application and the $100 application fee. In reviewing a loan application, the SBA and/or the lender will determine whether a reasonable assurance of repayment exists.

1. *Preliminary commitment applications.* Exporters may apply directly to the SBA for a preliminary commitment if the loan amount is less than or equal to $833,333. Exporters may apply directly to ExIm Bank for a preliminary commitment for loan amounts in excess of $833,333. Upon approval of the application, the SBA issues a preliminary commitment letter which outlines the terms and conditions under which the SBA is prepared to issue its guarantee to a lender. The exporter then has up to 60 days to find a lender and negotiate financing.

2. *Conversion of preliminary commitments.* Once the exporter has selected a lender, the lender submits an Application for Guarantee (SBA form 4-1) to the SBA. The lender must submit a completed application form and must comply with all the terms and conditions of the preliminary commitment, including any special conditions. An additional $100 application fee is not required to convert a preliminary commitment to an SBA guarantee.

3. *Applications submitted by lenders.* If an exporter and a lender have agreed to participate in the EWCP, the lender can bypass the preliminary commitment process by making the initial application to the SBA on behalf of the exporter. The lender may apply directly to the SBA for loan amounts less than or equal to $833,333. For loan amounts greater than $833,333,

the lender must send the application to ExIm Bank, (unless the loan is processed under the ExIm Bank Delegated Authority). In order to expedite processing time, the lender should submit its credit memorandum and financial analysis along with the other information required and Agreement of Loan Authorization (SBA form 529B) which outlines the terms and conditions of the guarantee.

4. *Renewal of existing revolving loans.* Revolving lines of credit under the EWCP are designed to finance groups of specifically identified transactions. While the specific transactions within a group will generally be limited to one year or less, the SBA can approve a line of credit facility for a term of up to 36 months, subject to annual renewals. A line of credit will be renewed unless there is an adverse change in the exporter's financial condition or operations that jeopardizes its ability to perform on export transactions. Should a line be terminated at a renewal period, no additional disbursements will be allowed and the lender should give the exporter a reasonable period of time to repay the loan.

H. *SBA fees.* In addition to the $100 application fee, the SBA charges the lender a guarantee fee of 0.25 percent of the guaranteed amount for loans of 12 months or less. The guarantee fee for loans with terms greater than 12 months is 2 percent. Guarantee fees for loans of 12 months or less must be submitted with the lender's application. The guarantee fee for loans greater than 12 months are due within 90 days of the date of the loan approval stated in the loan authorization.

I. *Loan servicing.* The lender is expected to monitor the loan in accordance with prudent lending standards. This includes receiving all payments of principle and interest, inspections of collateral, reviewing borrowing base of similar certificates, and performing all other necessary loan servicing.

J. *Expiration date for final disbursement.* The expiration date for final disbursement is the latest allowable date for loan disbursements. Any disbursements made after the expiration date are not covered under the guarantee. However, the guarantee remains in effect for disbursements made prior to the expiration date, subject to the terms and conditions of the guarantee agreement and the loan authorization agreement.

K. *Program and disbursement restrictions.* The SBA's program restrictions are outlined as follows:

1. *Defense and nuclear products and services.* If the SBA or the lender determine that ExIm Bank export credit insurance is required, the items to be exported must comply with ExIm Bank's guidelines on defense and nuclear products and services. Otherwise, the ExIm Bank guidelines do not apply.

2. *Inventory.* Inventory not eligible for EWCP financing is listed as follows:

   a. Inventory that is not located in the United States

    b. Demonstration inventory or inventory sold on consignment

    c. Defense articles or services if ExIm Bank insurance is required

    d. Inventory that is damaged, obsolete, returned, defective, recalled, or unfit for further processing

    e. Inventory that is to be incorporated into items destined for shipment to a foreign buyer in a country in which the SBA is legally prohibited from doing business as designated in ExIm Bank's country limitation schedule

    f. Inventory that is to be incorporated into items destined for shipment to a foreign buyer in a country in which ExIm Bank coverage is not available for commercial reasons, as designated in the country limitation schedule, unless and only to the extent that such inventory is sold to the foreign buyer on terms of an irrevocable letter of credit, confirmed by a bank acceptable to the SBA.

3. *Receivables.* Receivables not eligible for EWCP financing are listed as follows:

    a. Receivables with terms of greater than net 180 days

    b. Receivables more than 60 calendar days past the invoice due date unless insured through ExIm Bank export credit insurance for comprehensive commercial and political risk, or through SBA-approved private insurers for comparable coverage, in which case 90 calendar days shall apply

    c. Receivables from foreign buyers in countries in which the SBA is legally prohibited from doing business as set forth in the current ExIm Bank country limitation schedule

    d. Receivables from foreign buyers in countries where ExIm Bank coverage is not available for commercial reasons, as designated in the country limitation schedule, unless the export sale is supported by an irrevocable letter of credit, confirmed by a bank acceptable to the SBA.

    e. Receivables that the lender or the SBA, in its sole judgement, deem uncollectible or unacceptable for whatever reason

    f. Receivables denominated in non–U.S. currency, unless preapproved by SBA.

4. *U.S. Content.* If the SBA or the lender determine that ExIm Bank export credit insurance is required, the items to be exported must comply with ExIm Bank's guidelines on U.S. content. Otherwise, the ExIm Bank guidelines do not apply. Under ExIm Bank guidelines, when the cost of any item is made up of less than 50 percent U.S. content, then only the cost of the U.S. content may be eligible for financing. If the cost of any item is made up of at least 50 percent U.S. content, then the entire cost of that item may be eligible for financing, provided that the non–U.S. content portion is incorporated into

the item in the United States. *Note:* The term "item" means the finished goods or services that are intended for export.

5. *Other prohibited uses of disbursements.* Disbursements under the EWCP cannot be used to (a) acquire fixed assets or capital goods for use in the exporter's business; (b) acquire, equip, or rent commercial space overseas; (c) support staff in offices outside the United States; (d) finance professional export marketing advice or services, foreign business travel, or participation in trade events; or (e) repay preexisting debt or future indebtedness unrelated to the loan.

L. *Defaults and other events, acceleration and rescheduling, and claims.*

1. *Defaults and other events.* The lender is required to notify SBA in writing immediately upon receipt of information of any substantially adverse change in the financial or other condition of the exporter, including the exporter's failure to pay any amount due under the loan or any non–SBA-guaranteed loan; a borrowing base that, after a ten-day grace period, no longer supports the amount outstanding under the loan; a filing for bankruptcy or liquidation; any other uncured technical default; or any material litigation.

2. *Rescheduling and acceleration.* With the written consent of the SBA, a lender may waive a default, reschedule, or accelerate the maturity of the note if a default has not been cured within 60 days.

3. *Claims.* Lenders may request the SBA to honor its guarantee after the lender has liquidated collateral associated with an EWCP loan that has an uncured default in payment. Requests for guarantee purchase may be made as soon as 30 days after an uncured default in payment but not later than 120 days after default. For revolving loans, the period in which requests for guarantee purchase may be made is extended to one year after maturity. Lenders must establish that the cause of loss is not covered by ExIm Bank or other insurers' applicable postshipment insurance.

4. *Prohibition on litigation.* The lender shall not initiate litigation or other legal action against the exporter (or against the guarantors, if any) without the prior written consent of the SBA.

5. *Inventory liquidation.* The lender must liquidate the primary collateral associated with the export transaction financed by the EWCP loan. Unless the SBA determines otherwise, an EWCP Preferred Lender must also liquidate any additional collateral for the loan. A lender, if not a Preferred Lender, may liquidate any additional collateral for the loan subject to SBA approval. A lender who liquidates additional collateral for the loan must submit a liquidation plan to the SBA and follow the procedures set forth in the Code of Federal Regulation (13 CFR 120.405) and SBA Standard Operating Procedures 50-51.

III. EWCP Certified Lenders

   A. *Requirements.* Under the EWCP Certified Lender Program (CLP), approved lenders submit an application for guarantee, including a credit memorandum, to the SBA and usually receive a decision within three business days. The loan application must be approved by the lender prior to submission to the SBA. The lender's credit memorandum must contain the information covered in the SBA's EWCP loan officer's report guidelines, which is provided to participating lenders. In order to participate in the EWCP Certified Lender Program, the lender must meet the eligibility requirements for CLP lenders set forth in the Code of Federal Regulations (13 CFR 120, subpart E). In addition, the lender must meet the following requirements.

     1. At least one person on the lender's staff who will be involved in the EWCP Certified Lender Program must attend the SBA's export finance seminar. *Note:* the SBA may waive the training requirement for a lender with substantial experience with the EWCP.

     2. The lender must demonstrate an understanding of the EWCP by having successfully completed a minimum of two loans.

   B. *Documentation.* The SBA confers EWCP Certified Lender status through an EWCP supplemental guarantee agreement, which sets forth the SBA's agreement to provide the lender with a three-business-day response.

   C. *Certified lender limitation.* EWCP Certified Lender status does not entitle the lender to Certified Lender status for the SBA's regular 7(a) business loan program unless conferred separately for that purpose.

IV. EWCP Preferred Lender Program

   A. *Requirements.* A lender, which has been deemed eligible by the SBA pursuant to the general eligibility requirements set forth in the Code of Federal Regulations (13 CFR 120, subpart D), and has met the Certified Lender Program eligibility criteria, can apply to become an EWCP Preferred Lender. Under the Preferred Lender Program (PLP), a lender and the SBA enter into an agreement that allows the lender to approve loans and receive a guarantee from the SBA without obtaining prior SBA approval. *Note:* The maximum SBA guarantee under the EWCP Preferred Lender Program is 70 percent of the loan amount.

      EWCP participating lenders must apply for PLP status to the SBA district office where its EWCP loans are processed. The district office will forward recommendations for approval to the associate administrator of the Office of Financial Assistance, who will make the final determination on the application and notify the requesting district office.

      In making the determination of whether a lending institution shall be a Preferred Lender, the SBA shall consider, but is not limited to, the following factors:

1. The lender must have a successful history of providing trade finance to exporters (lender and loan officers).
2. The lender must have successful history with SBA demonstrating that it has the consistent ability to develop complete and well-analyzed loan packages. It must have been an active participant in the EWCP program for at least six consecutive months immediately prior to the SBA field office's recommendation. It must have submitted and the SBA must have approved at least five EWCP loans, which may have been approved on either a regular or CLP basis.

B. *Documentation.* The lender, before it can operate as a Preferred Lender, must execute an EWCP Preferred Lender Supplemental Agreement.

C. *Preferred lender limitation.* EWCP Preferred Lender status does not entitle the lender to Preferred Lender status for SBA's regular 7(a) business loan program unless conferred separately for that purpose.

V. **SBA-Approved Intermediaries**

A Certified Development Company (CDC), Small Business Development Center (SBDC), or other intermediary approved by the local SBA district office is available to help the exporter prepare and present its application for a preliminary commitment and/or application through a lender. Intermediaries are a resource to applicants; however, their use is not required. If an intermediary is used, the exporter and intermediary must enter into a written contract setting forth the terms and conditions of the arrangement. The executed contract must be included in the preliminary commitment or loan application. *Note:* The lender is not considered an intermediary for purposes of loan packaging. However, any fees charged by the lender for loan packaging must be disclosed when the lender applies to the SBA for guarantee.

Intermediaries may charge the exporter a one-time packaging fee not to exceed 1 percent of the loan amount. The fee is restricted to services rendered pursuant to the contract; however, the intermediary is not required to justify to the SBA, beyond the contract with the exporter, how the fee is used. The packaging fee is an eligible use of loan proceeds and is earned at the earlier of the issuance of a preliminary commitment or loan authorization.

VI. **Documentation**

A. *SBA/ExIm Bank joint application.* The SBA/ExIm Bank joint application sets forth the requested terms and conditions of the individual loan. This application must be submitted with all EWCP loan requests.

B. *Guarantee Agreements.* The Guarantee Agreement (SBA forms 750/750B), an agreement between the SBA and the lender, sets forth the rights and obligations of the lender and the SBA for guaranteed loans. Upon request, the SBA will forward to the lender the guarantee agreement, which must be duly executed by the lender prior to approval of the lender's first loan application.

C. *EWCP Supplemental Agreement.* The EWCP Supplemental Agreement (SBA form 750EX), an agreement between the SBA and the lender, sets forth the special eligibility requirements for a lender to participate in the EWCP.

D. *EWCP Certified Lender Supplemental Agreement.* The EWCP Certified Lender Program Supplemental Agreement (SBA form 1186EX), sets forth the SBA's agreement to provide the lender with a three-business-day response.

E. *EWCP Preferred Lender Supplemental Agreement.* The EWCP Preferred Lender Supplemental Agreement (SBA form 1347EX), an agreement between the SBA and the lender, governs the relationship between the SBA and the lender for the exercise of certain functions and responsibilities without prior SBA approval.

Upon the SBA's approval of a lender for EWCP Preferred Lender status, the SBA will forward to the lender an EWCP preferred lender supplemental agreement, which must be duly executed by the lender.

F. *Loan Authorization Agreement.* The Loan Authorization Agreement (SBA form 529B, which is available on diskette from the SBA) sets forth the SBA's approved terms and conditions for the loan. Upon approval of a loan, the SBA will issue to the lender a loan authorization agreement, which must be duly executed by the lender and borrower.

G. *Note.* The Note (SBA form 147) sets forth the specific terms and responsibilities of the exporter's obligation to repay the principal and interest on an SBA-guaranteed loan.

H. *Settlement Sheet.* The Settlement Sheet (SBA form 1050) is used to notify the SBA of the initial and all subsequent disbursements of a loan. The settlement sheet must be signed by the borrower and two copies submitted to the SBA.

I. *ExIm Bank Country Limitation Schedule.* The country limitation schedule indicates in which countries and under what conditions ExIm Bank is open for business. Compliance with the country limitation schedule is required for EWCP financing of accounts receivable that are insured by ExIm Bank.

J. *Preliminary Commitment.* The preliminary commitment is a conditional commitment issued to the exporter upon the SBA's approval of an application for a loan. It outlines the specific terms and conditions of the loan under which the SBA is prepared to issue its guarantee to an eligible lender.

VII. Inquiries

General program inquiries or requests for applications and EWCP literature should be directed to the U.S. Export Assistance Center or SBA office nearest you.

U.S. EXPORT ASSISTANCE CENTERS

BALTIMORE

World Trade Center
401 East Pratt Street, Suite 2432
Baltimore, MD 21202
(410) 962-4539

CHICAGO

Xerox Center
55 West Monroe Street, Suite 2440
Chicago, IL 60603
(312) 353-8040

LOS ANGELES

One World Trade Center
Suite 1670
Long Beach, CA 90831
(310) 980-4550

MIAMI

Trade Port Building
5600 NW 36th Street, 6th Floor
Miami, FL 33166
(305) 526-7425

For additional information on the EWCP contact: Wayne Foren, Office of Financial Assistance (202) 205-7502, or Shelly Snook, Office of International Trade (202) 205-6720.

REACH STRATEGIC VENTURE PARTNERS (RSVP)

SBA offers an on-line system for matching U.S. small businesses with potential international joint venture partners. Reach Strategic Venture Partners (RSVP) contains profiles of companies from around the world interested in developing partnerships with U.S. companies. RSVP is available through SBA OnLine, the SBA's electronic bulletin board at 1-900-463-4636 (9600, n, 8, 1).

14 Minority Enterprise Development Programs

The SBA offers special programs to assist members of minority groups who want to start or expand a small business. In this effort, the SBA has combined its own programs with those of private industry, local communities, and other federal agencies.

- *The 8(a) Program.* Under section 8(a) of the Small Business Act, the SBA works with procurement officials in other federal agencies and serves as the prime contractor for the purchase of goods and services for the federal government. The agency then subcontracts this work to small firms owned by socially and economically disadvantaged persons. The goal of the program is to help minority-owned firms become competitive by providing contracts for a limited number of years.

- *The 7(j) Program.* Under the 7(j) program, management and technical assistance is provided to 8(a) firms, other small disadvantaged businesses, low-income individuals, and small-business firms in either labor surplus areas or areas with a high proportion of low-income individuals. Assistance is provided in four major areas: accounting and finance, marketing, proposal/bid preparation, and industry-specific technical assistance. The SBA stewards cooperative agreements to both public and private organizations for the delivery of program services. Competitive and 8(a) set-aside program announcements are issued annually to solicit proposals to provide 7(j) services.

Note: This program is under legal attack from lawsuits filed in Washington D.C. and in New Mexico, which question its constitutionality. Recent Supreme Court rulings have made this program questionable, and major players are now challenging its constitutionality, but the program is still effective as of this writing.

8(a) PARTICIPANT LOANS

The SBA provides financial assistance to businesses participating in the 8(a) program. Loans may be made on a direct basis, or through lending institutions under the SBA's immediate participation or guarantee program.

Eligibility

Only applicants currently participating in the 8(a) program and therefore eligible for contractual assistance under that program are eligible.

Loan Amounts

The maximum SBA guarantee of a loan through a lending institution is $750,000. Direct and immediate participation loans are limited to an SBA share of $150,000.

Loan Proceeds

Loan proceeds are to be used within a reasonable time for plant construction, conversion or expansion, purchase of machinery and equipment, or facilities. Loan proceeds to manufacturers may be used for working capital purposes. For nonmanufacturers, working capital loan proceeds are limited to purchasing of inventory, supplies, and materials. No debt repayment is permitted.

Interest Rates

Interest rates on guarantee loans are negotiated with the lender, but may not exceed the SBA's maximum interest rates under its regular guarantee loan program. The interest rate on direct loans will be 1 percent less than the SBA direct loan rate, which changes each calendar quarter.

Maturity

The loan maturity depends on the ability of the business to repay the loan, subject to the requirements of prudent lending practices and the SBA's regulatory maximums. Machinery and equipment cannot be financed for periods longer than their conservative economic life. Real estate and construction loan maturities generally cannot exceed 25 years. Working capital maturities generally cannot exceed seven years.

Collateral

Collateral requirements for guaranteed loans are the same as for the SBA's regular loan program. Generally, collateral is required to the extent it is available and in value sufficient to secure the loan. Direct or immediate participation loans will be subordinate to perfected security interests held by financial institutions, arising from the borrowers past borrowing. This provision does not apply to past borrowings from individuals.

15 Handicapped Loan Program

The Handicapped Loan Program allows public or private nonprofit organizations for the employment of the handicapped (HAL-1) and disabled individuals (HAL-2) to get SBA financing for starting, acquiring, or operating a small business.

ELIGIBILITY

Public or Private Nonprofit Organizations (HAL-1)

Financial assistance is available to state- and federal-chartered organizations that operate in the interest of disabled individuals. Eligibility rules specify that the applying organization's net income cannot benefit any stockholder or other individual, and that at least 75 percent of the direct work involved must be done by handicapped persons.

To establish HAL-1 eligibility, applicants must provide evidence that the business is operated in the interest of handicapped individuals. The evidence may consist of copies of bylaws, incorporation papers, certification of tax-exempt status as determined by the Internal Revenue Service, or recognition and approval by the U.S. Secretary of Labor or a state vocational rehabilitation agency.

HAL-1 loan proceeds may be used for most business purposes. They may not be used for supportive service expenses such as subsidized wages of low producers, health and rehabilitation services, management, training, education and housing of handicapped workers, and other such uses.

Handicapped Individuals (HAL-2)

To be eligible for loans under the HAL-2 program, handicapped individuals must provide evidence of the following:

- The business is a for-profit operation and qualifies as small under the SBA's size standard criteria. Loans cannot be made to businesses, such as newspapers, magazines, and academic schools, involved in creating or distributing ideas or opinions, or businesses engaged in speculation or investment in rental real estate.

- The business must be 100 percent owned by one or more handicapped individuals. A handicapped individual is a person who has a permanent physical, mental, or emotional impairment, defect, ailment, disease, or major disability. Applicants must show that their disability keeps them from competing on a par with nonhandicapped competitors.

- The handicapped owner(s) must actively participate in managing the business. Applications that propose absentee ownership are not eligible.

Whether the business is organized as a proprietorship, a partnership, or a corporation is not a determining factor with respect to eligibility as a small business.

AMOUNT AND INTEREST RATES

The SBA can guarantee up to $750,000 of a loan made by a private lending institution. Direct loans from the SBA under this program are limited to $150,000. No direct loan can be approved if a guaranteed loan is available.

The SBA will not provide financial assistance if funds are otherwise available from the applicant's own resources, from a private lending institution or through financing by a government entity other than the SBA.

Interest rates on direct loans are 3 percent per year. Interest rates on guaranteed loans are set by the private lending institution and must be legal, reasonable, and within a maximum allowable rate established by the SBA.

MATURITY

The loan maturity depends on the business's ability to repay, subject to the requirements of prudent lending practices and the SBA's regulatory maximums. Machinery and equipment cannot be financed for periods longer than their conservative economic life. Real estate and construction loan maturities generally cannot exceed 25 years. Working capital maturities generally cannot exceed seven years.

COLLATERAL

Collateral requirements for all HAL loans are the same as for the SBA's regular program. Generally, collateral is required to the extent it is available and in value sufficient to secure the loan. Direct or immediate participation loans will be subordinate to perfected security interests held by financial institutions, arising from the borrower's past borrowing. This provision does not apply to past borrowing from individuals.

BASIS FOR LOAN APPROVAL

Nonprofit organizations must have the capability and experience to successfully produce or provide marketable goods and services. An evaluation of the experience, competency and ability of the owners and operators of the small business must indicate that they can operate it successfully and can repay the loan from business earnings.

16 Pollution Control Loans

The Pollution Control Loan Program provides financial assistance to small businesses for the planning, design, or installation of a "pollution control facility" for the applicant's own business. This term is rather loosely defined to include most real or personal property that will reduce pollution. The program has a maximum SBA exposure of $1,000,000 less any outstanding balance due the SBA on other loans. Note that there is nothing in this program that is different from the regular guarantee program, other than the maximum amount of the SBA's exposure and the fixed-asset-only use of proceeds aspect; therefore, this program is expected to be used when the financial need exceeds the $750,000 ceiling. Loans are made only through lenders participating in the SBA's guarantee loan program.

Eligible businesses must be for-profit operations. They also must qualify as small according to the SBA's size standards. An exception is provided for sheltered workshops qualifying under the Handicapped Assistance Loan Program. Loans cannot be made to businesses engaged in speculation or investment in rental real estate.

Maximum rates are based on the lowest prime rate on the date the SBA receives the application. For loans with maturities of less than seven years, the maximum rate is 2.25 percentage points above the prime rate. For loans with maturities of seven years or more, the maximum rate is 2.75 percentage points above the prime rate. For loans of $50,000 or less, slightly higher maximum interest rates are allowable. The interest rate may be fixed or variable, depending on negotiated loan agreements between the borrower and the lender.

A pollution control loan can be used only to finance the planning, design, or installation of a "pollution control facility." Such a facility is defined as

- A real or personal property that is likely to help prevent, reduce, abate, or control noise, air, or water pollution or contamination, by removing, altering, disposing of, or storing pollutants, contaminants, wastes, or heat; or

- A real or personal property that will be used for the collection, storage, treatment, utilization, processing, or final disposal of solid or liquid waste; or

• Any related recycling property when a local, state, or federal environmental regulatory agency says it will be useful for pollution control.

The SBA will guarantee up to $1 million of a loan to any one borrower. This maximum will be reduced by any amount owed by the borrower on a loan made under the regular SBA lending program.

Applicants must pledge adequate collateral and provide personal guaranties if required by the agency. Refusal to pledge available collateral may be sufficient reason for declining the loan.

The SBA analyzes projected cash flows to determine if the company can repay the proposed loan together with any other fixed obligations.

The loan maturity depends on the applicant's ability to repay the loan, subject to the requirements of prudent lending practices and the SBA's regulatory maximums. Machinery and equipment cannot be financed for periods longer than its conservative economic life. Real estate and construction loan maturities cannot exceed 25 years.

17 Microloan Program

With entrepreneurs starting up new businesses at a record rate, the need for start-up financing is greater now than ever before. Yet most banks do not make loans to businesses needing less than $25,000, in business for less than 2 years, and which lack acceptable collateral. While most start-ups end up getting their initial funds from savings and personal loans from friends and relatives, new businesses often need additional financing for working capital, or to continue to grow during the first and second years. The role of the SBA Microloan Program is to take promising new businesses and provide the financing to get them to the next stage.

The SBA Microloan Demonstration Program was authorized in October 1991, with the ratification of Public Law 102-140, section 609 (h). The program is referred to as the Microloan Program. The law is effective for five years and expires on October 23, 1996. Funding of the program is subject to availability of appropriations. Public Law 102-366, dated September 4, 1992, and known as the Commerce, Justice and State, the Judiciary, and Related Agencies Appropriations Act of 1992 provided substantive amendments to the Microloan Program.

Virtually all types of business are eligible for a microloan. To be eligible, the business must be operated for profit and fall within six standards set by the SBA (most businesses are well within the standards).

Money borrowed under this program can be used for the purchase of machinery and equipment, furniture and fixtures, inventory, supplies, and for working capital. You may not use it to pay existing debts. A microloan must be paid on the shortest term possible—no longer than six years—depending on the earnings of the business. The interest rate on these loans cannot be higher than 4 percentage points over the New York prime rate.

The loan applicant must demonstrate good character, enough management expertise and commitment for running a successful operation, and show that there is a reasonable assurance that the loan will be repaid. Each nonprofit lending organization will have its own requirements about collateral. However, the organization must at least take as collateral any assets that are bought with the microloan. In most cases, the personal guaranties of the business owners will also be required.

In 1992, the SBA unveiled this ''microloan'' program as designed to assist very small businesses, especially those run by women, minorities, and low-income entrepreneurs who often have serious trouble raising capital. It was also developed for those times when just a small loan can make the difference. Under this program, loans range from less than $100 to a maximum of $25,000, averaging about $10,000. In some cases, a good reputation in the community is the only collateral required.

Under this program the SBA has made funds available to nonprofit organizations for the purpose of lending to small businesses. For example, a Los Angeles nonprofit agency, the Coalition for Women's Economic Development, received a $750,000 SBA loan from which it makes microloans. These organizations can also provide management and technical assistance.

The Bush administration started this one-year pilot program to assist low-income people such as single mothers and public housing tenants toward self-employment. It was the first SBA program designed to help the poor become business owners.

Loans under this pilot program started flowing in July 1992. SBA Administrator Patricia Saiki said at the time, "I hope this program will give an opportunity to the small cottage industry . . . [to] people who haven't had a chance before. Home-based sole proprietorships, including 'homemakers who want to start something in the basement,' are a target of the microloan program."

The microloan idea is one of several domestic initiatives aimed at empowering the poor. The SBA experiment is modeled after several seed-loan programs run by nonprofit groups in recent years that have helped start businesses or fund going mom-and-pop operations.

The Microloan Program is part of the SBA's direct loan program, which offers direct loans at slightly below market rates to military veterans, disabled business owners, and those who want to start companies in economically depressed areas. Funds for such programs currently total $17 million annually and may be increased.

The program was introduced in a limited number of cities in the northeast to test its feasibility. News of the plan came as a surprise to some of those involved with existing non-SBA programs, such as Women's Economic Development Corp. (Wedco) in St. Paul, Minn. This microenterprise loan organization, founded by Ms. Kathryn Keeley, has offered self-employment loans for eight years, helped start over 900 businesses (of which 87 percent are still in operation), and served as one of the SBA's program models.

Another such program is operating in North Carolina. Scot Sanderson of Marshall, N.C., built his ABC Recycling Service, Inc. into a $180,000-a-year company after starting with a $2,500 microenterprise loan from the North Carolina Rural Economic Development Center. In business for about two years, the concern doubled in size every six months, and at last report had four employees and is handling 30 different classes of materials.

The North Carolina program began in the fall of 1989 and has made over 57 loans. It has a 90 percent repayment rate so far. Modeled in part after a peer-group lending program used by the Grameen Bank of Bangladesh, the program forms teams of five people with a shared interest in starting or developing their own businesses. The group chooses two of its members to receive the first loans, and no one else in that particular group can get a loan until the original recipients have made four consecutive payments. The loan amounts range from about $500 to $8,000 at market interest rates, but are made without collateral. Peer pressure and support from other members of the group are supposed to keep the payments coming. The program operates statewide, using local community organizations to provide business counseling services and a nonprofit credit union to handle the paper work on the loans. This program was started to reach small rural businesses that couldn't even qualify for credit union financing.

Although the money attracts people to the program—most banks don't consider very small loans worth the paper work, the biggest gain is reported to be the exchange of ideas with other business owners in a peer group established as part of the program. This group becomes a brain trust and a sounding board that multiplies members' capabilities four or five times. Everybody knows the statistics for small-business failure, but participants in this program are certain that if programs like it were to be established on a larger scale, the statistics would be reversed. Most would succeed rather than fail.

Veterans of other enterprise programs for low-income people express caution. They warn that without substantial counseling and guidance, this SBA direct loan program will not succeed. The SBA has taken these cautions to heart, and the program includes a demanding training and counseling process for applicants before they get a loan. Directors of the microloan programs that have served as models for the SBA effort claim their programs are both tough and successful.

Different participants participate differently. The Center for Southeast Asian Refugee Resettlement (CSEARR), licensed as a commercial lender by the State of California, makes loans from $5,000 to $25,000 to small businesses located in Alameda, Contra Costa, Marin, San Francisco, San Mateo, Santa Clara, Sonoma, Napa, and Solano counties. Businesses in other northern California counties will be considered on a case by case basis.

Since 1993, the CSEARR has been the sole operator of the SBA microloan program in San Francisco. More than 20 loans have been made to small businesses in industries ranging from fast food to insurance consulting to auto parts remanufacture. Although the loan program takes risks that most bank lenders avoid, a disciplined and detailed assessment of each loan applicant focusing on the abilities of the entrepreneur and the potential of the business to generate positive cash flows has resulted in no loan defaults to date. Loans are available to any qualifying small business.

This participant applies the basic SBA rule that borrowers seeking these loans of $15,000 to $25,000 must have been turned down by a regular commercial lender. For specific loan eligibility requirements, you must attend a loan application workshop. These are offered every Wednesday at 10:00 A.M.

Generally, the following criteria apply for applicants:

- Should have run the business for at least 6 months on a full-time basis, although start-ups will be considered if certain conditions are met.

- The business must be "small" under SBA 7(a) small-business guidelines.

- Collateral is required; business assets are acceptable as collateral in most cases.

- An equity contribution equal to at least one-half of the loan amount requested is required.

Applicants are required to demonstrate good credit and character, complete a loan package that demonstrates the viability of the business and adequate debt coverage, provide tax returns, personal financial statements, and other standard loan documents. The borrower(s) must be over 18 and a U.S. citizen, permanent resident, or have legal status to own and operate a U.S.-based business.

Participants in the microloan program have created new jobs for entrepreneurs and employees alike, sometimes in traditional areas, but other times, in areas of less obvious market opportunities including dog grooming and commercial art. Several loan recipients have built their businesses into highly profitable operations in less than six months.

The Coalition for Women's Economic Development (CWED) was founded as a nonprofit organization in 1988 to assist low-income women achieve self-sufficiency through self-employment. Although initially targeted for women, CWED now offers training, technical assistance, and loans to both women and men in the greater Los Angeles area. The program promotes self-employment and microbusiness ownership as a strategy to increase self-sufficiency and self-esteem. As the first program of its kind in southern California, CWED has become a leader in the emerging field of microenterprise and community development.

CWED offers two programs to its participants: Microbusiness Workshops, consisting of a five-week "get ready for business" workshop and a ten-week "business plan" workshop. These workshops are designed to help low-income entrepreneurs start, manage, and expand their own small businesses. The second program, Solidarity Circles, is a peer lending and credit training program for low-income entrepreneurs already in business. Both programs offer technical assistance and are offered in English and Spanish. Access to credit from the Revolving Loan Fund is available to participants who complete the training. The Revolving Loan Fund offers microloans to $25,000. Capital for this fund is provided by various private and public loan sources, as well as through the SBA Microloan Demonstration Program.

Since the inception of training programs in May 1989, over 5,000 women and men have attended orientation sessions on self-employment, and 200 loans have been issued, totaling approximately $600,000.

CWED's commitment to assisting low-income entrepreneurs also includes a commitment to changing local policies that present obstacles for low-income individuals who wish to become self-employed. CWED board and staff members have participated on the City of Lost Angeles Street Vending Task Force since 1989. On January 14, 1994, the City Council adopted a sidewalk vending ordinance to allow pilot districts for sidewalk vending. CWED is proud of its involvement with the task force and continues to work toward creating a more friendly business environment for low-income entrepreneurs.

Solidarity Circle Program. This program consists of a group lending model developed in the Grameen Bank in Bangladesh. Through mutual support and a shared risk, a circle of five business owners come together and go through an eight- to ten-week initiation period that incorporates business training and technical assistance. At the end of this initiation period, the circle is certified and its members begin to receive microloans. The loan review committee is composed of the five Solidarity Circle members and CWED staff. No collateral is required for these loans, rather the Circle members agree to assume each other's loan in case of default.

Get Ready for Business Workshop. This five-week workshop is designed for individuals who are at an idea or planning stage in their business or who have been operating their business for less than six months. This workshop is designed to assist an individual's potential to succeed in business and introduce basic business concepts, such as marketing, pricing, competition analysis, and feasibility. Graduates of the Get Ready for Business Workshop can enroll in CWED's Business Plan Workshop.

Business Plan Workshop. This ten-week workshop is designed for individuals who have an existing business. The workshop allows students to develop a business plan, and in the process learn how to successfully manage their business for stability. Topics covered include time and money management, business operations and management, market research and strategy, record keeping systems and financial documentation, and business plan preparation.

Loan Application Workshop. This two-hour workshop is designed to familiarize potential CWED borrowers with all loan requirements and to walk them through the actual loan application. It also has a business plan and loan application checklist which lists all the supporting documentation that is needed in order to review the loan application.

Revolving Loan Fund. The Revolving Loan Fund is the capital fund for CWED microbusiness owners. First stage ($500–$5,000) and second stage ($5,001–$25,000) loans are available through the CWED Revolving Loan Fund. This fund is designed as a single source use of funds and will loan to start-up and existing microbusinesses. Loan approval is based on either peer review (Solidarity Circle borrowers) or Loan Committee review (individual borrowers). All individual borrowers must develop a current business plan within six months of applying. CWED will review loan applications only from CWED Business Plan Workshop graduates or graduates from an affiliated training agency by written referral only.

The CWED 1994 program highlights include the following:

- *Orientation meetings.* These monthly, one-hour orientation meetings were held in both Spanish and English in different areas of Los Angeles County. These meetings served to introduce potential clients to the CWED programs, as well as provide an opportunity to inform people about business do's and don'ts, and other training and financing resources. The total number of people seen during 1994 was 1,051.

- *Solidarity Circle Program.* Eighty-two businesses participated in CWED's Solidarity Circle Program, the innovative noncollateral peer lending program. Of these businesses, ten received their first-time loans in 1994. The remaining 72 businesses are borrowers that had received their first and second loans in 1992 and 1993. These borrowers continued to receive loan management assistance through the Solidarity Circle Program. Total loans disbursed through the Solidarity Circle Program in 1994 amounted to $42,900. The average solidarity loan size for 1994 was $2,250.

- *Microbusiness Workshop Program.* Twenty-five Get Ready for Business Workshops, 15 Business Plan Workshops, and 4 Entrepreneurial Mentoring Workshop Programs (44 entrepreneurial training workshops) were offered in 1994. The Get Ready for Business and Business Plan Workshops were also offered in Spanish.

  - *Get Ready for Business Workshops (five-week workshops).* Beginning Enrollment = 351, Graduates = 256 (73%), Dropped = 44 (12%), No-shows = 51 (15%)
  - *Business Plan Workshops (12-week Workshops).* Beginning Enrollment = 234, Completed Training and Graduated = 141 (60%), Dropped = 52 (22%), No Shows = 41 (18%)

- *Preborrower Workshops.* CWED's Preborrower workshops include a six-hour Bookkeeping Workshop and a two-hour Loan Preparation Workshop that were designed to strengthen the potential applicant's loan package before final presentation to the Loan Review Committee. Bookkeeping Workshop enrollment was 140. Loan Preparation Workshop enrollment was 130.

- *CWED Loan Fund.* The CWED Loan Fund disbursed 27 loans in the 1994 calendar year, totaling $93,795. The Revolving Loan Fund is capitalized by various loan sources, including the SBA Microloan Demonstration Program. Nineteen loans were disbursed through the Solidarity Circle Program, totaling $42,900, while eight loans were disbursed to individuals who had graduated from the CWED Microbusiness Workshop program. These eight loans totaled $50,895. The average loan size for an individual borrower was $6,361, while the average Solidarity Circle loan was $2,250.

Valley Small Business Development Corporation (Valley) is organized as a nonprofit, public benefit corporation. Valley contracts with the State of California, Department of Commerce, Office of Small Business. Valley's primary service area is the central San Joaquin Valley, from Modesto to Bakersfield. Under the terms of the state contract, Valley administers several direct loan and loan guarantee programs.

When financing for a business start-up, deficiencies are identified relative to the adequacy of the borrower's management/business skills, or if the business has shown consistent profitability, the borrower must participate in a business course designed to remedy the deficiencies.

- *Valley Small Business Institute.* Valley offers a basic management and business skills training course conducted through video seminars designed to improve the borrower's chances of obtaining bank loans by providing a working knowledge of basic business skills and techniques. However, taking this course is not a guarantee that bank financing will occur.

  The course consists of instruction on accounting controls and reporting, construction of a budget, cash flow evaluation, preparation of a business plan, basic marketing, personnel management, licensing, taxation, and sources of capital. The fee for the VSBI business training course videos is $149.50.

- *Loan particulars.* Microloans shall receive normal and customary staff, loan committee, and board of directors review, just as for loans made under the guarantee loan program. However, the approval requirements are not as stringent.

  Valley may offer a guaranteed microloan through Clovis Community Bank or First Interstate Bank who have agreed to fund all loans having satisfactorily passed the loan committee and board review. The interest rate is 12.5 percent, fixed. Typically, the loans will be secured by all business assets. In all instances, personal assets must also be pledged as security for the loan. All loans must be repaid in full over no longer than a five-year period. The borrower may request interest-only payments for the first three months. Where applicable, loans are repaid through an automatic debit of the borrower's business checking account established with First Interstate Bank.

- *Loan fees.* Valley charges a 2 percent guarantee fee and a $250 processing fee for guaranteed loans. There are no fees on the SBA microloans. Any fees due are collected at the time the loan is made and can be paid with loan proceeds. However, the borrower is responsible for all out-of-pocket costs for security filings, credit reports, lien searches, and so forth.

As can be seen by the way the above participants describe their programs, they all are different—meeting the particular needs of the people in the serviced area. But they are also basically alike in that they are dedicated to meeting the needs of the very small entrepreneurial businessperson.

The $17 million SBA microloan program operated initially in 35 cities and towns. (The SBA and Congress have established this as a size limit for the program; see the list on page 239.) In each of these cities and towns, a nonprofit agency, chosen because of its familiarity with the local business scene, decides who qualifies for the SBA money and sets the terms of the loans. The maximum loan is $25,000, and the maximum term is six years. The negotiated interest rate can't exceed four percentage points over the prime lending rate charged by commercial banks. Asset collateral is required for larger loans. But for a loan in the $600 to $700 range, the lending requirement could be a character reference.

The 35 nonprofit groups from urban and rural areas use their own judgement about who gets the loan funds and for what purposes, although Congress requires that half the loans be made to small businesses in rural areas. The SBA stresses that the funds are not grants. The nonprofit agencies are expected to eventually repay these funds to the federal treasury, with interest. The microloan program is a risk venture to which the SBA has committed itself. The end result cannot be predicted, because the nonprofit agencies are the ones who will make it work or not. But reports to date are very positive.

Politics appeared to play a part in how the original funds were distributed. A total of $3 million, or 20 percent of the loan fund, was earmarked for agencies in the four states represented by the chair and ranking minority members of the House and Senate Small Business Committees. The Arkansas Enterprise Group in Arkadelphia received the maximum $750,000 to reloan. At the time, Sen. Dale Bumpers (D. Ark.) headed the Senate's small-business panel.

ELIGIBILITY REQUIREMENTS

Practically all types of businesses are eligible for a microloan. To be eligible, your business must be operated for profit and fall within size standards set by the SBA (most businesses are well within the standards).

USE OF FUNDS

Money borrowed under this program can be used for the purchase of machinery and equipment, furniture and fixtures, inventory, supplies, and for working capital. It may not be used to pay existing debts.

TERMS OF LOAN

A microloan must be repaid on the shortest term possible—no longer than six years—depending on the earnings of the business. The interest rate on these loans is competitive and based on the cost of money to the intermediary lender. *It cannot be higher than 4 percentage points over the New York prime rate.*

CREDIT REQUIREMENTS

The loan applicant must demonstrate good character and enough management expertise and commitment for running a successful operation, and show that there is a reasonable assurance that the loan will be repaid.

COLLATERAL REQUIREMENTS

Each nonprofit lending organization will have its own requirements about collateral. *However, the organization must at least take as collateral any assets that are bought with the microloan.* In most cases, the personal guarantees of the business owner(s) will also be required.

APPLYING FOR A MICROLOAN

The first step in applying for a microloan is to call or visit a participating lender (see the following list). Or, contact the regional office of the SBA and ask for a list of participating lenders. They can tell you if your company qualifies for a microloan and will explain what information you must supply and how to apply.

Remember, this program is designed primarily to assist women, low-income, and minority entrepreneurs, business owners, and others who show they can operate small businesses successfully. Most likely to benefit are new and existing part-time and home-based sole proprietorships.

The SBA provided the funds to the 35 preselected nonprofit agencies because of their familiarity with the local business community. These agencies decide who receives microloans and they set the loan terms. The agencies are expected to repay the SBA for the funds with interest within ten years. The following is a list of the 35 nonprofit agencies and the total amounts of loan money available from them.

Albuquerque, N. Mex., Women's Economic Self-Sufficiency Team, $80,000

Anchorage, Alaska, Community Enterprise Development of Alaska, $200,000

Arcata, Calif., Arcata Economic Development Corp., $200,000

Arkadelphia, Ark., The Arkansas Enterprise Group, $750,000

Athens, Ohio, Athens Small Business Center Inc., $250,000

Baltimore, Md., Council for Equal Business Opportunity, $345,000

Bozeman, Mont., Capital Opportunities, $60,000

Charleston, S.C., The Charleston Citywide Local Development Corp., $300,000

Chicago, Ill., The Neighborhood Institute and Women's Self-Employment Project, $750,000

Dallas, Tex., Southern Dallas Development Corp., $750,000

Denver, Colo., Greater Denver Local Development Corp., $250,000

Durham, N.C., Self-Help Ventures Fund, $500,000

Fond du Lac, Wis., Advocap Inc., $100,000

Greenfield, Mass., The Western Massachusetts Enterprise Fund, $125,000

Greenville, Miss., Delta Foundation, $500,000

Hayden, Idaho, Panhandle Area Council, $200,000

Indianapolis, Ind., Eastside Community Investments Inc., $175,000

London, Ky., Kentucky Highlands Investment Corp., $750,000

Los Angeles, Calif., Coalition for Women's Economic Development, $750,000

Manchester, N.H., Institute for Cooperative Community Development Inc., $500,000

Milwaukee, Wis., Women's Business Initiative Corp., $750,000

Pensacola, Fla., Community Equity Investments Inc., $500,000

Phoenix, Ariz., Chicanos Por La Causa Inc., $300,000

Providence, R.I., Elmwood Neighborhood Housing Services, $150,000

Rochester, N.Y., Rural Opportunities Inc., $400,000

Saranac Lake, N.Y., Adirondack Economic Development Corp., $500,000

Savannah, Ga., Small Business Assistance Corp., $175,000

Sioux City, Iowa, Siouxland Economic Development Corp., $200,000

Sisseton, S.D., Northeast South Dakota Energy Conservation Corp., $120,000

St. Johnsbury, Vt., Northern Community Investment Corp., $375,000

St. Paul, Minn., Women Venture, $500,000

Sterling, Ill., Greater Sterling Development Corp., $150,000

Virginia, Minn., Northeast Entrepreneur Fund Inc., $200,000

Walthill, Nebr., Rural Enterprise Assistance Project, $80,000

Wiscasset, Maine, Coastal Enterprises Inc., $750,000

As the program was initially conceived, the SBA was authorized to fund a maximum of 35 intermediaries. At least one, but not more than two, were to be named in each of the following states: Alaska, Arkansas, Arizona, California, Illinois, Indiana, Iowa, Kentucky, Maine, Minnesota, Mississippi, Missouri, New Hampshire, New York, North Carolina, Pennsylvania, South Carolina, Vermont, and Wisconsin. Organizations in all other states, territories, and the District of Columbia were eligible to compete. Original intermediaries were eligible for grant funding of up to 20 percent of their loan amount. The SBA was also authorized to fund two grants to microenterprise development organizations for the provision of technical assistance and training to low-income individuals for the purpose of increasing the chances of viability for their businesses. The original 35 lenders and two grantees were announced on June 10, 1992. Since that time, the program has grown to its current level of 101 intermediaries and 25 nonlending technical assistance grantees.

The purpose of the program was and is the following:

- To assist women, low-income, and minority entrepreneurs, business owners, and other individuals possessing the capability to operate successful business concerns; and to assist small business concerns in those areas suffering from a lack of credit due to economic downturn

- To make loans to eligible intermediaries for the provision of small-scale loans, particularly in amounts averaging $7,500 or less, to start-up, newly established, or growing small-business concerns for working capital or acquisition of materials, supplies or equipment

- To make grants to eligible intermediaries that, together with nonfederal matching funds, will enable them to provide intensive marketing, management, and technical assistance to microloan borrowers

- To make grants to eligible nonprofit entities that, together with nonfederal matching funds, will enable them to provide intensive marketing, management, and technical assistance to low-income entrepreneurs and other low-income individuals with the goal of obtaining private sector financing for their businesses.

In addition, the SBA reports to the Congressional Committees of Small Business regarding program effectiveness, and the advisability and feasibility of nationwide implementation.

There are three levels of participation. An entity can participate as an intermediary lender, providing loans and technical assistance. An entity can take part as a nonlending technical assistance provider. Or, an entity can participate as a capacity builder, providing technical assistance to those acting as intermediaries or having the potential to do so. No more than four such entities may be authorized in each state.

- *Participation Level One.* An organization is eligible to apply to become an intermediary lender if it

  1. Is a private, nonprofit entity (or consortium of same); a private, nonprofit community development corporation (or a consortium of same); or a quasi-governmental economic development entity, other than a state, county, or municipal government, or any agency thereof, only if no application is received from an otherwise eligible organization, or the needs of a region or geographical area are not or cannot be adequately served by an otherwise eligible organization that has applied to participate or has previously been accepted for participation in the program; and
  2. Has a minimum of one year of experience, of itself, making and servicing microloans to start-up, newly established, or growing small-business concerns; and
  3. Has a minimum of one year of experience, of itself, providing as an integral part of its lending program, technical assistance and training to its microloan borrowers.

An eligible organization applying to take part as an intermediary lender may qualify, based on information submitted in its proposal, according to criteria set forth in a current Program Announcement/Request for Proposals. An intermediary lender may borrow up to $750,000 during its first year of participation and receive a grant of up to 25 percent of the amount of the loan that the SBA disburses. Grant funds must be used to provide technical assistance to program-funded microloan borrowers. A 15 percent, cash, matching contribution is required for loan funds. A 25 percent, cash or in kind, matching contribution is required for grant funds.

A business in need of a microloan must apply directly to the intermediary lender serving its geographic location.

A small business is eligible to apply for a microloan if it is a for-profit business that meets SBA-type business requirements and size eligibility standards at the time of application.

The maximum term for a microloan is six years. Intermediary lenders may charge interest based on the size of the microloans. Maximum interest rates are 8.50 percent above the intermediary's cost of funds for microloans less than or equal to $7,500, or 7.75 percent above the intermediary's cost of funds for microloans over $7,500.

- *Participation Level Two.* Under the program, the SBA may make grants to nonprofit entities participating exclusively as technical assistance providers. Such organizations must provide marketing, management, and technical assistance to low-income individuals seeking to start or enlarge their small-business concerns. Organizations wishing to participate in this manner, who deem themselves qualified to provide the required assistance and who are not participating, or seeking to participate, as intermediary lenders may apply for such grants under a current Program Announcement/Request for Proposals. A maximum of 25 such grants will be awarded annually during the life of the program. The maximum grant amount per participant is $125,000 per year. A matching contribution of 20 percent, cash or in kind, is required.

- *Participation Level Three.* Qualification procedures and requirements are currently being developed for those organizations interested in participating as providers of technical assistance to other microenterprise development organizations. Application procedures will be issued in the near future.

The SBA is authorized to make direct loans to eligible and qualified intermediary lenders, who will use the proceeds to make short-term fixed interest rate microloans to start-up, newly established, and growing small-business concerns.

The SBA is authorized to make grants to such intermediary lenders to be used to provide intensive marketing, management, and technical assistance to their microloan borrowers.

The SBA is authorized to make six grants to nonintermediary, nonprofit entities who will provide intensive marketing, management, and technical assistance to qualified small-business concerns and will help these concerns to obtain loans up to $15,000. Such grants cannot exceed $125,000.

INTERMEDIARY QUALIFICATIONS

- The intermediary must be a private, nonprofit entity or a private, nonprofit community development corporation, or a quasi-governmental development entity other than a state, county, or municipal government or any agency thereof.

- Two or more private, nonprofit organizations pooling human and other resources, and applying for participation in the microloan program is considered to be a single entity. This precludes any such organization from participating singly in the operation of the program.

- The intermediary must have a minimum of one year of experience, of itself, making and servicing microloans to start-up, newly established, or growing small-business concerns.

- The intermediary must have a minimum of one year of experience, of itself, providing, as an integral part of its microloan program, intensive marketing, management, and technical assistance to its microloan borrowers.

- An intermediary may not conduct its operations under this program outside of the geographical area approved by the SBA.

Legislation governing the Microloan Demonstration Program was ratified on October 22, 1994. Under PL 104-140, effective March 1995, several program changes were provided which await finalization or new regulations. Highlights of the legislation include the following:

Section 201. Up to twenty intermediaries will receive loans under a deferred participation (guarantee) pilot. Each organization will borrow its loan funding from local financial institutions. The SBA will then guarantee those loans as opposed to offering direct financing. These loans will be designed as revolving lines of credit during the first five years of a ten-year maturity. During the first year, no interest or principal will be due on funds drawn down. During the second through fifth years, interest payments will be required. During the sixth through tenth years, full amortization of principal and interest will be required.

Section 202. Agencies of, or nonprofit entities established by, Native American tribal governments will now be eligible to participate as intermediary lenders.

Section 204. Expansion to a maximum of 200 intermediaries will be allowed with population-based limitations on funding.

Section 206. Within limitations, intermediaries will be allowed to borrow up to $2.5 million (up from $1.25 million).

Section 207. Intermediaries will be able to spend up to 15 percent of their grant funding for "prospective borrowers" as opposed to the 10 percent previously allowed.

Section 208. Availability of the 5 percent "bonus" grant has been expanded to include intermediaries making 50 percent or more of their loans in economically distressed areas.

Section 611. The program will be prohibited from providing financial or technical assistance to any business whose products or services are deemed to be obscene.

Section 612. Recipients of financial assistance will be required to certify that they are not more than 60-days delinquent in child support payments.

FUNDING

Loan Limitation

Loan amounts from the SBA to an intermediary lender(s) shall not exceed the following:

$750,000 to any one intermediary lender in the first year of the lender's participation in the program

$1,250,000 to any one intermediary lender, for all the years of the lender's participation in the program

$1,500,000 to *all* intermediary lenders selected within a state in the first year of such state's participation in the program

$2,500,000 to *all* intermediary lenders selected within a state for all the years of such state's participation in the program

Funds are disbursed quarterly by the SBA to an intermediary requesting funds. The written request must be accompanied by the quarterly report and a projection showing the need for these funds. In no case should the first request exceed 35 percent of the total loan approved.

Cost of Money

Loans made to an intermediary by the SBA will bear a rate of interest equal to the rate applicable to five-year obligations of the U.S. Treasury, adjusted to the nearest one-eighth of 1 percent, less 1.25 percent.

Maturity

Any loan made by the SBA to an intermediary under this program shall be for a term of ten years.

An intermediary shall not be required to make any repayment of principal and interest during the first year of any loan made under this program. However, interest will accrue on the outstanding balance during such time period.

Amortization will be over a nine-year period (or 108 monthly payments of principal and interest). Monthly payments due the SBA will start on the first day of the thirteenth month from the date of the note.

Fees

The SBA may charge only normal routine closing fees, and the closing will be facilitated by the local SBA office.

Collateral

The SBA shall have security interest with first lien position on the following:

1. Notes receivable due to an intermediary from its microloan borrowers under this program
2. The bank accounts of the intermediary

Matching Contribution

Each intermediary will be required to contribute, *from nonfederal sources,* 15 percent of the loan amount and deposit same in an account called the Microloan Revolving Fund Account (MRF). Such contributions must be in cash, and no portion thereof can be borrowed funds. This account may be used also for normal business transactions.

LOANS TO BORROWERS

Eligibility

The microloan borrower must be a for-profit business concern, must meet SBA size standards, and must be located within the geographical area served by the intermediary lender.

Use of Proceeds

Microloan proceeds shall be used by microloan borrowers exclusively for working capital, inventory, supplies, furniture, fixtures, machinery, and/or equipment. In no case shall the proceeds of a microloan be used for down payment purposes.

Servicing

Loan applications should be filed directly with the intermediary, who has sole responsibility for making eligibility determination, credit decisions, closing and disbursing approved loans, and for servicing its microloan portfolio. The SBA will not review microloan applications.

Terms

Generally, a microloan made under this program should not be for more than $10,000. An intermediary lender may make a microloan of more than $15,000 only if the borrower demonstrates that it is unable to obtain credit elsewhere at comparable rates. In no case may a loan exceed $25,000, nor can an intermediary have more than $25,000 outstanding and committed to any one borrower.

The average loan in the portfolio of an intermediary should not exceed $7,500. There is a discount available to intermediaries (for funds borrowed from SBA) who stay within this parameter.

Maturity

The maximum maturity of microloans made under this program is six years.

Interest Rate

If the amount of a microloan is $7,500 or less, the maximum interest rate is 8.5 percentage points *above* the cost of money to the intermediary lender. If the amount of a microloan is more than $7,500, the maximum interest rate is 7.75 percentage points above the cost of money to the intermediary lender.

Loan Loss Reserve Fund

Each intermediary must establish a deposit account called the Loan Loss Reserve Fund (LLRF) account. The LLRF account, and all earnings thereon, shall be maintained until all obligations owed to the SBA under this program are repaid. In the first year of an intermediary's participation in this program, the LLRF account must be maintained in an amount equal to 15 percent of the outstanding balance of notes receivable owed to the intermediary under this program. For subsequent years, the LLRF account should be maintained at a level that reflects the intermediary's total loss experience in this program, as determined by the SBA on a case by case basis.

TECHNICAL ASSISTANCE GRANTS

General

A microloan borrower shall be entitled to receive intensive marketing, management, and technical assistance from the intermediary lender. Any intermediary that receives a loan from the SBA under this program shall be eligible to receive a grant from the SBA, the proceeds of which must be used to provide the services mentioned above. An intermediary is prohibited from contracting for or engaging the services of another entity, on a fee basis, for the provision of such marketing, management, and technical assistance.

Amount of Grant

An intermediary lender may receive a yearly grant of not more than 25 percent of the total outstanding balance of loans made to it under this program. A specialized intermediary (one who maintains an average portfolio of $7,500) may be eligible for an additional 5 percent of the outstanding balance of its SBA loan.

Matching Contribution

Each intermediary that receives a grant will be required to provide a matching contribution, solely from nonfederal sources, equal to 25 percent of the amount of its SBA grant. The matching contribution may include cash, indirect costs, or in-kind contributions paid for under nonfederal programs. A matching contribution is not required for the specialized intermediaries who obtain the additional 5 percent grant.

MICROLOAN PROGRAM STATISTICAL INFORMATION AS OF MARCH 31, 1995

Program Participants

Intermediary lenders selected	103
Intermediary loans closed	135
Intermediary lenders withdrawn	2
Total current intermediaries	101
Total $ Intermediary loans approved	$48,700,000

Microloans Made to Small Business

# of loans made to small business		2760
$ of loans made to small business		$29,422,847
Average loan amount		$10,660
Average interest rate		10.35%
Average loan maturity in months		44
Loans made in urban areas	1543	55.91%
Loans made in rural areas	1150	41.67%
Nonresponsive	67	2.42%
TOTAL	2760	100.00%
Loans made for business start-up	1114	40.36%
Loans to existing businesses	1601	58.01%
Nonresponsive	45	1.63%
TOTAL	2760	100.00%
Loans made to manufacturing bus.	406	14.71%
Loans made to wholesale bus.	140	5.07%
Loans made to retail bus.	758	27.46%
Loans made to service bus.	956	34.64%
Loans made to other bus.	386	13.99%
Nonresponsive	114	4.13%
TOTAL	2760	100.00%
Loans to 100% women-owned bus.	955	34.60%
Loans to 51% women-owned bus.	204	7.39%
TOTAL	1159	41.99%
Loans to nonveterans	2077	75.25%
Loans to Vietnam-era veterans	168	6.09%
Loans to other veterans	188	6.81%
Nonresponsive	327	11.85%
TOTAL	2760	100.00%

Ethnic Breakdown

Black	654	23.70%
Hispanic	117	4.24%
White	1734	62.83%
Puerto Rican	81	2.93%
Asian or P. Islander	27	.98%
Multi-group	43	1.56%
American Indian	44	1.59%
Eskimo/Aleut	7	.25%
Nonresponsive	53	1.92%
TOTAL	2760	100.00%

Use of Proceeds of Loans Made to small Business

Working capital	41%
Materials	4%
Supplies	6%
Equipment	32%
Inventory	17%

18 LowDoc Loans

LowDoc is the program that the SBA has implemented to help those who feel overwhelmed by the paperwork and red tape when applying for a loan: a low-documentation lending program for small business.

The program attempts to accomplish the following purposes:

- LowDoc provides an easy, one-page SBA application (SBA form 4-L, see Figure 18.1).
- LowDoc simplifies the application process.
- LowDoc provides a rapid response from SBA—usually only two or three days.
- LowDoc focuses on character, credit, and experience.

This makes small-business financing faster and easier.

HOW IT WORKS

- LowDoc is for small business loans of $100,000 or less.
- The SBA guarantees up to 90 percent of the loan.
- The applicant completes the front of a one-page SBA application; the lender completes the back. Lenders may require additional information from the applicant.
- For loans over $50,000, the applicant includes a copy of federal income tax Schedule C or the front page of the corporate or partnership returns for the past three years. Or, the applicant may sign a waiver and the SBA will get the tax information direct from the IRS.
- Personal financial statements are required for all guarantors.

WHO'S ELIGIBLE

- Entrepreneurs starting a new business

- Businesses whose average annual sales for the preceding three years do not exceed $5 million and who employ 100 or less, including affiliates
- Businesses that satisfy other statutory criteria

INTEREST RATES

- Applicants negotiate terms with the lender.
- Interest rates are tied to the prime rate and may be fixed or variable; however, they cannot exceed SBA maximums as follows:
  - For loans of less than seven years the maximum is 2.25 percentage points over prime.
  - For loans of seven years or longer the maximum is 2.75 percentage points over prime.
  - Loans under $50,000 may be subject to slightly higher rates.

MATURITY

Length of time for repayment depends on

- The ability to repay; and
- The use of the loan proceeds; however
- It may not exceed 25 years for fixed assets or 10 years for all other uses.

COLLATERAL

- All loans are to be adequately secured, but loans generally are not declined where inadequate collateral is the only unfavorable factor.
- Normally, business assets are pledged; pledging of personal assets may occasionally be required.
- Personal guarantees of the principals are required.

THE APPLICATION

Following is an example of the LowDoc application form.

COMPLETING THE LOWDOC APPLICATION

The first two lines of the LowDoc application form 4-L are for your corporate name (if any) and your trade name and street address. If you do not have a corporate name write in the business name you'll be operating under as it appears on your business bank account. The street address is the address

U.S. SMALL BUSINESS ADMINISTRATION
APPLICATION FOR BUSINESS LOAN (UP TO $100,000)
It is not necessary to hire outside assistance for preparation of the application.

Corporate Name (If any) Trade Name & Street Address	Home Phone ( ) Bus. Phone ( )	Ownership in any other business? Yes ____ No ____ #Employees (Including Subsidiaries & Affiliates)Include Owners & Managers
		Before Loan After Loan
City _____ County _____ State ____ Zip _____		Bank of Business Account:
Mailing Address (if different)		IRS Tax ID #
Type of Business	Date Established	

MANAGEMENT (Proprietor, partners, officers, directors owning 20% or more of the company)—Must account for 100% of ownership of the business.

Name	SOCIAL SECURITY #	Complete Address	% Owned	Y/N	*Military Service From To	*Race	*Sex

*This data is collected for statistical purposes only. It has no bearing on the credit decision to approve or decline this application. Disclosure is voluntary.

U.S. Citizen? Yes ____ No ____ If no, include a copy of Alien Registration Card (Form I 151 or I 551)   Alien Registration #

Are any of the above individuals (a) presently under indictment, on parole or probation, or have they ever been (b) charged for any criminal offense other than a minor vehicle violation, or convicted, placed on pretrial diversion, or placed on any form of probation including adjudication withheld pending probation for any criminal offense other than a minor vehicle violation?   Yes ____ No ____ If yes, loan request

must be submitted under regular 7(a) loan program.

Have you employed anyone to prepare this application? Yes ____ No ____ If yes, how much have you paid? $ _____   How much do you owe? $ _____

Have you or any officer of your company ever been involved in bankruptcy or insolvency proceedings? Yes ____ No ____ If yes, provide details to bank.

Are you or your business involved in any pending lawsuits? Yes ____ No ____ If yes, provide details to bank.

DESCRIBE YOUR BUSINESS OPERATION:

IS BUSINESS ENGAGED IN EXPORT TRADE? Yes ____ No ____   DO YOU INTEND TO BEGIN EXPORTING AS A RESULT OF THIS LOAN?   Yes ____ No ____

SUMMARY OF MANAGEMENT'S BUSINESS EXPERIENCE, EDUCATION, AND TRAINING:

LOAN REQUEST: HOW MUCH, FOR WHAT, WHY IT IS NEEDED

INDEBTEDNESS: Furnish information on ALL BUSINESS debts, contracts, notes, and mortgages payable.   Indicate by an (*) items to be paid with loan proceeds.

To Whom Payable	Original Amount	Original Date	Present Balance	Rate of Interest	Maturity Date	Monthly Payment	Collateral	Current or Past Due
	$		$			$		
	$		$			$		
	$		$			$		
	$		$			$		

PREVIOUS SBA OR OTHER GOVERNMENT FINANCING: If you or any principals or affiliates have ever requested Government Financing complete the following:

Name of Agency	Loan Number	Date Approved	$ Amount	Loan Balance	Status

If you knowingly make a false statement or overvalue a security to obtain a guaranteed loan from SBA you can be fined up to $10,000 or imprisoned for not more than five years or both under 18 USC 1001.

I hereby certify that all information contained in this document and any attachments is true and correct to the best of my knowledge.

If applicant is a proprietor or general partner, sign here: By: _____   Title _____   Date _____

If corporation sign below: Corporate Name

By: _____   Date: _____ Attested By: _____
    Signature of President   Signature of Corporate Secretary

---

Figure 18.1a

152

FOR BANK USE ONLY

LENDER'S APPLICATION FOR Guarantee

Name of Lender
Telephone(A/C)   Fax #   Address

Date of Guarantee Agreement (SBA Form 750)

Applicant's Trade Name

We request SBA to guarantee   % of a loan in the amount of $ for   years, with monthly (P&I payments of $ / principal
payments of $ plus interest) beginning   month(s) from date of note. (If applicable: Interest only payment to begin   months from date
of note).
The interest rate is to be fixed at _____ % OR variable with a base rate of _____ %, spread _____ %, and an adjustment period of _____ .

Lender's Experience with Applicant and Assessment of Management's Character and Capability:

CREDIT REPORTS (CR):   CR Company _____   Risk Score _____   SIC Code _____   Summary of Business Credit:

OWNERS, GUARANTORS, AND CO-SIGNERS:
Owners of 20% or more of business must guarantee the note. Lender must obtain personal credit reports on all owners, guarantors, and co-signers.
Name (Indicate co-signers with *)   Address   Individual Credit Reports Analysis

Personal F/S: Lender should obtain signed personal financial statements for all owners, guarantors, and co-signers.
                     Do owners' personal unpledged liquid assets exceed $50,000 (not including IRA, CV Life Insurance, or savings for education)? Yes   No
                     Comments on personal resources, including any supplementary or outside sources of income available for debt service or to secure loan:

P&L: Average annual gross sales, including all affiliates, for the last 3 years (if applicable) $
       Year end cash flow last 3 years (if applicable)   FY   , $, FY   , $, FY   , $

       One year projected cash flow after owner's compensation $ Total annual debt service (including interest) after the loan $
       Comments on repayment ability:

Pro Forma Balance Sheet: Debt/NW Ratio   Current Ratio (CA/CL)   Comments on balance sheet:

IF NEW BUSINESS OR FOR PURCHASE OF EXISTING BUSINESS, AMOUNT OF APPLICANT INJECTION - CASH $ OTHER $

Lender's Analysis of Risk (If there are affiliates, submit analysis of financial condition of affiliate and potential impact on applicant business. Affiliates include all businesses owned by applicant or spouse of applicant, even though not in a related business. Comment on bankruptcies and pending lawsuits. Include lien position on collateral.)	Collateral Market Value *
	Inventory $
	Equipment $
	A/R $
	R/E ** $
	                  $
	
	* Value determined by:
	   Lender ____ Appraisal ____
	
	   Other (specify)_____
	** Furnish Legal Description
		Use of Proceeds:
		Inventory $
		Fixed Assets $
		Real Estate $
		Note Payment $
		Working Capital $
		SBA Payoff $
		                  $
		                  $
		
		TOTAL $

For loans over $50,000 and up to $100,000, the following must be submitted:
  1. Lender's internal loan report, including cash flow analysis and pro forma balance sheet
  2. Income tax schedule C or front page of corporate returns for past 3 years (if applicable)
  3. Personal F/S's for all guarantors
	IF LOAN IS TO PURCHASE AN EXISTING BUSINESS Include copy of terms of sale and F/S on the existing business. Also, comment on any benefit to the business as a result of the change of ownership. Are buyer & seller related? Yes No State relationship

I submit this application to SBA for approval subject to the terms and conditions outlined above. Without the participation of SBA to the extent applied for we would not be willing to make this loan, and in our opinion the financial assistance applied for is not otherwise available on reasonable terms. I certify that none of the Lender's employees, officers, director or substantial stockholders (more than 10%) have a financial interest in the applicant.

Signature of Lender Official: Title
                              Date

Figure 18.1b

where you will be transacting business. This could be your home address if you are operating from your home.

Home phone. Insert the home phone number of the principle operating person.

Business phone. Insert the phone number that will be receiving calls for the business.

City. Insert the name of the city where your business is located.

County. Insert the name of the county or township where your business is located.

State. Insert the name of the state where your business is located.

Zip. Insert the zip code (5 + 4 if available) of your business location.

Mailing address (if different). If you have a post office box or other mail receiving point other than the one stated above write it in here.

Type of business. Note the type of business you're in (i.e. retail, wholesale, auto repair, gift shop, etc.). The Standard Industrial Classification (SIC) code of your business would be handy here.

Date established. Enter the date you started the business. It's good to have a date at least two years prior to the current application date, but be sure you can prove that date of existence with your tax records.

Ownership in any other business? Merely check the appropriate yes or no blank.

Number of employees (including subsidiaries and affiliates), include owners and managers before loan and after loan. Enter the current number of employees in your business including yourself and all others *earning full-time wages from the business.* Then enter the number of employees you anticipate having after receiving the funds from the loan.

Bank of business account. Enter the name and address of the bank where you have your business account established.

IRS tax ID number. Enter your business tax number or, if you do not currently have one, enter your personal social security number. Some municipalities require a tax ID number before they will issue a business permit, others do not require a tax ID number and will accept your social security number if your business is a sole proprietorship.

Management. List the names of all persons having signing authority for the business and/or a 20 percent or more ownership interest in the business. You must list each person's name, social security number, complete address, and business ownership percentage (the total must equal 100 percent). Supplying the remainder of the information is optional; you don't have to provide it. If you do include it, state whether each person served in the military or not and the dates of that service, racial extraction of each person, and sex of each person. If necessary, continue this list on a separate paper and attach it to the completed application.

U.S. citizen? Merely check the appropriate yes or no blank as it applies to the principle owner and operator of the business. However, if "no" is indicated you must attach a copy of that person's alien registration card (form I 151 or I 551) and provide that person's alien registration number in the blank provided.

The next series of questions on the form pertains to the principle owner/operator of the business's judicial standing. If you are involved in any legal proceedings of a criminal nature other than a minor vehicle (traffic) violation (i.e., parking, speeding, improper turn) you must indicate "yes" here. This will disqualify you from the LowDoc program, but you can submit a loan request under the regular 7(a) loan program which is a bit more involved and lengthy to apply for than the LowDoc program. If you are not involved in legal proceedings as just described, indicate "no" here.

Have you employed anyone to prepare this application? Merely indicate "yes" or "no" as appropriate. If you indicate "yes," state the full amount paid for this service; if a balance is still owing, indicate that amount.

Have you or any officer of your company ever been involved in bankruptcy or insolvency proceedings? Merely indicate "yes" or "no" as appropriate. If "yes" is indicated, prepare a detailed explanation of such proceedings on a separate page or pages for presentation to the bank if so requested.

Are you or your business involved in any pending lawsuits? Indicate "yes" or "no" as appropriate. If "yes" is indicated, prepare a detailed explanation of such proceedings on a separate page or pages for presentation to the bank if so requested.

Describe your business operation. Write a very short, general description of your business here. It is a good idea to have a business plan written and make a note that the "business plan is available."

Is business engaged in export trade? Merely indicate "yes" or "no" as appropriate. Be consistent with your written business plan.

Do you intend to begin exporting as a result of this loan? Merely indicate "yes" or "no" as appropriate. Be consistent with your written business plan.

Summary of management's business experience, education, and training. If yours is a single proprietor business, a short statement about your prior business experience, education, and training can be inserted here. However, if your business consists of more than one principle manager, such as in a corporation, it is good to have brief resumes of each of these principles attached to the application.

Loan request: how much, for what, why it is needed. Again, refer to your business plan and remain consistent with the plan. Merely write a short statement stating the amount needed, what it's to be used for, and why that use is necessary.

Indebtedness. Furnish information on all *business* debts, contracts, notes, and mortgages payable. Indicate by an asterisk items to be paid with loan proceeds. Write in the current status of each financial liability of your company. If necessary, use another sheet of paper, but present the information in the same format as presented on this section of the application form. This makes it easier for the loan officer to read and thus makes him/her look more favorably toward the loan.

Previous SBA or other government financing. If you or any principals or affiliates have ever requested government financing, complete this section. Be sure that each principle of the business submits full particulars of any past or present government financing that he/she has or is a signing party to. Write those particulars here and, if necessary, use another sheet of paper, but present the information in the same format as presented on this section of the application form. This makes it easier for the loan officer to read and thus makes him/her look more favorably toward the loan.

The note at the bottom of the form stating "If you knowingly make a false statement or overvalue a security to obtain a guaranteed loan from SBA you can be fined up to $10,000 or [be] imprisoned for not more than five years or both under 18 USC 1001," means exactly what it says. The SBA is now auditing loan requests and prosecuting cases where false statements are found, especially those related to business income. They are now obtaining tax records to verify the claimed income directly from the IRS. So, be sure your figures and statements are as accurate as possible.

The remainder of the application form is a certification by the applicant(s) as to the correctness of the information contained on the application. You should sign this as appropriate for your situation. As a single proprietor or partnership, the owner or general partner merely signs at the "By:" blank, notes his/her title (owner, general partner, president, etc.) and dates the application certification. As a corporation, the person signing should skip to the line starting with "If corporation sign below:" and fill in the business (corporate) name, his/her signature, date the document, and have the corporate secretary, if any, sign in the "Attested By:" blank.

The lending bank's loan officer will complete the second page of the application and then submit the application to the SBA for approval after the bank loan committee has reviewed the lending officer's analysis and recommendations and that committee has approved the loan request.

As you can see, if you read this page, the lender will require personal financial statements from each of the principals, owners, guarantors, and cosigners of the loan request, as well as credit reports of each of these people. These will help verify the statements made on the application and help in the evaluation process.

Profit and loss statements for the last three years along with year-end cash flow statements and a one year projected cash flow statement will also be required. Also, an analysis of your total annual debt service (with interest) after the loan has been approved must be submitted.

Also, you should prepare a "pro forma" (this means projected or estimated for the future) balance sheet. The loan officer will use this to calculate the critical business ratios for evaluation purposes. These ratios are total debt divided by net worth, and current assets divided by current liabilities, (known as the "current ratio") which are compared to the standard ratios for comparable businesses. If these ratios are noticeably above or below the standards you will be asked for clarification as to why your business ratios are so different.

If this is a new business or the purchase of an existing business, the lender wants to know how much cash or other contributions you are putting into the business. Other contributions can consist of items such as inventory, capital equipment, accounts receivable, notes receivable, and so forth, but this amount must have a verifiable dollar value given.

With this information the lending officer can proceed with the processing of the loan. And, if everything is in order, the loan will be completed in a minimum of time.

19 Greenline Revolving Line of Credit

New to the SBA's lending programs in 1994, the GreenLine Revolving Line of Credit provides flexibility to finance the cash cycle of a small business. Many businesses use this type of financing throughout their entire existence. Over a period of as much as five years, the SBA provides a term commitment for a revolving line of credit that supplies the capital to cover the cyclical, recurring, and short-term needs that so many businesses experience. Borrowers draw and repay as the cash cycle dictates, up to the approved amount of the GreenLine account throughout the term of the loan.

The new GreenLine program could greatly expand the use of a highly flexible financing tool by capital-hungry small businesses. Revolving loans permit companies to draw on a credit line only when they need money to fund increases in receivables and inventory. Term loans, which the SBA has traditionally guaranteed, lock a borrower into fixed monthly payments.

The SBA has taken unprecedented steps to protect itself against repayment problems in this new program, because revolving loans are riskier than term loans. For the first time, the agency has third parties monitor the collateral that secures the newly guaranteed loans. Revolving loans pose more risks than term loans because they are secured by receivables and inventory, which are less reliable collateral than the real estate, buildings, and machinery that typically secure term loans. Small businesses normally find they can't get or afford revolving loans in the general finance market.

Some lenders aren't enthusiastic about this new SBA program, however. There is no secondary market for revolving loans. Thus, banks aren't able to sell the guaranteed portion of the revolving credit line while still servicing it for a fee. They can possibly do that now with the SBA backing these term loans.

And since the less-permanent nature of a revolving credit line's collateral makes it riskier to secure such debt, SBA lenders will need to be more careful about monitoring their loans. If not, they will set themselves and the SBA up for losses. That's why the agency has authorized lenders to use firms that specialize in managing loans' collateral. Their methods include employing agents who watch over inventory that secures the debt, sometimes releasing it to a debtor only after a creditor receives its payment.

The GreenLine program, a revamped version of two troubled regional pilot projects begun in 1992, guarantees revolving credit lines of as much as $750,000 per loan. The SBA guarantee lasts as long as five years and covers 75 percent of a loan, which can bear an interest rate of as much as 2.75 percent above the prime rate.

Virtually all types of businesses are eligible for GreenLine. Applicants must meet the same eligibility criteria applicable to other SBA 7(a) guarantee loans. The business must be operated for profit and meet SBA size standards. Loan proceeds can be used for operating capital, inventory, and consolidation of short-term debt. Advances can be made any time prior to maturity provided the borrower is not in default.

A GreenLine must be secured by a first lien on the assets being financed (i.e., inventory, receivables, contracts, etc.). Personal guarantees will be required. Secondary liens on machinery and equipment, real estate, and personal assets may be required. The degree to which collateral assets are to be monitored or controlled by the lender will be based on a determination of the credit risk inherent in each individual GreenLine. Borrowers will generally be required to report cash flow as often as monthly.

A GreenLine applicant must be of good character, demonstrate sufficient management ability, experience, and commitment necessary for a successful and viable operation, demonstrate the capability to perform and collect payment for that performance, have a feasible business plan, have adequate equity or investment in the business, and pledge sufficient assets to adequately secure the loan. The applicant must also submit SBA form GL-4 with the standard form 4 application (see Figure 19.1).

The SBA can guarantee up to $750,000 of a GreenLine loan. The lender will request a maximum of 75 percent of the loan to be guaranteed by the SBA. The maximum initial maturity is five years; specific circumstances may lend themselves to establishing a shorter initial maturity. No advances can be made after the loan matures. The rate of interest to be charged will be negotiated between the borrower and the lender, but won't exceed the prime rate plus 2.25 percentage points. Revenues from the cash cycle of the business operation—sale of inventory, performance of service, performance on contract, collection of receivables—constitute the primary source of repayment of a properly operating GreenLine. SBA guarantee fees for GreenLine are the same as for all other SBA 7(a) guarantee loans.

ADDITIONAL GREEN LINE APPLICATION QUESTIONS

TO BE INCLUDED WITH SBA FORM 4

THE INFORMATION ON THIS FORM SHOULD BE COMPLETED AND INCLUDED WITH THE SBA FORM 4 TO COMPLETE THE GREENLINE APPLICATION

NAME OF BUSINESS: _____

BUSINESS ADDRESS: _____

ACCOUNTS RECEIVABLES:

1.   DO YOU SELL PRODUCT(S) ON CREDIT?   YES: NO:

     IF YES, ANSWER ALL PARTS OF QUESTION 1:

1A. WHAT PERCENTAGE OF YOUR TOTAL SALES ID FOR CREDIT?   %

1B. WHAT ARE THE CREDIT TERMS YOU PROVIDE YOUR CUSTOMERS?

1C. DESCRIBE THE PROCEDURES YOUR BUSINESS USES WHEN EXTENDING CREDIT/TERMS TO ITS CUSTOMERS?

     _____

     _____

1D. DO ANY OF YOUR CREDIT CUSTOMERS ACCOUNT FOR OVER 10% OF YOUR TOTAL CREDIT SALES?

     YES _____ NO _____ IF YES, LIST THESE CUSTOMERS:

     _____

1E. DO YOU MAINTAIN CREDIT INSURANCE TO COVER YOUR RECEIVABLES?   YES: _____ NO: _____

     IF YES, WHAT PERCENTAGE OF TOTAL SALES ARE COVERED BY THIS INSURANCE?   %

1F. DESCRIBE THE DISCOUNT POLICY OF YOUR BUSINESS.

     _____

     _____

1G. THE TOTAL DOLLAR AMOUNT OF RECEIVABLES WRITTEN OFF LAST FISCAL YEAR WAS: $_____

2.   DESCRIBE THE WARRANTS. GUARANTIES, OR OTHER DEVICES PROVIDED BY YOUR BUSINESS TO SUPPORT PRODUCT QUALITY.

     _____

     _____

3.   FOR YOUR BUSINESS MOST RECENTLY COMPLETED FISCAL YEAR:

     TOTAL CREDIT SALES WERE: $_____   TOTAL RETURNS WERE: $_____

     TOTAL ALLOWANCES WERE: $_____   TOTAL CREDITS WERE: $_____

4.   DO YOU SELL TO OTHER BUSINESSES ON CREDIT WHICH ALSO SELL TO YOU?   YES: _____ NO: _____

5.   DO YOU SELL OVERSEAS?   YES: _____ NO: _____

6.   DESCRIBE THE PRIMARY INDUSTRY(S) TO WHOM YOU SELL ON CREDIT.

SBA Form GL-4   June 27, 1994

Figure 19.1

20 Disaster Loan Programs

In the wake of hurricanes, floods, earthquakes, wildfires, tornados, and other physical disasters, the SBA plays a major role. The SBA's disaster loans are the primary form of federal assistance for nonfarm, private sector disaster losses. For this reason, the disaster loan program is the only form of SBA assistance not limited to small businesses. Disaster loans from the SBA help homeowners, renters, businesses of all sizes, and nonprofit organizations fund rebuilding. The SBA's disaster loans are a critical source of economic stimulation in disaster-ravaged communities, helping to spur employment and stabilize tax bases.

The SBA was given a mandate to provide financial assistance to victims of disasters. By providing disaster assistance in the form of loans that are repaid to the Treasury, the SBA disaster loan program helps reduce federal disaster costs compared to other forms of assistance, such as grants. When disaster victims need to borrow to repair uninsured damages, the low interest rates and long terms available from the SBA make recovery affordable. Because the SBA tailors the repayment of each disaster loan to each borrower's financial capability, unnecessary interest subsidies paid by the taxpayers are avoided. Moreover, providing disaster assistance in the form of loans rather than grants avoids creating an incentive for property owners to underinsure against risk. Disaster loans require borrowers to maintain appropriate hazard and flood insurance coverage, thereby reducing the need for future disaster assistance.

TYPES OF DISASTER LOANS

- *Home disaster loans.* These are loans to homeowners or renters to repair or replace disaster-related damage to homes or personal property that is owned by the applicant. Renters are eligible for personal property loans.

- *Business physical disaster loans.* These are loans to businesses to repair or replace disaster-related damaged property owned by the business, including inventory and supplies.

- *Economic injury disaster loans.* Working capital loans (referred to as EIDL) to small businesses and to small agricultural cooperatives assist these businesses through the disaster recovery period. These loans are available only if the business or its owners cannot obtain this type of assistance from nongovernment sources. This determination is made by the SBA.

The need for SBA disaster loans is as unpredictable as the weather. In the aftermath of the Northridge earthquake, the SBA approved more than 125,000 loans for more than $4.1 billion in fiscal year 1994. In the aftermath of the Midwest floods, hurricanes Andrew and Iniki, the Los Angeles riots, and other recent disasters, the SBA approved 58,644 disaster loans for $1.67 billion during fiscal year 1993, and another 23,417 disaster loans for $794.6 million in fiscal year 1992. Since the inception of the program in 1953, the SBA has approved more than 1,274,000 disaster loans for more than $22.4 billion.

The SBA is authorized by the Small Business Act to make two types of disaster loans:

- Physical disaster loans are a primary source of funding for permanent rebuilding and replacement of uninsured disaster damages to privately owned real and/or personal property. The SBA's physical disaster loans are available to homeowners, renters, nonfarm businesses of all sizes, and nonprofit organizations.
- Economic injury disaster loans provide necessary working capital until normal operations resume after a physical disaster. The law restricts economic injury disaster loans to small businesses only.

The disaster program is the SBA's largest direct-loan program, and the only SBA program for entities other than small businesses. By law, neither governmental units nor agricultural enterprises are eligible; agricultural producers may seek disaster assistance from specialized programs at the U.S. Department of Agriculture.

Disaster victims must repay the SBA disaster loans. The SBA can approve loans only to applicants with a reasonable ability to repay the loan and other obligations from earnings. The terms of each loan are established in accordance with each borrower's ability to repay. The law gives the SBA several powerful tools to make disaster loans affordable: low interest rates (around 4 percent), long terms (up to 30 years), and refinancing of prior debts (in some cases). As required by law, the interest rate for each loan is based on the SBA's determination of whether each applicant does or does not have credit available elsewhere (the ability to borrow or use their own resources to overcome the disaster). Generally, over 90 percent of the SBA's disaster loans are to borrowers without credit available elsewhere and have an interest rate of around 4 percent.

For disasters occurring on or after January 1, 1994, the following interest rates were applied:

	CREDIT AVAILABLE ELSEWHERE	CREDIT NOT AVAILABLE ELSEWHERE
Home loans (includes personal property loans)	7.250%	3.625%
Business loans	4.000%	7.700%
Nonprofit organizations	4.000%	7.125%
Economic injury loans	4.000%	Not available

Physical loss loans in excess of $10,000 and EIDL loans in excess of $5,000 must be secured with collateral. Generally, for individuals, that will include a lien on the applicant's real estate. However, loans will not be declined for lack of a fixed amount of collateral.

SBA delivers disaster loans through four specialized Disaster Area Offices located in Niagara Falls, N.Y., Atlanta, Ga., Ft. Worth, Tex., and Sacramento, Calif.

Economic Injury Disaster Loans for Small Businesses (SBA Publication DAD-3, 5/95)

If, as a direct result of a physical disaster, or as the result of an agricultural production disaster designated by the Secretary of Agriculture, a business has suffered substantial economic injury, with or without actual physical damage, it may be eligible for an Economic Injury Disaster Loan (EIDL). Substantial economic injury is the inability of a business to meet its obligations as they mature and to pay its ordinary and necessary operating expenses. These loans, however, are limited to small businesses and to small agricultural cooperatives.

The purpose of the loan is to permit the business to meet necessary financial obligations that the business could have met had the disaster not occurred. EIDLs are working capital loans and are made only to provide relief from economic injury caused directly by the disaster and to permit the business to maintain a reasonable working capital position during the period affected by the disaster.

No EIDL assistance can be made to a business that is determined by the SBA to be able to obtain credit elsewhere. EIDL assistance to businesses is limited to a maximum of $1,500,000 (together with any business physical disaster loan for damage from the same disaster). However, the actual amount of the loan will be based upon the business's actual economic injury and its financial needs. The interest rate on EIDLs may not exceed 4 percent per year. The term of these loans may not exceed 30 years. However, the actual term will be set depending upon the ability of the business to repay the loan.

Physical Disaster Business Loans
(SBA Publication DAD-2, 5/95)

The SBA is authorized to make loans up to $1,500,000 to a business of any size to repair or replace the business's property to its predisaster condition. Repair or replacement of real property, machinery, equipment, fixtures, inventory, and leasehold improvements may be included in a loan.

Any business that is located in a declared disaster area and has suffered damage as a result of a physical disaster is eligible to apply for a physical disaster loan to help repair or replace damaged property to its predisaster condition. In addition, disaster loans to repair or restore real property or leasehold improvements may be increased by as much as 20 percent to protect the damaged real property from possible future disasters of the same type.

SBA loans will cover uninsured physical damage. If the business is required to apply insurance proceeds to an outstanding mortgage on the damaged property, the amount applied can be included in the disaster loan. The interest rate that the agency charges on its disaster loans is determined by the business's ability to obtain credit elsewhere, that is, from nonfederal sources.

If the SBA determines that the business (or nonprofit organization) is unable to obtain credit elsewhere (considering the cash flow and assets of the business, its principals, and affiliates), the interest rate that will be charged on a loan will not exceed 4 percent per year.

The maximum maturity for such business disaster loans is 30 years. However, the actual maturity of a loan is set depending upon the ability of the business to repay the loan.

If the SBA determines that the business does have the ability to obtain credit elsewhere, the agency can make a loan at an interest rate that will not exceed that being charged in the private market at the time of the physical disaster, or 8 percent, whichever is less. The maturity of this loan may not exceed 3 years. *Note:* Charitable, religious, nonprofit and similar organizations with the ability to obtain credit elsewhere are eligible for physical disaster loans for up to 30 years at an interest rate based upon a different statutory formula. The nearest SBA disaster office can supply the interest rate.

Disaster Loans for Homes and Personal Property
(SBA Publication DAD-, 1/94)

Do not let the name, "U.S. Small Business Administration," confuse you. A homeowner or a person who owns personal property may apply to the SBA for a loan to help recover from a declared disaster. Where it is practical, assistance with the application process will be available, and the applicant will be told how to obtain this assistance when requesting an application.

For an individual, there is one basic loan, with two purposes, available as follows:

- *Personal Property Loan.* This loan is limited to $40,000 and is meant to help repair or replace the personal property lost in the disaster, such as clothing, furniture, automobiles, and so forth. As a rule of thumb, personal property is anything that is not considered real estate or a part of the actual structure. This loan may not be used to replace extraordinarily expensive or irreplaceable items, such as antiques, collections, pleasure boats, recreational vehicles, fur coats, and so forth.

- *Real Property Loan.* Homeowners may apply for a loan of up to $200,000 to repair or restore their primary home to its predisaster condition. The loan may not be used to upgrade the home or make additions to it. However, in the event that city or county building codes require structural improvements, the loan may be used to comply with these requirements. Also, loans may be increased by as much as 20 percent to protect the damaged real property from possible future disasters of the same kind. *Note:* A renter may apply only for a personal property loan.

Insurance Proceeds

If there is insurance coverage on the personal property/home, the amount received from the insurance company will be deducted from the total damage to the property in order to determine the amount for which the owner is eligible to apply to the SBA.

If a homeowner is required to apply insurance proceeds against an outstanding mortgage, the amount applied can be included in the disaster loan. But, if the application of insurance proceeds against an outstanding mortgage is voluntary, the amount applied cannot be included in the disaster loan.

If a settlement has not been reached with the insurance company, then application for a loan may be made in the full amount of the damages. An assignment will be given to the SBA on any insurance proceeds to be received.

INTEREST RATES

The law requires a test of the applicant's ability to obtain funds elsewhere in order to determine the rate of interest that will be charged on your loan. This "credit elsewhere" test also applies to applicants for personal property loans.

Applicants Determined to Be Able to Obtain Credit Elsewhere. The interest rate to be charged is based on the cost of money to the U.S. government, but will not be more than 8 percent per year.

Applicants Determined to Be Unable to Obtain Credit Elsewhere. The interest rate to be charged will be one-half of the interest rate applied to those able to obtain credit elsewhere, but will not be more than 4 percent per year.

LOAN AMOUNT

For homeowners and renters, loans up to $200,000 for repair or replacement of real estate, and loans up to $40,000 for repair or replacement of personal property are available. The loan amount is limited to the amount of uninsured, SBA-verified losses, but may be increased by up to 20 percent for mitigating devices for damaged real property.

For business physical disaster loans, up to 100 percent of the uninsured, SBA-verified loss not to exceed $1,500,000 is available. Within this limit, the loan may be increased by up to 20 percent for mitigating devices for damaged real property.

Any insurance proceeds that are required to be applied against outstanding mortgages may be included in disaster loan eligibility. Any insurance proceeds that are voluntarily applied against outstanding mortgages by the owner may not be included in disaster loan eligibility.

Refinancing of existing mortgages on homes and business property is possible in some circumstances. Consult an SBA representative for further information.

For economic injury, loan amounts up to $500,000 are available. The total loan amount to any one business entity (including affiliates for combined economic injury and business disaster loans) cannot exceed $1,500,000.

LOAN TERM

For businesses with credit available elsewhere, the maximum term is three years. For all other borrowers, loan terms not to exceed 30 years are available. Loan terms are determined individually based upon what is reasonable in consideration of the applicant's repayment capability.

LOAN LIMITATIONS

The following limitations apply to all SBA disaster loans.

- No loans are made available for damages to secondary homes.
- No loans are made available for damage to personal pleasure boats, planes, recreational vehicles, antiques, collections, and so forth.
- There are limitations on loan amounts for landscaping, family swimming pools, and so forth.

FLOOD INSURANCE REQUIREMENTS

Applicants who have SBA loans that require them to maintain flood insurance are not eligible for loans if they have not maintained their insurance.

If the applicant's property is located in a special flood hazard area, flood insurance must be purchased and maintained for the insurable value of the property, regardless of the amount of the loan.

21 Special Assistance Programs

QUALIFIED EMPLOYEE TRUST PROGRAM

This program was created to allow a trust to reloan funds to its employer concern or to permit the employees to buy the employer concern.

Eligible employee trusts are those that meet the SBA's size and policy requirements and are part of a plan sponsored by their employer concern and qualified under either the Internal Revenue Code (as an Employee Stock Ownership Plan (ESOP), or the Department of Labor (under the Employee Retirement Income Security Act (ERISA)). The trust must exist prior to application.

Loan proceeds may be used by the employee trust for either of the following:

1. *Growth and development loans,* whereby the trust reloans the loan proceeds to the employer by purchasing qualifying employer securities (not necessarily voting stock)
2. *Change of Ownership Loans,* whereby employees acquire controlling interest in the employer concern

Collateral will include the assets of the employer concern. Maturities will be consistent with the borrower's ability to repay, but will not exceed 25 years.

SURETY BOND GUARANTEE PROGRAM

The SBA makes the bonding process accessible to small contractors who find commercial bonding unavailable to them. The agency will guarantee to a qualified surety up to 80 percent of losses incurred under bid, payment, or performance bonds issued to contractors on contracts valued up to $1.25 million. The contracts may be used for construction, supplies, or services provided for government or nongovernment work.

Eligibility

Businesses in the construction and service industries can meet the SBA's size eligibility standards if their average annual receipts, including those of their affiliates, for the last three fiscal years do not exceed $5 million. Local SBA offices can answer questions dealing with size standard eligibility.

Types of Eligible Bonds

Any contract bond (bid, performance, or payment) is eligible for an SBA guarantee if the bond conforms to the following requirements:

- It is covered by the Contract Bonds section of the *Surety Association of America Rating Manual.*
- It is required by the invitation to bid.
- It is executed by a surety company that is acceptable to the U.S. Treasury (Circular 570) and qualified by the SBA.

Some noncompetitive negotiated contracts are eligible if they are in accord with appropriate federal regulations.

Size of Eligible Contracts

The SBA can guarantee bonds for contracts up to $1.25 million.

SBA Guarantee

The SBA guarantees surety companies against a percentage of losses sustained on contracts up to $1.25 million in face value.

Duties of Contractor

Contractors should apply for a specific bond with a surety company of their choice, providing background, credit, and financial information required by the surety company and the SBA.

The contractor must use the following forms, which are available from the SBA.

- SBA form 994: Application for Surety Bond Guarantee Assistance
- SBA form 912: Statement of Personal History (on first application and once every two calendar years thereafter)
- SBA form 994F: Schedule of Uncompleted Work on Hand (required initially and then at least quarterly)

Duties of Surety Company

After an applicant completes the forms and furnishes the surety company with sufficient underwriting information, the surety company processes and underwrites the application in the same manner as any other contract bond application. The surety company decides whether to:

- Execute the bond without the SBA's guarantee;
- Execute the bond only with the SBA's guarantee; or
- Decline the bond even with the SBA's guarantee.

If the surety company determines an SBA guarantee is required in order to provide the bond, it must then complete an SBA form 994B (Underwriting Review) and the SBA form 990 (Guarantee Agreement). These forms—and supporting documents—are submitted along with the forms 994, 912, and 994F to the appropriate SBA office. If the application is for a final bond, the contractor's guarantee fee check must be attached.

Duties of the SBA

The SBA determines an applicant's ability to complete the contract based on the information, documentation, and underwriting rationale provided by the surety company. If the review establishes performance capacity, and all other aspects of the application are approved, a duly authorized SBA official signs a guarantee agreement and returns it to the surety company. If the review fails to establish performance capacity, the SBA seeks clarification from the surety underwriter. If performance capacity cannot be reasonably assured, the SBA rejects the application.

Cost of an SBA-Guaranteed Bond

The SBA charges fees to both the contractor and the surety company, as described in the most recent edition of 13 CFR 115.

- The small business pays the SBA a guarantee fee of $6 per $1,000 of the contract amount.
- When the bond is issued, the small business pays the surety company's bond premium. This charge cannot exceed the level approved by the appropriate state regulatory body.
- The surety company pays the SBA a guarantee fee as determined by the SBA.

SMALL BUSINESS INVESTMENT COMPANY PROGRAM

Congress created the Small Business Investment Company (SBIC) Program in 1958 to fill the gap between the availability of venture capital and the needs of small businesses in start-up and growth situations. SBICs, licensed and regulated by the SBA, are privately owned and managed investment firms that use their own capital, plus funds borrowed at favorable rates with an SBA guarantee, to make venture capital investments in small businesses.

An SBIC, approved and licensed by the SBA, may provide equity capital or working capital exceeding the agency's $750,000 statutory maximum. To be eligible for SBIC financing, at least half of the small business's assets and operations must be in the United States. Unlike the SBA, SBICs can invest in export trading companies in which banks have equity participation, as long as other SBIC requirements are met.

Virtually all SBICs are profit-motivated businesses. They provide equity capital, long-term loans, debt-equity investments, and management assistance to qualifying small businesses. Their incentive is the chance to share in the success of the small business as it grows and prospers. There are two types of SBICs: regular SBICs and Specialized SBICs, also known as 301(d) SBICs. Specialized SBICs invest in small businesses owned by entrepreneurs who are socially or economically disadvantaged, mainly members of minority groups.

The program makes funding available to all types of manufacturing and service industries. Many investment companies seek out small businesses with new products or services because of the strong growth potential of such firms. Some SBICs specialize in the field in which their management has special knowledge or competency. Most, however, consider a wide variety of investment opportunities.

Eligibility

Only firms defined by the SBA as small are eligible for SBIC financing. The SBA defines small businesses as companies whose net worth is $6 million or less and whose average net (after tax) income for the preceding two years does not exceed $2 million. For businesses in those industries for which the above standards are too low, alternative size standards are available. In determining whether or not a business qualifies, its parent, subsidiaries, and affiliates must also be considered.

If you own or operate a small business and would like to obtain SBIC financing, you should first identify and investigate existing SBICs that may be interested in financing your company. You should also consider whether or not the SBIC can offer you management services appropriate to your needs.

The SBA publishes a regularly updated directory listing all current SBIC licensees. The amount of each SBIC's private capital and the amount of government leverage it has received are listed, as well as information on each SBIC's type of ownership and investment policy.

Plan in Advance

The business owner should research SBICs and determine the company's needs well in advance—long before actually needing the money. Research takes time.

When the SBICs that appear best suited for financing the company have been identified, prepare for a presentation. This initial presentation will play a major role in successfully obtaining financing. It's up to you to demonstrate that an investment in your firm is worthwhile. The best way to achieve this is to present a detailed and comprehensive business plan, or prospectus. This should include at a minimum the following information about the business:

- Identification

  Name of the business as it appears on the official record of the state or community in which it operates

  City, county, and state of the principal location and any branch offices or facilities

  Business organization; if a corporation, date and state of incorporation

- Product or service

  Description of the business performed, including the principal products sold or services rendered

  History of the development of the products and/or service during the past five years or since inception

  Relative importance of each product or service to the volume of the business and to its profits

- Marketing

  Detailed information about the business's customer base, including potential customers. Indicate the percentage of gross revenue accounted for by your five largest customers.

  Marketing survey and/or economic feasibility study

  Distribution system by which products or services are provided to customers

- Competition

  Competitive conditions in the industry in which your business is engaged, including your company's position relative to its largest and smallest competitors

  Full explanation and summary of your business's pricing policies

- Management

  Brief resumes of management and principal owners, including their ages, education, and business experience

  Banking, business, and personal references for each member of management and for the principal owners

- Financial statements

  Balance sheets and profit and loss statements for the last three fiscal years or from your business's inception

  Detailed projections of revenues, expenses, and net earnings for the coming year

  Amount of funding you are requesting and the time requirement for the funds

  Reasons for your request for funds and a description of the proposed uses

  Benefits you expect your business to gain from the financing (e.g., improvement of financial position, increases in revenues, expense reduction, increase in efficiency)

- Production facilities and property

    Description of real and physical property and adaptability to new or existing business ventures

    Description of technical attributes of production facilities.

Additional Information

You may obtain the Directory of Operating Small Business Investment Companies by visiting the SBA regional or district office nearest you, or by writing to:

    Associate Administrator for Investment
    U.S. Small Business Administration
    409 Third Street, S.W.
    Washington, DC 20416

CERTIFIED DEVELOPMENT COMPANY PROGRAM (504)

This is a program for financing the fixed asset requirements of small businesses through a guarantee of loans made by SBA Certified Development Companies. Development companies are charged with the responsibilities of identifying eligible small businesses, performing credit analysis, recommending loan approval, and closing and servicing the loans it originates. Since the program is intended to finance the expansion needs of small business, a main eligibility consideration involves the extent to which new jobs are to be created or retained via the financing. The present rule requires that one job be created or retained for each $35,000 of guaranteed 504 loan proceeds.

The financing structure of a 504 proposal is different from a regular SBA guarantee. Typically, a lender will fund 50 percent of the total fixed asset needs of the small business, taking as collateral a senior position on those assets financed. The SBA will provide a 100 percent guarantee of a loan made by the Certified Development Company for the next 40 percent, which would be secured by a second position on the project assets. The small concern itself would contribute a minimum of 10 percent of the total project cost. Other business and/or personal assets may also be required by the lender and/or the SBA as collateral.

The maximum loan amount on 504 loans is $750,000, except in situations where significant public policy goals are involved, in which cases the maximum amount is $1,000,000. These goals are expansion of exports, business district revitalization, expansion of minority business development, rural development, enhanced economic development (often hi-tech), fostering of a sound environment, and expansion or location in areas adversely affected by federal budget cutbacks, such as military base closings and the like.

The maturity on 504 loans is either 10 or 20 years, depending on the useful life of the assets being financed. The private sector lender's loan is required to have a maturity of at least 10 years, when the 504 loan has a 20-year maturity, and 7 years when the 504 loan has a 10-year maturity.

The interest rate on the 504 loan is a fixed rate set in relation to the return on other U.S. government debt instruments with similar maturities, virtually always resulting in a rate lower than the prevailing market rate. The lender in the first position is free to negotiate its own rate with the small business.

Size standards used to determine eligibility of the applicant business include either those used for the regular guarantee loan program or the following: (a) average net profit for the past two years shall not exceed $2 million, and (b) net worth may not exceed $6 million. The applicant is eligible if both of these two or the regular criteria are met.

Certain fees are associated with this program, none of which are borne by the lender of the first 50 percent. Keep in mind that the CDC's 504 loan is guaranteed by the SBA, not the lender's first mortgage loan.

SBA form 1244 must be included with a 504 loan package. An example is shown in Figure 21.1.

DEFENSE LOAN AND TECHNICAL ASSISTANCE (DELTA)

The Clinton administration is committed to helping small businesses that are adversely affected by defense reductions to restructure so they can survive, grow, and become less dependent on defense contracts. To that end, the Defense Loan and Technical Assistance (DELTA) Program was created. It is set up to guarantee $1 billion in loans to defense industry–dependent companies. The SBA makes the loan guarantees, and the Defense Department provides the $30 million needed to meet the reserve requirements for the guarantees.

The DELTA program will guarantee loans up to $1.25 million. Borrowers must meet requirements for either of two older SBA lending programs, the 7(a) and 504 programs. In addition, the companies must derive at least 25 percent of their revenue from defense contracts or subcontracts involving either the Defense Department or the Energy Department. Officials said borrowers must have business plans consistent with any of three government objectives as follows:

- Job retention for workers whose employment is threatened by defense cutbacks
- Job creation in communities already hurt by the cutbacks
- Plant retooling or expansion to enable companies to remain qualified to handle defense-related work

The loans can be used to provide working capital or to finance machinery and equipment purchases, plant renovations, and other capital projects. Loans are available to businesses throughout the United States. However, the program is particularly well-suited to many businesses in New York, California, Texas, Florida, and South Carolina, states that have been hit hardest by defense cuts.

The SBA notes that DELTA loans require special handling because of complex credit analyses. Applicants may not be able to show the ability to

PART C

Statements Required by Laws and Executive Orders

Federal executive agencies, including the Small Business Administration, are required to withhold or limit financial assistance, to impose special conditions on approved loans, to provide special notices to applicants or borrowers, and to require special reports and data from borrowers in order to comply with legislation passed by Congress, by Executive Orders issued by the President and by the provisions of various inter-agency agreements. SBA has issued regulations and procedures that implement these laws and executive orders, and they are contained in Parts 112, 113, 116, 117, and 140, Title 13 Code of Federal Regulations, Chapter 1, or Standard Operating Procedures. This form contains a brief summary of the various laws and executive orders that affect SBA's state and local development company loan programs and gives applicants and borrowers the notices required by law or otherwise.

Freedom of Information Act

(5 U.S.C. 552)

This law provides, with some exceptions, that SBA must supply information reflected in agency files and records to a person requesting it. Information about approved loans that will be automatically released includes, among other things, statistics on our loan programs (individual borrowers are not identified in the statistics) and other information such as the names of the borrowers (and their officers, stockholders or partners), the collateral pledged to secure the loan, the amount of the loan, its purpose in general terms, and the maturity. Proprietary data on a borrower would not routinely be made available to third parties. All requests under this Act are to be addressed to the nearest SBA office and must be identified as a Freedom of Information request.

Right to Financial Privacy Act of 1978

(12 U.S.C. 3401)

This is notice to you, as required by the Right to Financial Privacy Act of 1978, of SBA's access rights to financial records held by financial institutions that are, or have been, doing business with you or your business, including any financial institution participating in a loan or loan guaranty. The law provides that SBA shall have a right of access to your financial records in connection with its consideration or administration of assistance to you in the form of a Government loan or loan guaranty agreement. SBA provides a certification of its compliance with the Act to a financial institution in connection with its first request for access to your financial records, after which no further certification is required for subsequent access. The law also provides that SBA's access rights continue for the term of any approved loan or loan guaranty agreement. No further notice to you of SBA's access rights is required during the term of any such agreement. The law also authorizes SBA to transfer to another Government authority any financial records included in an application for a loan, or concerning an approved loan or loan guaranty, as necessary to process, service or foreclose on a loan or loan guaranty or to collect on a defaulted loan or loan guaranty. No other transfer of your financial records to another Government authority will be permitted by SBA except as required or permitted by law.

Privacy Act of 1974 Information

Certain information such as personal balance sheets are used to evaluate your application. Such information may be given to Federal, state or local agencies for law enforcement purpose. Omission of an item means your application might not receive full consideration.

Equal Credit Opportunity Act

(15 U.S.C. 1691)

The Federal Equal Credit Opportunity Act prohibits creditors from discriminating against credit applicants on the basis of race, color, religion, national origin, sex, marital status or age (provided that the applicant has the capacity to enter into a binding contract); because all or part of the applicant's income derives from any public assistance program, or because the applicant has in good faith exercised any right under the Consumer Credit Protection Act. The Federal agency that administers compliance with this law concerning this creditor is the Federal Trade Commission, Equal Credit Opportunity, Washington, D.C. 20580.

Civil Rights Legislation

All businesses receiving SBA financial assistance must agree not to discriminate in any business practice, including employment practices and services to the public, on the basis of categories cited in 13 C.F.R., Parts 112, 113 and 117 of SBA regulations. This includes making their goods and services available to handicapped clients or customers. All business borrowers will be required to display the "Equal Employment Opportunity Poster" prescribed by SBA.

SBA Form 1244 (3-92) Previous Edition is Obsolete   - 1 -

Figure 21.1a

Certification as to Compliance with Nondiscrimination Laws

I give the assurance that I will comply with Sections 112, 113, and 117 of Title 13 of the Code of Federal Regulations, which prohibit discrimination on the grounds of race, color, sex, religion, marital status, handicap, age or national origin by recipients of Federal financing assistance and require appropriate reports and access to books and records. These requirements are applicable to anyone who buys or takes control of the business. I realize that if I do not comply with these nondiscrimination requirements, SBA can call, terminate, or accelerate repayment or suspend any or all Federal financial assistance provided by SBA.

Immigration Reform and Control Act of 1986

(Pub. L. 99-603)

If you are an alien who was in this country illegally since before January 1, 1982, you may have granted lawful temporary resident status by the United States Immigration and Naturalization Service pursuant to the Immigration Reform and Control Act of 1986 (Pub. L. 99-603). For five years from the date you are granted such status, you are not eligible for financial assistance from the SBA in the form of a loan or guaranty under Section 7(a) of the Small Business Act or Section 504 of the Small Business Investment Act unless you are disabled or a Cuban or Haitian entrant. When you sign this document, you are making the certification that the Immigration Reform and Control Act of 1986 does not apply to you, or if it does apply, more than five years have elapsed since you have been granted lawful temporary resident status pursuant to such 1986 legislation.

Occupational Safety and Health Act

(15 U.S.C. 651 et seq.)

This legislation authorizes the Occupational Safety and Health Administration in the Department of Labor to require businesses to modify facilities and procedures to protect employees or pay penalty fees. In some instances the business can be forced to cease operations or be prevented from starting operations in a new facility. Therefore, in some instances SBA may require additional information from an applicant to determine whether the business will be in compliance with OSHA regulations and allowed to operate its facility after the loan is approved and disbursed.

Flood Disaster Protection Act

(42 U.S.C. 4011)

Regulations have been issued by the Federal Insurance Administration (FIA) and by SBA implementing this Act and its amendments. These regulations prohibit SBA from making certain loans in an FIA designated floodplain unless Federal flood insurance is purchased as a condition of the loan. Failure to maintain the required level of flood insurance makes the applicant ineligible for any future financial assistance from SBA under any program, including disaster assistance.

Executive Orders -- Floodplain Management and Wetland Protection

(42 F.R. 26951 and 42 F.R. 26961)

The SBA discourages any settlement in or development of a floodplain or a wetland. This statement is to notify all SBA loan applicants that such actions are hazardous to both life and property and should be avoided. The additional cost of flood prevention construction must be considered in addition to the possible loss of all assets and investments in future floods.

Executive Order 11736 -- Environmental Protection

(38 F.R. 25161)

The Executive Order charges SBA with administering its loan programs in a manner that will result in effective enforcement of the Clean Air Act, the Federal Water Pollution Act and other environmental protection legislation. SBA must, therefore, impose conditions on some loans. By acknowledging receipt of this form and presenting the application, the principals of all small businesses borrowing $100,00 or more in direct funds stipulate to the following:

1. That any facility used, or to be used, by the subject firm is not cited on the EPA list of violating facilities.
2. That subject firm will comply with all the requirements of Section 114 of the Clean Air Act (42 U.S.C. 7414) and Section 308 of the Water Act (33 U.S.C. 1318) relating to inspection, monitoring, entry, reports and information, as well as all other requirements specified in Section 114 and Section 308 of the respective Acts, and all regulations and guidelines issued thereunder.
3. That subject firm will notify SBA of the receipt of any communication from the Director of the Environmental Protection Agency indicating that a facility utilized, or to be utilized, by subject firm is under consideration to be listed on the EPA list of violating facilities.

Lead-Based Paint Poisoning Prevention Act

(42 U.S.C. 4821 et seq.)

Borrowers using SBA funds for the construction or rehabilitation of a residential structure are prohibited from using lead-based paint (as defined in SBA regulations) on all interior surfaces, whether accessible or not, and exterior surfaces, such as stairs, decks, porches, railings, windows and doors, which are readily accessible to children under 7 years of age. A "residential structure" is any home, apartment, hotel, motel, orphanage, boarding school, dormitory, day care center, extended care facility, college or other school housing, hospital, group practice or community facility and all other residential or institutional structures where persons reside.

SBA Form 1244 (3-92) Previous Edition is Obsolete   - 2 -

Figure 21.1b

Agreement of Nonemployment of SBA Personnel

I agree that if SBA approves this application, I will not for at least two years hire an employee or consult anyone who was employed by the SBA during the one year period prior to the disbursement of the debenture.

Certification as to Payment for Financial Assistance

I certify: I have not paid anyone connected with the Federal government for help getting this financial assistance. I also agree to report to the SBA Office of Inspector General, 409 Third Street SW, Washington, D.C. 20416, any Federal government employee who offers in return for any type of compensation to help get this application approved. I understand that I need not pay anybody to deal with SBA. I also understand that a Certified Development Company may charge the applicant a percentage of the loan proceeds as set forth in SBA regulations as a fee for preparing and processing loan applications.

Certification as to Non-relocation

Regulations issued by SBA prohibit the making of loans that will result in a significant increase of unemployment in any area of the country (13 CFR 108.3(a)). In the event that proceeds from this loan are used to provide a facility for relocation of the beneficiary small business concern (including any affiliate, subsidiary or other business entity under direct, indirect or common control), the undersigned certifies that such relocations will not significantly increase unemployment in the area of the original location.

Debarment, Suspension, Ineligibility and Voluntary Exclusion for Lower Tier Covered Transactions

This certification is required by the regulations implementing Executive Order 12549, Debarment and Suspension, 13 CFR 145.

1. The prospective lower tier participant certifies, by submission of this loan application, that neither it nor its principals are presently debarred, suspended, proposed for debarment, declared ineligible, or voluntarily excluded from participation in this transaction by any Federal department or agency.

2. Where the prospective lower tier participant is unable to certify to any of the statements in this certification, such prospective participant shall attach an explanation to the loan application.

Certification as to Application Accuracy

All information in this application, including exhibits, is true and complete to the best of my knowledge and is submitted to SBA so that SBA can decide whether to approve this application. I agree to pay for or reimburse SBA for the cost of any surveys, title or mortgage examinations, appraisals, etc., performed by non-SBA personnel provided that I have given my consent. Whoever makes any statement knowing it to be false, or whoever willfully overvalues any security, for the purpose of obtaining any loan, or substitution of security therefor, or for the purpose of influencing in any way the action of SBA, or for the purpose of obtaining money, property, or anything of value, under the Small Business Investment Act, as amended, may be punished by a fine of not more than $5,000 or by imprisonment for not more than two years, or both, pursuant to the Federal law at 15 U.S.C. 645.

Whoever in any matter within the jurisdiction of any department or agency of the United States knowingly and willfully falsifies, conceals or covers up a material fact by any trick, scheme or device, or makes any false, fictitious or fraudulent statements or representations, or makes or uses any false writings or documents knowing the same to contain any false, fictitious or fraudulent statement or entry may be fined up to $10,000 or imprisoned for up to 5 years, or both, pursuant to the Federal law at 18 U.S.C. 1001.

Debt Collection Act of 1982 and Deficit Reduction Act of 1984

(31 U.S.C. 3701 et seq. and other titles)

These laws require SBA to aggressively collect any loan payments which become delinquent. SBA must obtain your taxpayer identification number when you apply for a loan. If you receive a loan, and do not make payments as they come due, SBA may take one or more of the following actions:

*Report the status of your loan(s) to credit bureaus.
*Hire a collection agency to collect your loan.
*Offset your income tax refund or other amounts due to you from the Federal Government.
*Suspend or debar you or your company from doing business with the Federal Government.
*Refer your loan to the Department of Justice or other attorneys for litigation.
*Foreclose on collateral or take other action permitted in the loan instruments.
*Disclose the status of your loan(s) to other Federal agencies for the purpose of computer matching. Matching may be used to initiate offsets or limit your access to Federal benefits.

Figure 21.1c

CONFLICTS OF INTEREST

No overlapping relationship exists between the small business concern, including its associates, and the CDC, including its associates, or any other lender providing financing for the project that could create an appearance of a conflict of interest as defined in 13 CFR 120.102-10 or violate 13 CFR 108.4(d). No such relationships existed within six months of this application or will be permitted to exist while the assistance is outstanding.

OTHER AGREEMENTS AND CERTIFICATIONS

I authorize disclosure of all information submitted in connection with this application to the financial institution agreeing to participate with SBA's guaranteed debenture.

I waive all claims against SBA and its consultants for any management and technical assistance that may be provided.

In consideration for assistance from the Small Business Administration, I hereby agree that I will comply with all Federal laws and regulations to the extent that they are applicable to such assistance, including conditions set forth in this application.

I, my spouse, or any member of my household, or anyone who owns, manages, or directs the business or their spouses or members of their households do not work for the SBA, Small Business Advisory Council, SCORE or ACE, any Federal agency, or the participating lender. If someone does, the name and address of such person and where employed is provided on an attached page.

Applicant Notifications

I or any of the officers of my company ◯ have/ ◯ have not been involved in bankruptcy or insolvency proceedings. If so, I have attached copies of the proceedings.

I or my business ◯ is/ ◯ is not involved in any pending lawsuits. If so, I have attached a description.

Applicant's Acknowledgment

My signature acknowledges receipt of this form, that I have read it and that I have a copy for my files. My signature represents my agreement to comply with the requirements the Small Business Administration makes in connection with the approval of my loan request and to comply, whenever applicable, with the limitations contained in this notice.

(Each Proprietor, each General Partner, each Limited Partner or Stockholder owning 20% or more, and each Guarantor must sign. Each person should only sign once.)

If Applicant is a proprietor or partnership, sign below:

If Applicant is a corporation, sign below:

_____

Name of Business

_____

Corporate Name

By: _____ Date _____

By: _____ Date _____

Attested by: _____ (seal if required)

Additional Proprietors, Partners, Stockholders or Guarantors as required.

_____

Signature

_____

Date

_____

Signature

_____

Date

_____

Signature

_____

Date

_____

Signature

_____

Date

SBA Form 1244 (3-92) Previous Edition is Obsolete   - 4 -

Figure 21.1d

repay based on past operations. But the SBA has the authority to resolve reasonable doubts in favor of DELTA applicants.

SBA DIRECT LOANS

Direct loans from the SBA are available to eligible small businesses that are unable to obtain the needed credit through either conventional loans or the SBA's guarantee loan program. Direct loan funds are very limited and are presently available to Vietnam-era veterans, handicapped and sheltered workshops, 8a-certified companies, and those owned by low-income individuals or those located in low-income or labor surplus areas.

Eligible businesses are those that present a letter of decline from a lender in communities with a population of 200,000 or less. Letters of decline are necessary from two unaffiliated lenders if the population exceeds 200,000. These letters should include the name and telephone number of the persons contracted at the lender, the amount and terms of the loan requested, the reasons for decline, and a statement that the lender will not extend the requested credit with or without the SBA's guarantee. The SBA anticipates that lenders will issue decline letters based on their policies and analysis of the credit factors, not as an accommodation. Applicants must also meet, as a minimum, the same credit, size, and eligibility requirements that applicants for guarantee loans must meet.

Loan amounts are generally limited to $150,000 to any one borrower for any combination of direct loans.

WOMEN'S DEMONSTRATION PROGRAM

The Women's Demonstration Program was established through the Women's Business Ownership Act of 1988 and was reauthorized through the Women's Business Development Act of 1991. Administered by the SBA's Office of Women's Business Ownership, it establishes centers around the country to train and counsel women in the skills necessary to launch their own businesses. In particular, the program targets socially and economically disadvantaged women.

A number of the sites have developed a loan pool based on the Grameen Bank model. The loan pool allows participating members to borrow money based on group consensus accompanied by long-term counseling and financial and management training. More than 47,000 women have benefitted from the program's training and counseling.

There are currently 54 sites in 28 states and the District of Columbia; all the centers offer financial, management, marketing, and technical assistance to current and potential women business owners. Each center tailors its style and offerings to the particular needs of its community. Some sites target minorities such as Native Americans, African-Americans, Hispanics, and Asian-Americans.

The National Academy of Public Administration (a national federal program evaluator) has reported to Congress that "During the ... years of assessing the effectiveness of projects throughout the United States, the Academy panel and project staff found these organizations ... to be dynamic groups whose services are making a difference for the women who used them."

U.S. Small Business Administration's Office of Women's Business
Ownership's Demonstration Program Women's Business Centers
409 3rd Street, S.W.
Washington, DC 20416
(202) 205-6673
Acting Assistant Administrator Sherre Henry,
Contracting Representative Harriet Fredman

ALABAMA

Women's Business Assistance Center
Kathryn Cariglino, Director
1301 Azalea Road, Suite 111-A
Mobile, AL 36693
(205) 660-2725   (205) 660-8854 Fax
Mailing address: P.O. Box 6021, Mobile, AL 36660

ARIZONA

National Center for American Indian Enterprise Development
Vera Pooyouma, Marilyn Andrews, Steven L.A. Stallings
953 East Juanita Avenue
Mesa, AZ 85204
(602) 831-7524   (602) 491-1332 Fax
Serving Arizona, Washington, and California

CALIFORNIA

American Woman's Economic Development Corporation (AWED)
Phil Borden, Regional Director
100 West Broadway, Suite 500
Long Beach, CA 90802
(310) 983-3747   (310) 983-3750 Fax

American Woman's Economic Development Corporation (AWED)
Linda Harasin, Acting Executive Director
2301 Campus Drive, Suite 20
Irvine, CA 92715
(714) 474-2933   (714) 474-7416 Fax

WEST Company (Not Funded)
Parent Organization to WEST Co. in Fort Bragg, CA
Sheilah Rogers, Director
367 North State Street, Suite 206
Ukiah, CA 95482
(707) 468-3553   (707) 462-8945 Fax

WEST Company–A Women's Economic Self-Sufficiency
Training Program
    Carol Steele
    340 North Main Street
    Fort Bragg, CA 95437
    (707) 964-7571   (707) 961-1340 Fax

Women's Initiative for Self Employment (WISE) (Not Funded)
Parent Organization for WISE in Oakland, CA
    Etienne LeGrand, Executive Director
    450 Mission Street, Suite 402
    San Francisco, CA 94102
    (415) 247-9473   (415) 247-9471 Fax

WISE Oakland
    Helen Branham, Project Director
    519 17th Street, Suite 520
    Oakland, CA 94612
    (510) 208-9473   (510) 208-9471 Fax

Women Business Owners Corporation
    Kathleen Schwallie
    18 Encanto Drive
    Rolling Hills Estates, CA 90274
    (310) 530-0582   (310) 530-1483 Fax

COLORADO

Mi Casa Business Center for Women (BCW)
    Luz Cofresi-Howe, Wendy Krajewski-Kenar
    571 Galapago Street
    Denver, CO 80204
    (303) 573-1302   (303) 595-0422 Fax

CONNECTICUT

American Woman's Economic Development Corporation (AWED)
    Fran Polak, Connecticut Manager
    2001 W. Main Street, Suite 140
    Stamford, CT 06902
    (203) 326-7914   (203) 326-7916 Fax

DISTRICT OF COLUMBIA

American Woman's Economic Development Corporation (AWED)
    Susan Bari, Regional Director
    1250 24th Street, N.W., Room 120
    Washington, DC 20037
    (202) 857-0091   (202) 223-2775 Fax

FLORIDA

Women's Business Development Center
Christine Kurtz-White, Director
Florida International University, OET-3
Miami, FL 33199
(305) 348-3951, 3903   (305) 348-2931 Fax

GEORGIA

Coalition of 100 Black Women
Leah Creque-Harris, Project Director
The Candler Building
Atlanta, GA 30303
(404) 659-4008   (404) 659-3001 Fax

ILLINOIS

Women's Business Development Center (Not Funded)
Parent Organization for WBDC Florida
Linda Darragh, Hedy Ratner, Co-Directors
8 South Michigan Avenue, Suite 400
Chicago, IL 60603
(312) 853-3477   (312) 853-0145 Fax

LOUISIANA

Women Entrepreneurs for Economic Development Inc. (WEED)
Paula Pete
817 N. Claiborne Avenue
New Orleans, LA 70116
(504) 827-1066   (504) 949-8885 Fax

Southeast Louisiana Black Chamber of Commerce (works with WEED)
Valentine Pierce
1600 Canal Street, Suite 606
New Orleans, LA 70112
(504) 539-9450(1)   (504) 539-9499 Fax

MAINE

Coastal Enterprises, Inc.
Ellen Golden
P.O. Box 268
Wiscasset, ME 04578
(207) 882-7552   (207) 882-7308 Fax

MASSACHUSETTS

Center for Women & Enterprise, Inc.
Andrea Silbert, Susan Hammond
48A Coolidge Street
Brookline, MA 02146
(617) 734-2241   (617) 731-9303 Fax

MICHIGAN

Ann Arbor Community Development Corporation
Michelle Vasquez
2008 Hogback Road, Suite 2A
Ann Arbor, MI 48105
(313) 677-1400   (313) 677-1465 Fax

EXCEL!
Carol Lopucki, Executive Director
% Prangley, Marks & Co.
Bridgewater Place, 11th Floor
Grand Rapids, MI 49504
(616) 458-4783   (616) 774-9081 Fax

EXCEL! Midwest Women Business Owners Development Team
Mary Burt, Executive Director
600 W. Lafayette
Detroit, MI 48226
(313) 961-4748   (313) 961-5434 Fax

MINNESOTA

Bi-County Community Action Programs, Inc.
Lucille Moe, Kimberle Nagle, Anne McGill
P.O. Box 579
Bemidji, MN 56601
(218) 751-4631   (218) 751-8452 Fax

Women's Business Center White Earth Reservation Tribal Council
Mary Turner, Director
North Main Street
P.O. Box 478
Mahnomen, MN 56557
(218) 935-2827   (218) 935-2390 Fax

MISSISSIPPI

National Council of Negro Women
Eleanor Hinton-Hoytt
10001 G Street, N.W., Suite 800
Washington, DC 20001
(202) 628-0015 x20   (202) 628-0233 Fax
Servicing rural Mississippi

MISSOURI

NAWBO of St. Louis
Irina Bronstein, Project Director
222 S. Bemiston, Suite 216
St. Louis, MO 63105
(313) 863-0046   (314) 863-2079 Fax

MONTANA

Montana Women's Capital Fund
Kelly Flaherty
54 North Last Chance Gulch
Helena, MT 59624
(406) 443-3144   (406) 442-1789 Fax

Women's Opportunity & Resource Development Inc.
Kelly Rosenleaf, Director
Rosalie Cates, Project Director
127 N. Higgins
Missoula, MT 59802
(406) 543-3550   (406) 721-4584 Fax

NEVADA

Nevada Self-Employment Trust
Janice Barbour, Director
Marguerite Mathis, Project Director
560 Mill Street
Reno, NV 89502
(702) 329-6789   (702) 329-6738 Fax

NEW JERSEY

New Jersey NAWBO EXCEL
Harriet Nazarete, Project Director
120 Finderne Avenue
Bridgewater, NJ 08807
(908) 707-0173   (908) 707-1213 Fax

NEW MEXICO

Women's Economic Self-Sufficiency Team (WESST Corp.)
Agnes Noonan, Executive Director
414 Silver Southwest
Albuquerque, NM 87102
(505) 848-4760   (505) 848-2368 Fax

WESST Corp. Taos, NM
Yolanda Nunez, Project Director
Taos County Economic Development
P.O. Box 1389
Taos, NM 87571
(505) 758-3099   (505) 758-8153 Fax

NEW YORK

American Woman's Economic Development Corporation
(Not Funded)
    Parent Organization to AWED Washington DC and CT
    Suzanne Tufts, President and CEO
    71 Vanderbilt Avenue, Suite 320
    New York, NY 10169
    (212) 692-9100   (212) 688-2718 Fax

Asian American Professional Women Inc.
    Mei Chan, Bonnie Wong
    125 Lafayette Street
    New York, NY 10013
    (212) 966-7888   (212) 966-8988 Fax

NORTH DAKOTA

Women's Business Institute
    Penny Retzer, Director
    901 Page Drive
    Fargo, ND 58106
    (701) 235-6488   (701) 235-8284 Fax

OHIO

Ohio Women's Business Resource Network (OWBRN)
    Mary Ann McClure, Coordinator
    77 South High Street, 28th Floor
    Columbus, OH 43266
    (614) 466-2682   (614) 466-0829 Fax

Chamber Women's Business Initiative
    Linda Steward, Director
    37 North High Street
    Columbus, OH 43215
    (614) 225-6082   (614) 469-8250 Fax

Women's Development Center
    Tina Macon, Director
    300 N. Abbe Road
    Elyria, OH 44035
    (216) 366-0770   (216) 366-0769 Fax

Enterprise Center/Women's Business Center
    Betty Reese, Coordinator
    129 E. Main Street
    Hillsboro, OH 45133
    (513) 393-9599   (513) 393-8159 Fax

Northwest Ohio Women's Entrepreneurial Network
  Linda Fayerweather, Director
  Toledo Area Chamber of Commerce
  300 Madison Avenue, Suite 200
  Toledo, OH 43604
  (419) 243-8191   (419) 241-8302 Fax

Women Entrepreneurs Inc. (not funded by SBA)
  Peg Moertl, Executive Director
  Bartlett Building
  36 East 4th Street
  Cincinnati, OH 45202
  mailing address: P.O. Box 2662, Cincinnati, OH 45201
  (513) 684-0700   (513) 665-2052 Fax

EMPOWER Pyramid Career Services
  Andrea Zalantis, Director
  2400 Cleveland Avenue NW
  Canton, OH 44709
  (216) 453-3767   (216) 453-6079 Fax

Women's Business Resource Program of S.E. Ohio
  Debra McBride, Project Director
  Technology & Enterprise Building, Suite 190
  20 East Circle Drive
  Athens, OH 45701
  (614) 593-1797   (614) 593-1795 Fax

Women's Entrepreneurial Growth Organization (WEGO) (not funded
by SBA)
  Susan Hale, Director
  58 West Center Street
  Akron, OH 44309
  mailing address: P.O. Box 544, Akron, OH 44309
  (216) 535-9346   (216) 535-4523 Fax

Women's Network, Inc.
  Marlene Miller, Director of Mentoring Programs
  1540 West Market Street, Suite 100
  Akron, OH 44313
  (216) 864-5636   (216) 864-6526 Fax

OKLAHOMA

Working Women's Money University
  Lori Smith
  3501 NW 63rd, Suite 609
  Oklahoma City, OK 73116
  (405) 842-1196   (405) 842-5067 Fax

OREGON

> Southern Oregon Women's Access to Credit
> Mary O'Kief
> 33 North Central, Suite 410
> Medford, OR 97510
> (503) 779-3992   (503) 779-3992 Fax

PENNSYLVANIA

> National Association of Women Business Owners Pittsburgh
> Carmelle Nickens, Director
> 5604 Solway Street, Suite 207
> Pittsburgh, PA 15217
> (412) 521-4735 x4736   (412) 521-4737 Fax

> Women's Business Development Center
> Geri Swift, Ellen Fisher
> 8 Station Lane
> Philadelphia, PA 19118
> (215) 248-7999   (215) 248-1846 or (610) 446-2607 Fax

SOUTH DAKOTA

> Watertown Area Career Learning Center
> Ann Taecker, Kay Tschakert
> P.O. Box 81
> Watertown, SD 57201
> (605) 235-6488   (605) 235-8284 Fax

TEXAS

> Center for Women's Business Enterprise
> Susan Spencer, Austin Site Coordinator
> 508 Ladin Lane
> Austin, TX 78734
> (512) 261-8525   (512) 261-8525 Fax

> Center for Women's Business Enterprise (CWBE)
> Linda Schneider, Coordinator
> 2425 West Loop South, Suite 1004
> Houston, TX 77027
> (713) 552-1267   (713) 578-7061 Fax

> North Texas Women's Business Development Center, Inc.
> Bill J. Priest Institute for Economic Development
> Kay Cole, Project Director
> Lou Bettes, Billie Bryant, Sharon Venable, Heather Day Ballinger
> 1402 Corinth Street
> Dallas, TX 75215-2111
> (214) 855-4378   (214) 855-4378 Fax

UTAH

Utah Technology Finance Corporation
Susan Bastian
177 East 100 South
Salt Lake City, UT 84111
(801) 364-4346   (801) 364-4361 Fax

WISCONSIN

Women's Business Initiative Corporation (WBIC)
Wendy K. Werkmeister, President
3112 West Highland Blvd.
Milwaukee, WI 53208
(414) 933-3231   (414) 933-2515 Fax

Wisconsin Women Entrepreneurs, Inc.
Karen Hendrickson, Project Manager
2830 North 48th Street
Milwaukee, WI 53210
(414) 873-0687   (414) 873-9360 Fax

Section Six

22 SBA Field Offices

The following is a listing of all SBA field offices.

ALABAMA

TYPE	CITY	STATE	ZIP CODE	ADDRESS	PHONE NUMBER
RO	ATLANTA	GA	30367	1375 PEACHTREE ST., NE	(404) 347-2797
DO	ATLANTA	GA	30309	1720 PEACHTREE RD., NW	(404) 347-4749
DO	BIRMINGHAM	AL	35203-2398	2121 8TH AVE. N.	(205) 731-1344
DO	CHARLOTTE	NC	28202	200 N. COLLEGE ST.	(704) 344-6563
DO	COLUMBIA	SC	29201	1835 ASSEMBLY ST.	(803) 765-5376
DO	JACKSON	MS	39201	101 W. CAPITOL ST.	(601) 965-5325
DO	JACKSONVILLE	FL	32256-7504	7825 BAYMEADOWS WAY	(904) 443-1900
DO	LOUISVILLE	KY	40202	600 DR. M.L. KING JR PL	(502) 582-5976
DO	CORAL GABLES	FL	33146-2911	1320 S. DIXIE HGWY.	(305) 536-5521
DO	NASHVILLE	TN	37228-1500	50 VANTAGE WAY	(615) 736-5881
BO	GULFPORT	MS	39501-7758	1 HANCOCK PLAZA	(601) 863-4449
POD	STATESBORO	GA	30458	52 N. MAIN ST.	(912) 489-8719
POD	TAMPA	FL	33602-3945	501 E. POLK ST.	(813) 228-2594
POD	W. PALM BEACH	FL	33407-2044	5601 CORPORATE WAY	(407) 689-3922

RO = REGIONAL OFFICE   DO = DISTRICT OFFICE   BO = BRANCH OFFICE   POD = POST OF DUTY

ALASKA

TYPE	CITY	STATE	ZIP CODE	ADDRESS	PHONE NUMBER
RO	SEATTLE	WA	98121	2615 4TH AVENUE	(206) 553-5676
DO	ANCHORAGE	AK	99513	222 WEST 8TH AVENUE	(907) 271-4022
DO	BOISE	ID	83702	1020 MAIN STREET	(208) 334-1096
DO	PORTLAND	OR	97201	222 S.W. COLUMBIA	(503) 326-5223
DO	SEATTLE	WA	98174	915 SECOND AVENUE	(206) 553-1420
DO	SPOKANE	WA	99204	WEST 601 FIRST AVE	(509) 353-2810

RO = REGIONAL OFFICE   DO = DISTRICT OFFICE

ARIZONA

TYPE	CITY	STATE	ZIP CODE	ADDRESS	PHONE NUMBER
DO	SAN FRANCISCO	CA	94105	71 STEVENSON STREET	(415) 744-6402
DO	FRESNO	CA	93727	2719 N. AIR FRESNO DR	(209) 487-5189
DO	HONOLULU	HI	96850	300 ALA MOANA BLVD	(808) 541-2990
DO	LAS VEGAS	NV	89125	301 EAST STEWART ST	(702) 388-6611
DO	GLENDALE	CA	91203	330 N. BRAND BLVD	(213) 894-2956
DO	PHOENIX	AZ	85004	2828 N. CENTRAL AVE	(602) 640-2316
DO	SAN DIEGO	CA	92188	880 FRONT STREET	(619) 557-7252
DO	SAN FRANCISCO	CA	94105	211 MAIN STREET	(415) 744-6820
DO	SANTA ANA	CA	92703	901 W. CIVIC CENTER DR	(714) 836-2494
BO	AGANA	GM	96910	238 ARCHBISHOP FC FLORES ST	(671) 472-7277
BO	SACRAMENTO	CA	95814	660 J STREET	(916) 551-1426
POD	RENO	NV	89505	50 SOUTH VIRGINIA ST	(702) 784-5268
POD	TUCSON	AZ	85701	300 WEST CONGRESS ST	(602) 670-4759
POD	VENTURA	CA	93003	6477 TELEPHONE ROAD	(805) 642-1866

DO = DISTRICT OFFICE   BO = BRANCH OFFICE   POD = POST OF DUTY

ARKANSAS

TYPE	CITY	STATE	ZIP CODE	ADDRESS	PHONE NUMBER
RO	DALLAS	TX	75235	8625 KING GEORGE DR	(214) 767-7635
DO	ALBUQUERQUE	NM	87102	625 SILVER AVENUE, SW	(505) 766-1870
DO	DALLAS	TX	75242	1100 COMMERCE STREET	(214) 767-0600
DO	EL PASO	TX	79935	10737 GATEWAY WEST	(915) 541-5676
DO	HOUSTON	TX	77054	2525 MURWORTH	(713) 660-4401
DO	LITTLE ROCK	AR	72202	2120 RIVERFRONT DRIVE	(501) 324-5278
DO	HARLINGEN	TX	78550	222 EAST VAN BUREN ST	(512) 427-8533
DO	LUBBOCK	TX	79401	1611 TENTH STREET	(806) 743-7462
DO	NEW ORLEANS	LA	70112	1661 CANAL STREET	(504) 589-2744
DO	OKLAHOMA CITY	OK	73102	200 NORTH WEST 5TH ST	(405) 231-4301
DO	SAN ANTONIO	TX	78216	7400 BLANCO ROAD	(512) 229-4535
BO	CORPUS CHRISTI	TX	78476	606 NORTH CARANCAHUA	(512) 888-3301
BO	FT. WORTH	TX	76102	819 TAYLOR STREET	(817) 334-3777
POD	AUSTIN	TX	78701	300 EAST 8TH STREET	(512) 482-5288
POD	MARSHALL	TX	75670	505 EAST TRAVIS	(903) 935-5257
POD	SHREVEPORT	LA	71101	500 FANNIN STREET	(318) 226-5196

RO = REGIONAL OFFICE   DO = DISTRICT OFFICE   BO = BRANCH OFFICE
POD = POST OF DUTY

CALIFORNIA

TYPE	CITY	STATE	ZIP CODE	ADDRESS	PHONE NUMBER
DO	SAN FRANCISCO	CA	94105	71 STEVENSON STREET	(415) 744-6402
DO	FRESNO	CA	93727	2719 N. AIR FRESNO DR	(209) 487-5189
DO	HONOLULU	HI	96850	300 ALA MOANA BLVD	(808) 541-2990
DO	LAS VEGAS	NV	89125	301 EAST STEWART ST	(702) 388-6611
DO	GLENDALE	CA	91203	330 N. BRAND BLVD	(213) 894-2956
DO	PHOENIX	AZ	85004	2828 N. CENTRAL AVE	(602) 640-2316
DO	SAN DIEGO	CA	92188	880 FRONT STREET	(619) 557-7252

DO	SAN FRANCISCO	CA	94105	211 MAIN STREET	(415) 744-6820
DO	SANTA ANA	CA	92703	901 W. CIVIC CENTER DR	(714) 836-2494
BO	AGANA	GM	96910	238 ARCHBISHOP FC FLORES ST	(671) 472-7277
BO	SACRAMENTO	CA	95814	660 J STREET	(916) 551-1426
POD	RENO	NV	89505	50 SOUTH VIRGINIA ST	(702) 784-5268
POD	TUCSON	AZ	85701	300 WEST CONGRESS ST	(602) 629-6715
POD	VENTURA	CA	93003	6477 TELEPHONE ROAD	(805) 642-1866

DO = DISTRICT OFFICE   BO = BRANCH OFFICE   POD = POST OF DUTY

COLORADO

TYPE	CITY	STATE	ZIP CODE	ADDRESS	PHONE NUMBER
RO	DENVER	CO	80202	999 18TH STREET	(303) 294-7021
DO	CASPER	WY	82602	100 EAST B STREET	(307) 261-5761
DO	DENVER	CO	80201	721 19TH STREET	(303) 844-3984
DO	FARGO	ND	58108	657 2ND AVE NORTH	(701) 239-5131
DO	HELENA	MT	59626	301 SOUTH PARK	(406) 449-5381
DO	SALT LAKE CITY	UT	84138	125 SOUTH STATE ST.	(801) 524-5800
DO	SIOUX FALLS	SD	57102	101 SOUTH MAIN AVENUE	(605) 330-4231

RO = REGIONAL OFFICE   DO = DISTRICT OFFICE

CONNECTICUT

TYPE	CITY	STATE	ZIP CODE	ADDRESS	PHONE NUMBER
RO	BOSTON	MA	02110	155 FEDERAL ST.	(617) 451-2023
DO	BOSTON	MA	02222-1093	10 CAUSEWAY ST.	(617) 565-5590
DO	AUGUSTA	ME	04330	40 WESTERN AVE.	(207) 622-8378
DO	CONCORD	NH	03302-1257	143 N. MAIN ST.	(603) 225-1400
DO	HARTFORD	CT	06106	330 MAIN ST.	(203) 240-4700
DO	MONTPELIER	VT	05602	87 STATE ST.	(802) 828-4422
DO	PROVIDENCE	RI	02903	380 WESTMINISTER MALL	(401) 528-4561
BO	SPRINGFIELD	MA	01103	1550 MAIN ST.	(413) 785-0268

RO = REGIONAL OFFICE   DO = DISTRICT OFFICE   BO = BRANCH OFFICE

DELAWARE

TYPE	CITY	STATE	ZIP CODE	ADDRESS	PHONE NUMBER
RO	KING OF PRUSSIA	PA	19406	475 ALLENDALE RD.	(215) 962-3700
DO	BALTIMORE	MD	21202	10 N. CALVERT ST.	(410) 962-4392
DO	CLARKSBURG	WV	26301	168 W. MAIN ST.	(304) 623-5631
DO	KING OF PRUSSIA	PA	19406	475 ALLENDALE RD.	(215) 962-3804
DO	PITTSBURGH	PA	15222	960 PENN AVE.	(412) 644-2780
DO	RICHMOND	VA	23240	400 N. 8TH ST.	(804) 771-2400
DO	WASHINGTON	DC	20036	1111 18TH ST., N.W.	(202) 634-1500
BO	CHARLESTON	WV	25301	550 EAGAN ST.	(304) 347-5220
BO	HARRISBURG	PA	17101	100 CHESTNUT ST.	(717) 782-3840
BO	WILKES-BARRE	PA	18702	20 N. PENNSYLVANIA AVE.	(717) 826-6497
BO	WILMINGTON	DE	19801	920 N. KING ST.	(302) 573-6295

RO = REGIONAL OFFICE   DO = DISTRICT OFFICE   BO = BRANCH OFFICE

DISTRICT OF COLUMBIA

TYPE	CITY	STATE	ZIP CODE	ADDRESS	PHONE NUMBER
RO	KING OF PRUSSIA	PA	19406	475 ALLENDALE RD.	(215) 962-3700
DO	BALTIMORE	MD	21202	10 N. CALVERT ST.	(410) 962-4392
DO	CLARKSBURG	WV	26301	168 W. MAIN ST.	(304) 623-5631
DO	KING OF PRUSSIA	PA	19406	475 ALLENDALE RD.	(215) 962-3804
DO	PITTSBURGH	PA	15222	960 PENN AVE.	(412) 644-2780
DO	RICHMOND	VA	23240	400 N. 8TH ST.	(804) 771-2400
DO	WASHINGTON	DC	20036	1111 18TH ST., N.W.	(202) 634-1500
BO	CHARLESTON	WV	25301	550 EAGAN ST.	(304) 347-5220
BO	HARRISBURG	PA	17101	100 CHESTNUT ST.	(717) 782-3840
BO	WILKES-BARRE	PA	18702	20 N. PENNSYLVANIA AVE.	(717) 826-6497
BO	WILMINGTON	DE	19801	920 N. KING ST.	(302) 573-6295

RO = REGIONAL OFFICE   DO = DISTRICT OFFICE   BO = BRANCH OFFICE

FLORIDA

TYPE	CITY	STATE	ZIP CODE	ADDRESS	PHONE NUMBER
RO	ATLANTA	GA	30367	1375 PEACHTREE ST., NE	(404) 347-2797
DO	ATLANTA	GA	30309	1720 PEACHTREE RD., NW	(404) 347-4749
DO	BIRMINGHAM	AL	35203-2398	2121 8TH AVE. N.	(205) 731-1344
DO	CHARLOTTE	NC	28202	200 N. COLLEGE ST.	(704) 344-6563
DO	COLUMBIA	SC	29201	1835 ASSEMBLY ST.	(803) 765-5376
DO	JACKSON	MS	39201	101 W. CAPITOL ST.	(601) 965-5325
DO	JACKSONVILLE	FL	32256-7504	7825 BAYMEADOWS WAY	(904) 443-1900
DO	LOUISVILLE	KY	40202	600 DR. M.L. KING JR PL	(502) 582-5976
DO	CORAL GABLES	FL	33146-2911	1320 S. DIXIE HGWY.	(305) 536-5521
DO	NASHVILLE	TN	37228-1500	50 VANTAGE WAY	(615) 736-5881
BO	GULFPORT	MS	39501-7758	1 HANCOCK PLAZA	(601) 863-4449
POD	STATESBORO	GA	30458	52 N. MAIN ST.	(912) 489-8719
POD	TAMPA	FL	33602-3945	501 E. POLK ST.	(813) 228-2594
POD	W. PALM BEACH	FL	33407-2044	5601 CORPORATE WAY	(407) 689-3922

RO = REGIONAL OFFICE   DO = DISTRICT OFFICE   BO = BRANCH OFFICE   POD = POST OF DUTY

GEORGIA

TYPE	CITY	STATE	ZIP CODE	ADDRESS	PHONE NUMBER
RO	ATLANTA	GA	30367	1375 PEACHTREE ST., NE	(404) 347-2797
DO	ATLANTA	GA	30309	1720 PEACHTREE RD., NW	(404) 347-4749
DO	BIRMINGHAM	AL	35203-2398	2121 8TH AVE. N.	(205) 731-1344
DO	CHARLOTTE	NC	28202	200 N. COLLEGE ST.	(704) 344-6563
DO	COLUMBIA	SC	29201	1835 ASSEMBLY ST.	(803) 765-5376
DO	JACKSON	MS	39201	101 W. CAPITOL ST.	(601) 965-5325
DO	JACKSONVILLE	FL	32256-7504	7825 BAYMEADOWS WAY	(904) 443-1900
DO	LOUISVILLE	KY	40202	600 DR. M.L. KING JR PL	(502) 582-5976
DO	CORAL GABLES	FL	33146-2911	1320 S. DIXIE HGWY.	(305) 536-5521
DO	NASHVILLE	TN	37228-1500	50 VANTAGE WAY	(615) 736-5881
BO	GULFPORT	MS	39501-7758	1 HANCOCK PLAZA	(601) 863-4449
POD	STATESBORO	GA	30458	52 N. MAIN ST.	(912) 489-8719

POD	TAMPA	FL	33602-3945	501 E. POLK ST.	(813) 228-2594
POD	W. PALM BEACH	FL	33407-2044	5601 CORPORATE WAY	(407) 689-3922

RO = REGIONAL OFFICE   DO = DISTRICT OFFICE   BO = BRANCH OFFICE   POD = POST OF DUTY

HAWAII

TYPE	CITY	STATE	ZIP CODE	ADDRESS	PHONE NUMBER
DO	SAN FRANCISCO	CA	94105	71 STEVENSON STREET	(415) 744-6402
DO	FRESNO	CA	93727	2719 N. AIR FRESNO DR	(209) 487-5189
DO	HONOLULU	HI	96850	300 ALA MOANA BLVD	(808) 541-2990
DO	LAS VEGAS	NV	89125	301 EAST STEWART ST	(702) 388-6611
DO	GLENDALE	CA	91203	330 N. BRAND BLVD	(213) 894-2956
DO	PHOENIX	AZ	85004	2828 N. CENTRAL AVE	(602) 640-2316
DO	SAN DIEGO	CA	92188	880 FRONT STREET	(619) 557-7252
DO	SAN FRANCISCO	CA	94105	211 MAIN STREET	(414) 744-6820
DO	SANTA ANA	CA	92703	901 W. CIVIC CENTER DR	(714) 836-2494
BO	AGANA	GM	96910	238 ARCHBISHOP FC FLORES ST	(671) 472-7277
BO	SACRAMENTO	CA	95814	660 J STREET	(916) 551-1426
POD	RENO	NV	89505	50 SOUTH VIRGINIA ST	(702) 784-5268
POD	TUCSON	AZ	85701	300 WEST CONGRESS ST	(602) 629-6715
POD	VENTURA	CA	93003	6477 TELEPHONE ROAD	(805) 642-1866

DO = DISTRICT OFFICE   BO = BRANCH OFFICE   POD = POST OF DUTY

IDAHO

TYPE	CITY	STATE	ZIP CODE	ADDRESS	PHONE NUMBER
RO	SEATTLE	WA	98121	2615 4TH AVENUE	(206) 553-5676
DO	ANCHORAGE	AK	99513	222 WEST 8TH AVENUE	(907) 271-4022
DO	BOISE	ID	83702	1020 MAIN STREET	(208) 334-1096
DO	PORTLAND	OR	97201	222 S.W. COLUMBIA	(503) 326-5223
DO	SEATTLE	WA	98174	915 SECOND AVENUE	(206) 553-1420
DO	SPOKANE	WA	99204	WEST 601 FIRST AVE	(509) 353-2810

RO = REGIONAL OFFICE   DO = DISTRICT OFFICE

ILLINOIS

TYPE	CITY	STATE	ZIP CODE	ADDRESS	PHONE NUMBER
RO	CHICAGO	IL	60606-6611	300 S. RIVERSIDE PLAZA	(312) 353-5000
DO	CHICAGO	IL	60661-1093	500 W. MADISON ST.	(312) 353-4528
DO	CLEVELAND	OH	44199	1240 E. 9TH ST.	(216) 552-4180
DO	COLUMBUS	OH	43215	85 MARCONI BLVD.	(614) 469-6860
DO	DETROIT	MI	48226	477 MICHIGAN AVE.	(313) 226-6075
DO	INDIANAPOLIS	IN	46204-1873	429 N. PENNSYLVANIA	(317) 226-7272
DO	MADISON	WI	53703	212 E. WASHINGTON AVE.	(608) 264-5261
DO	MINNEAPOLIS	MN	55403-1563	100 N. 6TH ST.	(612) 370-2324
BO	CINCINNATI	OH	45202	525 VINE ST.	(513) 684-2814
BO	MILWAUKEE	WI	53203	310 W. WISCONSIN AVE	(414) 297-3941
BO	MARQUETTE	MI	49885	300 S. FRONT ST.	(906) 225-1108
BO	SPRINGFIELD	IL	62704	511 W. CAPITOL ST.	(217) 492-4416

RO = REGIONAL OFFICE   DO = DISTRICT OFFICE   BO = BRANCH OFFICE

INDIANA

No Data Available

IOWA

TYPE	CITY	STATE	ZIP CODE	ADDRESS	PHONE NUMBER
RO	KANSAS CITY	MO	64106	911 WALNUT STREET	(816) 426-3608
DO	CEDAR RAPIDS	IA	52402	373 COLLINS ROAD, NE	(319) 393-8630
DO	DES MOINES	IA	50309	210 WALNUT STREET	(515) 284-4422
DO	KANSAS CITY	MO	64105	323 WEST 8TH STREET	(816) 374-6708
DO	OMAHA	NE	68154	11145 MILL VALLEY RD	(402) 221-3604
DO	ST. LOUIS	MO	63101	815 OLIVE STREET	(314) 539-6600
DO	WICHITA	KS	67202	100 EAST ENGLISH ST	(316) 269-6273
BO	SPRINGFIELD	MO	65802	620 S. GLENSTONE ST	(417) 864-7670

RO = REGIONAL OFFICE   DO = DISTRICT OFFICE   BO = BRANCH OFFICE

KANSAS

TYPE	CITY	STATE	ZIP CODE	ADDRESS	PHONE NUMBER
RO	KANSAS CITY	MO	64106	911 WALNUT STREET	(816) 426-3608
DO	CEDAR RAPIDS	IA	52402	373 COLLINS ROAD, NE	(319) 393-8630
DO	DES MOINES	IA	50309	210 WALNUT STREET	(515) 284-4422
DO	KANSAS CITY	MO	64105	323 WEST 8TH STREET	(816) 374-6708
DO	OMAHA	NE	68154	11145 MILL VALLEY RD	(402) 221-3604
DO	ST. LOUIS	MO	63101	815 OLIVE STREET	(314) 539-6600
DO	WICHITA	KS	67202	100 EAST ENGLISH ST	(316) 269-6273
BO	SPRINGFIELD	MO	65802	620 S. GLENSTONE ST	(417) 864-7670

RO = REGIONAL OFFICE   DO = DISTRICT OFFICE   BO = BRANCH OFFICE

KENTUCKY

TYPE	CITY	STATE	ZIP CODE	ADDRESS	PHONE NUMBER
RO	ATLANTA	GA	30367	1375 PEACHTREE ST., NE	(404) 347-2797
DO	ATLANTA	GA	30309	1720 PEACHTREE RD., NW	(404) 347-4749
DO	BIRMINGHAM	AL	35203-2398	2121 8TH AVE. N.	(205) 731-1344
DO	CHARLOTTE	NC	28202	200 N. COLLEGE ST.	(704) 344-6563
DO	COLUMBIA	SC	29201	1835 ASSEMBLY ST.	(803) 765-5376
DO	JACKSON	MS	39201	101 W. CAPITOL ST.	(601) 965-5325
DO	JACKSONVILLE	FL	32256-7504	7825 BAYMEADOWS WAY	(904) 443-1900
DO	LOUISVILLE	KY	40202	600 DR. M.L. KING JR PL	(502) 582-5976
DO	CORAL GABLES	FL	33146-2911	1320 S. DIXIE HGWY.	(305) 536-5521
DO	NASHVILLE	TN	37228-1500	50 VANTAGE WAY	(615) 736-5881
BO	GULFPORT	MS	39501-7758	1 HANCOCK PLAZA	(601) 863-4449
POD	STATESBORO	GA	30458	52 N. MAIN ST.	(912) 489-8719
POD	TAMPA	FL	33602-3945	501 E. POLK ST.	(813) 228-2594
POD	W. PALM BEACH	FL	33407-2044	5601 CORPORATE WAY	(407) 689-3922

RO = REGIONAL OFFICE   DO = DISTRICT OFFICE   BO = BRANCH OFFICE   POD = POST OF DUTY

LOUISIANA

TYPE	CITY	STATE	ZIP CODE	ADDRESS	PHONE NUMBER
RO	DALLAS	TX	75235	8625 KING GEORGE DR	(214) 767-7635
DO	ALBUQUERQUE	NM	87102	625 SILVER AVENUE, SW	(505) 766-1870
DO	DALLAS	TX	75242	1100 COMMERCE STREET	(214) 767-0600
DO	EL PASO	TX	79935	10737 GATEWAY WEST	(915) 541-5676
DO	HOUSTON	TX	77054	2525 MURWORTH	(713) 660-4401
DO	LITTLE ROCK	AR	72202	2120 RIVERFRONT DRIVE	(501) 324-5278
DO	HARLINGEN	TX	78550	222 EAST VAN BUREN ST	(512) 427-8533
DO	LUBBOCK	TX	79401	1611 TENTH STREET	(806) 743-7462
DO	NEW ORLEANS	LA	70112	1661 CANAL STREET	(504) 589-2744
DO	OKLAHOMA CITY	OK	73102	200 NORTH WEST 5TH ST	(405) 231-4301
DO	SAN ANTONIO	TX	78216	7400 BLANCO ROAD	(512) 229-4535
BO	CORPUS CHRISTI	TX	78476	606 NORTH CARANCAHUA	(512) 888-3301
BO	FT. WORTH	TX	76102	819 TAYLOR STREET	(817) 334-3777
POD	AUSTIN	TX	78701	300 EAST 8TH STREET	(512) 482-5288
POD	MARSHALL	TX	75670	505 EAST TRAVIS	(903) 935-5257
POD	SHREVEPORT	LA	71101	500 FANNIN STREET	(318) 226-5196

RO = REGIONAL OFFICE   DO = DISTRICT OFFICE   BO = BRANCH OFFICE
POD = POST OF DUTY

MAINE

TYPE	CITY	STATE	ZIP CODE	ADDRESS	PHONE NUMBER
RO	BOSTON	MA	02110	155 FEDERAL ST.	(617) 451-2023
DO	BOSTON	MA	02222-1093	10 CAUSEWAY ST.	(617) 565-5590
DO	AUGUSTA	ME	04330	40 WESTERN AVE.	(207) 622-8378
DO	CONCORD	NH	03302-1257	143 N. MAIN ST.	(603) 225-1400
DO	HARTFORD	CT	06106	330 MAIN ST.	(203) 240-4700
DO	MONTPELIER	VT	05602	87 STATE ST.	(802) 828-4422
DO	PROVIDENCE	RI	02903	380 WESTMINISTER MALL	(401) 528-4561
BO	SPRINGFIELD	MA	01103	1550 MAIN ST.	(413) 785-0268

RO = REGIONAL OFFICE   DO = DISTRICT OFFICE   BO = BRANCH OFFICE

MARYLAND

TYPE	CITY	STATE	ZIP CODE	ADDRESS	PHONE NUMBER
RO	KING OF PRUSSIA	PA	19406	475 ALLENDALE RD.	(215) 962-3700
DO	BALTIMORE	MD	21202	10 N. CALVERT ST.	(410) 962-4392
DO	CLARKSBURG	WV	26301	168 W. MAIN ST.	(304) 623-5631
DO	KING OF PRUSSIA	PA	19406	475 ALLENDALE RD.	(215) 962-3804
DO	PITTSBURGH	PA	15222	960 PENN AVE.	(412) 644-2780
DO	RICHMOND	VA	23240	400 N. 8TH ST.	(804) 771-2400
DO	WASHINGTON	DC	20036	1111 18TH ST., N.W.	(202) 634-1500
BO	CHARLESTON	WV	25301	550 EAGAN ST.	(304) 347-5220
BO	HARRISBURG	PA	17101	100 CHESTNUT ST.	(717) 782-3840
BO	WILKES-BARRE	PA	18702	20 N. PENNSYLVANIA AVE.	(717) 826-6497
BO	WILMINGTON	DE	19801	920 N. KING ST.	(302) 573-6295

RO = REGIONAL OFFICE   DO = DISTRICT OFFICE   BO = BRANCH OFFICE

MASSACHUSETTS

TYPE	CITY	STATE	ZIP CODE	ADDRESS	PHONE NUMBER
RO	BOSTON	MA	02110	155 FEDERAL ST.	(617) 451-2023
DO	BOSTON	MA	02222-1093	10 CAUSEWAY ST.	(617) 565-5590
DO	AUGUSTA	ME	04330	40 WESTERN AVE.	(207) 622-8378
DO	CONCORD	NH	03302-1257	143 N. MAIN ST.	(603) 225-1400
DO	HARTFORD	CT	06106	330 MAIN ST.	(203) 240-4700
DO	MONTPELIER	VT	05602	87 STATE ST.	(802) 828-4422
DO	PROVIDENCE	RI	02903	380 WESTMINISTER MALL	(401) 528-4561
BO	SPRINGFIELD	MA	01103	1550 MAIN ST.	(413) 785-0268

RO = REGIONAL OFFICE   DO = DISTRICT OFFICE   BO = BRANCH OFFICE

MICHIGAN

TYPE	CITY	STATE	ZIP CODE	ADDRESS	PHONE NUMBER
RO	CHICAGO	IL	60606-6611	300 S. RIVERSIDE PLAZA	(312) 353-5000
DO	CHICAGO	IL	60661-1093	500 W. MADISON ST.	(312) 353-4528
DO	CLEVELAND	OH	44199	1240 E. 9TH ST.	(216) 522-4180
DO	COLUMBUS	OH	43215	85 MARCONI BLVD.	(614) 469-6860
DO	DETROIT	MI	48226	477 MICHIGAN AVE.	(313) 226-6075
DO	INDIANAPOLIS	IN	46204-1873	429 N. PENNSYLVANIA	(317) 226-7272
DO	MADISON	WI	53703	212 E. WASHINGTON AVE.	(608) 264-5261
DO	MINNEAPOLIS	MN	55403-1563	100 N. 6TH ST.	(612) 370-2324
BO	CINCINNATI	OH	45202	525 VINE ST.	(513) 684-2814
BO	MILWAUKEE	WI	53203	310 W. WISCONSIN AVE	(414) 297-3941
BO	MARQUETTE	MI	49885	300 S. FRONT ST.	(906) 225-1108
BO	SPRINGFIELD	IL	62704	511 W. CAPITOL ST.	(217) 492-4416

RO = REGIONAL OFFICE   DO = DISTRICT OFFICE   BO = BRANCH OFFICE

MINNESOTA

TYPE	CITY	STATE	ZIP CODE	ADDRESS	PHONE NUMBER
RO	CHICAGO	IL	60606-6611	300 S. RIVERSIDE PLAZA	(312) 353-5000
DO	CHICAGO	IL	60661-1093	500 W. MADISON ST.	(312) 353-4528
DO	CLEVELAND	OH	44199	1240 E. 9TH ST.	(216) 522-4180
DO	COLUMBUS	OH	43215	85 MARCONI BLVD.	(614) 469-6860
DO	DETROIT	MI	48226	477 MICHIGAN AVE.	(313) 226-6075
DO	INDIANAPOLIS	IN	46204-1873	429 N. PENNSYLVANIA	(317) 226-7272
DO	MADISON	WI	53703	212 E. WASHINGTON AVE.	(608) 264-5261
DO	MINNEAPOLIS	MN	55403-1563	100 N. 6TH ST.	(612) 370-2324
BO	CINCINNATI	OH	45202	525 VINE ST.	(513) 684-2814
BO	MILWAUKEE	WI	53203	310 W. WISCONSIN AVE	(414) 297-3941
BO	MARQUETTE	MI	49885	300 S. FRONT ST.	(906) 225-1108
BO	SPRINGFIELD	IL	62704	511 W. CAPITOL ST.	(217) 492-4416

RO = REGIONAL OFFICE   DO = DISTRICT OFFICE   BO = BRANCH OFFICE

MISSISSIPPI

TYPE	CITY	STATE	ZIP CODE	ADDRESS	PHONE NUMBER
RO	ATLANTA	GA	30367	1375 PEACHTREE ST., NE	(404) 347-2797
DO	ATLANTA	GA	30309	1720 PEACHTREE RD., NW	(404) 347-4749
DO	BIRMINGHAM	AL	35203-2398	2121 8TH AVE. N.	(205) 731-1344
DO	CHARLOTTE	NC	28202	200 N. COLLEGE ST.	(704) 344-6563
DO	COLUMBIA	SC	29201	1835 ASSEMBLY ST.	(803) 765-5376
DO	JACKSON	MS	39201	101 W. CAPITOL ST.	(601) 965-5325
DO	JACKSONVILLE	FL	32256-7504	7825 BAYMEADOWS WAY	(904) 443-1900
DO	LOUISVILLE	KY	40202	600 DR. M.L. KING JR PL	(502) 582-5976
DO	CORAL GABLES	FL	33146-2911	1320 S. DIXIE HGWY.	(305) 536-5521
DO	NASHVILLE	TN	37228-1500	50 VANTAGE WAY	(615) 736-5881
BO	GULFPORT	MS	39501-7758	1 HANCOCK PLAZA	(601) 863-4449
POD	STATESBORO	GA	30458	52 N. MAIN ST.	(912) 489-8719
POD	TAMPA	FL	33602-3945	501 E. POLK ST.	(813) 228-2594
POD	W. PALM BEACH	FL	33407-2044	5601 CORPORATE WAY	(407) 689-3922

RO = REGIONAL OFFICE   DO = DISTRICT OFFICE   BO = BRANCH OFFICE   POD = POST OF DUTY

MISSOURI

TYPE	CITY	STATE	ZIP CODE	ADDRESS	PHONE NUMBER
RO	KANSAS CITY	MO	64106	911 WALNUT STREET	(816) 426-3608
DO	CEDAR RAPIDS	IA	52402	373 COLLINS ROAD, NE	(319) 393-8630
DO	DES MOINES	IA	50309	210 WALNUT STREET	(515) 284-4422
DO	KANSAS CITY	MO	64105	323 WEST 8TH STREET	(816) 374-6708
DO	OMAHA	NE	68154	11145 MILL VALLEY RD	(402) 221-3604
DO	ST. LOUIS	MO	63101	815 OLIVE STREET	(314) 539-6600
DO	WICHITA	KS	67202	100 EAST ENGLISH ST	(316) 269-6273
BO	SPRINGFIELD	MO	65802	620 S. GLENSTONE ST	(417) 864-7670

RO = REGIONAL OFFICE   DO = DISTRICT OFFICE   BO = BRANCH OFFICE

MONTANA

TYPE	CITY	STATE	ZIP CODE	ADDRESS	PHONE NUMBER
RO	DENVER	CO	80202	999 18TH STREET	(303) 294-7021
DO	CASPER	WY	82602	100 EAST B STREET	(307) 261-5761
DO	DENVER	CO	80201	721 19TH STREET	(303) 844-3984
DO	FARGO	ND	58108	657 2ND AVE NORTH	(701) 239-5131
DO	HELENA	MT	59626	301 SOUTH PARK	(406) 449-5381
DO	SALT LAKE CITY	UT	84138	125 SOUTH STATE ST.	(801) 524-5800
DO	SIOUX FALLS	SD	57102	101 SOUTH MAIN AVENUE	(605) 330-4231

RO = REGIONAL OFFICE   DO = DISTRICT OFFICE

NEBRASKA

No Data Available

NEVADA

TYPE	CITY	STATE	ZIP CODE	ADDRESS	PHONE NUMBER
DO	SAN FRANCISCO	CA	94105	71 STEVENSON STREET	(415) 744-6402
DO	FRESNO	CA	93727	2719 N. AIR FRESNO DR	(209) 487-5189
DO	HONOLULU	HI	96850	300 ALA MOANA BLVD	(808) 541-2990
DO	LAS VEGAS	NV	89125	301 EAST STEWART ST	(702) 388-6611
DO	GLENDALE	CA	91203	330 N. BRAND BLVD	(213) 894-2956
DO	PHOENIX	AZ	85004	2828 N. CENTRAL AVE	(602) 640-2316
DO	SAN DIEGO	CA	92188	880 FRONT STREET	(619) 557-7252
DO	SAN FRANCISCO	CA	94105	211 MAIN STREET	(415) 744-6820
DO	SANTA ANA	CA	92703	901 W. CIVIC CENTER DR	(714) 836-2494
BO	AGANA	GM	96910	238 ARCHBISHOP FC FLORES ST	(671) 472-7277
BO	SACRAMENTO	CA	95814	660 J STREET	(916) 551-1426
POD	RENO	NV	89505	50 SOUTH VIRGINIA ST	(702) 784-5268
POD	TUCSON	AZ	85701	300 WEST CONGRESS ST	(602) 629-6715
POD	VENTURA	CA	93003	6477 TELEPHONE ROAD	(805) 642-1866

DO = DISTRICT OFFICE   BO = BRANCH OFFICE   POD = POST OF DUTY

NEW HAMPSHIRE

TYPE	CITY	STATE	ZIP CODE	ADDRESS	PHONE NUMBER
RO	BOSTON	MA	02110	155 FEDERAL ST.	(617) 451-2023
DO	BOSTON	MA	02222-1093	10 CAUSEWAY ST.	(617) 565-5590
DO	AUGUSTA	ME	04330	40 WESTERN AVE.	(207) 622-8378
DO	CONCORD	NH	03302-1257	143 N. MAIN ST.	(603) 225-1400
DO	HARTFORD	CT	06106	330 MAIN ST.	(203) 240-4700
DO	MONTPELIER	VT	05602	87 STATE ST.	(802) 828-4422
DO	PROVIDENCE	RI	02903	380 WESTMINISTER MALL	(401) 528-4561
BO	SPRINGFIELD	MA	01103	1550 MAIN ST.	(413) 785-0268

RO = REGIONAL OFFICE   DO = DISTRICT OFFICE   BO = BRANCH OFFICE

NEW JERSEY

TYPE	CITY	STATE	ZIP CODE	ADDRESS	PHONE NUMBER
RO	NEW YORK	NY	10278	26 FEDERAL PLAZA	(212) 264-1450
DO	BUFFALO	NY	14202	111 WEST HURON ST.	(716) 846-4301
DO	NEWARK	NJ	07102	60 PARK PLACE	(201) 645-2434
DO	NEW YORK	NY	10278	26 FEDERAL PLAZA	(212) 264-2454
DO	HATO REY	PR	00918	CARLOS CHARDON AVE.	(809) 766-5572
DO	SYRACUSE	NY	13260	100 S. CLINTON ST.	(315) 423-5383
BO	ELMIRA	NY	14901	333 EAST WATER ST.	(607) 734-8130
BO	MELVILLE	NY	11747	35 PINELAWN RD.	(516) 454-0750
BO	ROCHESTER	NY	14614	100 STATE ST.	(716) 263-6700
POD	ALBANY	NY	12207	445 BROADWAY	(518) 472-6300
POD	CAMDEN	NJ	08104	2600 MT. EPHRAIN DR.	(609) 757-5183
POD	ST. CROIX	VI	00820	4200 UNITED SHOP. PLAZA	(809) 778-5380
POD	ST. THOMAS	VI	00802	VETERANS DR.	(809) 774-8530

RO = REGIONAL OFFICE   DO = DISTRICT OFFICE   BO = BRANCH OFFICE   POD = POST OF DUTY

NEW MEXICO

TYPE	CITY	STATE	ZIP CODE	ADDRESS	PHONE NUMBER
RO	DALLAS	TX	75235	8625 KING GEORGE DR	(214) 767-7635
DO	ALBUQUERQUE	NM	87102	625 SILVER AVENUE, SW	(505) 766-1870
DO	DALLAS	TX	75242	1100 COMMERCE STREET	(214) 767-0600
DO	EL PASO	TX	79935	10737 GATEWAY WEST	(915) 541-5676
DO	HOUSTON	TX	77054	2525 MURWORTH	(713) 660-4401
DO	LITTLE ROCK	AR	72202	2120 RIVERFRONT DRIVE	(501) 324-5278
DO	HARLINGEN	TX	78550	222 EAST VAN BUREN ST	(512) 427-8533
DO	LUBBOCK	TX	79401	1611 TENTH STREET	(806) 743-7462
DO	NEW ORLEANS	LA	70112	1661 CANAL STREET	(504) 589-2744
DO	OKLAHOMA CITY	OK	73102	200 NORTH WEST 5TH ST	(405) 231-4301
DO	SAN ANTONIO	TX	78216	7400 BLANCO ROAD	(512) 229-4535
BO	CORPUS CHRISTI	TX	78476	606 NORTH CARANCAHUA	(512) 888-3301
BO	FT. WORTH	TX	76102	819 TAYLOR STREET	(817) 334-3777
POD	AUSTIN	TX	78701	300 EAST 8TH STREET	(512) 482-5288
POD	MARSHALL	TX	75670	505 EAST TRAVIS	(903) 935-5257
POD	SHREVEPORT	LA	71101	500 FANNIN STREET	(318) 226-5196

RO = REGIONAL OFFICE   DO = DISTRICT OFFICE   BO = BRANCH OFFICE   POD = POST OF DUTY

NEW YORK

TYPE	CITY	STATE	ZIP CODE	ADDRESS	PHONE NUMBER
RO	NEW YORK	NY	10278	26 FEDERAL PLAZA	(212) 264-1450
DO	BUFFALO	NY	14202	111 WEST HURON ST.	(716) 846-4301
DO	NEWARK	NJ	07102	60 PARK PLACE	(201) 645-2434
DO	NEW YORK	NY	10278	26 FEDERAL PLAZA	(212) 264-2454
DO	HATO REY	PR	00918	CARLOS CHARDON AVE.	(809) 766-5572
DO	SYRACUSE	NY	13260	100 S. CLINTON ST.	(315) 423-5383
BO	ELMIRA	NY	14901	333 EAST WATER ST.	(607) 734-8130
BO	MELVILLE	NY	11747	35 PINELAWN RD.	(516) 454-0750
BO	ROCHESTER	NY	14614	100 STATE ST.	(716) 263-6700
POD	ALBANY	NY	12207	445 BROADWAY	(518) 472-6300
POD	CAMDEN	NJ	08104	2600 MT. EPHRAIN DR.	(609) 757-5183
POD	ST. CROIX	VI	00820	4200 UNITED SHOP. PLAZA	(809) 778-5380
POD	ST. THOMAS	VI	00802	VETERANS DR.	(809) 774-8530

RO = REGIONAL OFFICE   DO = DISTRICT OFFICE   BO = BRANCH OFFICE   POD = POST OF DUTY

NORTH CAROLINA

TYPE	CITY	STATE	ZIP CODE	ADDRESS	PHONE NUMBER
RO	ATLANTA	GA	30367	1375 PEACHTREE ST., NE	(404) 347-2797
DO	ATLANTA	GA	30309	1720 PEACHTREE RD., NW	(404) 347-4749
DO	BIRMINGHAM	AL	35203-2398	2121 8TH AVE. N.	(205) 731-1344
DO	CHARLOTTE	NC	28202	200 N. COLLEGE ST.	(704) 344-6563
DO	COLUMBIA	SC	29201	1835 ASSEMBLY ST.	(803) 765-5376
DO	JACKSON	MS	39201	101 W. CAPITOL ST.	(601) 965-5325
DO	JACKSONVILLE	FL	32256-7504	7825 BAYMEADOWS WAY	(904) 443-1900
DO	LOUISVILLE	KY	40202	600 DR. M.L. KING JR PL	(502) 582-5976

DO	CORAL GABLES	FL	33146-2911	1320 S. DIXIE HGWY.	(305) 536-5521
DO	NASHVILLE	TN	37228-1500	50 VANTAGE WAY	(615) 736-5881
BO	GULFPORT	MS	39501-7758	1 HANCOCK PLAZA	(601) 863-4449
POD	STATESBORO	GA	30458	52 N. MAIN ST.	(912) 489-8719
POD	TAMPA	FL	33602-3945	501 E. POLK ST.	(813) 228-2594
POD	W. PALM BEACH	FL	33407-2044	5601 CORPORATE WAY	(407) 689-3922

RO = REGIONAL OFFICE   DO = DISTRICT OFFICE   BO = BRANCH OFFICE   POD = POST OF DUTY

NORTH DAKOTA

TYPE	CITY	STATE	ZIP CODE	ADDRESS	PHONE NUMBER
RO	DENVER	CO	80202	999 18TH STREET	(303) 294-7021
DO	CASPER	WY	82602	100 EAST B STREET	(307) 261-5761
DO	DENVER	CO	80201	721 19TH STREET	(303) 844-3984
DO	FARGO	ND	58108	657 2ND AVE NORTH	(701) 239-5131
DO	HELENA	MT	59626	301 SOUTH PARK	(406) 449-5381
DO	SALT LAKE CITY	UT	84138	125 SOUTH STATE ST.	(801) 524-5800
DO	SIOUX FALLS	SD	57102	101 SOUTH MAIN AVENUE	(605) 330-4231

RO = REGIONAL OFFICE   DO = DISTRICT OFFICE

OHIO

TYPE	CITY	STATE	ZIP CODE	ADDRESS	PHONE NUMBER
RO	CHICAGO	IL	60606-6611	300 S. RIVERSIDE PLAZA	(312) 353-5000
DO	CHICAGO	IL	60661-1093	500 W. MADISON ST.	(312) 353-4528
DO	CLEVELAND	OH	44199	1240 E. 9TH ST.	(216) 552-4180
DO	COLUMBUS	OH	43215	85 MARCONI BLVD.	(614) 469-6860
DO	DETROIT	MI	48226	477 MICHIGAN AVE.	(313) 226-6075
DO	INDIANAPOLIS	IN	46204-1873	429 N. PENNSYLVANIA	(317) 226-7272
DO	MADISON	WI	53703	212 E. WASHINGTON AVE.	(608) 264-5261
DO	MINNEAPOLIS	MN	55403-1563	100 N. 6TH ST.	(612) 370-2324
BO	CINCINNATI	OH	45202	525 VINE ST.	(513) 684-2814
BO	MILWAUKEE	WI	53203	310 W. WISCONSIN AVE	(414) 297-3941
BO	MARQUETTE	MI	49885	300 S. FRONT ST.	(906) 225-1108
BO	SPRINGFIELD	IL	62704	511 W. CAPITOL ST.	(217) 492-4416

RO = REGIONAL OFFICE   DO = DISTRICT OFFICE   BO = BRANCH OFFICE

OKLAHOMA

TYPE	CITY	STATE	ZIP CODE	ADDRESS	PHONE NUMBER
RO	DALLAS	TX	75235	8625 KING GEORGE DR	(214) 767-7635
DO	ALBUQUERQUE	NM	87102	625 SILVER AVENUE, SW	(505) 766-1870
DO	DALLAS	TX	75242	1100 COMMERCE STREET	(214) 767-0600
DO	EL PASO	TX	79935	10737 GATEWAY WEST	(915) 541-5676
DO	HOUSTON	TX	77054	2525 MURWORTH	(713) 660-4401
DO	LITTLE ROCK	AR	72202	2120 RIVERFRONT DRIVE	(501) 324-5278
DO	HARLINGEN	TX	78550	222 EAST VAN BUREN ST	(512) 427-8533
DO	LUBBOCK	TX	79401	1611 TENTH STREET	(806) 743-7462
DO	NEW ORLEANS	LA	70112	1661 CANAL STREET	(504) 589-2744

DO	OKLAHOMA CITY	OK	73102	200 NORTH WEST 5TH ST	(405) 231-4301
DO	SAN ANTONIO	TX	78216	7400 BLANCO ROAD	(512) 229-4535
BO	CORPUS CHRISTI	TX	78476	606 NORTH CARANCAHUA	(512) 888-3301
BO	FT. WORTH	TX	76102	819 TAYLOR STREET	(817) 334-3777
POD	AUSTIN	TX	78701	300 EAST 8TH STREET	(512) 482-5288
POD	MARSHALL	TX	75670	505 EAST TRAVIS	(903) 935-5257
POD	SHREVEPORT	LA	71101	500 FANNIN STREET	(318) 226-5196

RO = REGIONAL OFFICE   DO = DISTRICT OFFICE   BO = BRANCH OFFICE   POD = POST OF DUTY

OREGON

TYPE	CITY	STATE	ZIP CODE	ADDRESS	PHONE NUMBER
RO	SEATTLE	WA	98121	2615 4TH AVENUE	(206) 553-5676
DO	ANCHORAGE	AK	99513	222 WEST 8TH AVENUE	(907) 271-4022
DO	BOISE	ID	83702	1020 MAIN STREET	(208) 334-1096
DO	PORTLAND	OR	97201	222 S.W. COLUMBIA	(503) 326-5223
DO	SEATTLE	WA	98174	915 SECOND AVENUE	(206) 553-1420
DO	SPOKANE	WA	99204	WEST 601 FIRST AVE	(509) 353-2810

RO = REGIONAL OFFICE   DO = DISTRICT OFFICE

PENNSYLVANIA

TYPE	CITY	STATE	ZIP CODE	ADDRESS	PHONE NUMBER
RO	KING OF PRUSSIA	PA	19406	475 ALLENDALE RD.	(215) 962-3700
DO	BALTIMORE	MD	21202	10 N. CALVERT ST.	(410) 962-4392
DO	CLARKSBURG	WV	26301	168 W. MAIN ST.	(304) 623-5631
DO	KING OF PRUSSIA	PA	19406	475 ALLENDALE RD.	(215) 962-3804
DO	PITTSBURGH	PA	15222	960 PENN AVE.	(412) 644-2780
DO	RICHMOND	VA	23240	400 N. 8TH ST.	(804) 771-2400
DO	WASHINGTON	DC	20036	1111 18TH ST., N.W.	(202) 634-1500
BO	CHARLESTON	WV	25301	550 EAGAN ST.	(304) 347-5220
BO	HARRISBURG	PA	17101	100 CHESTNUT ST.	(717) 782-3840
BO	WILKES-BARRE	PA	18702	20 N. PENNSYLVANIA AVE.	(717) 826-6497
BO	WILMINGTON	DE	19801	920 N. KING ST.	(302) 573-6295

RO = REGIONAL OFFICE   DO = DISTRICT OFFICE   BO = BRANCH OFFICE

RHODE ISLAND

TYPE	CITY	STATE	ZIP CODE	ADDRESS	PHONE NUMBER
RO	BOSTON	MA	02110	155 FEDERAL ST.	(617) 451-2023
DO	BOSTON	MA	02222-1093	10 CAUSEWAY ST.	(617) 565-5590
DO	AUGUSTA	ME	04330	40 WESTERN AVE.	(207) 622-8378
DO	CONCORD	NH	03302-1257	143 N. MAIN ST.	(603) 225-1400
DO	HARTFORD	CT	06106	330 MAIN ST.	(203) 240-4700
DO	MONTPELIER	VT	05602	87 STATE ST.	(802) 828-4422
DO	PROVIDENCE	RI	02903	380 WESTMINISTER MALL	(401) 528-4561
BO	SPRINGFIELD	MA	01103	1550 MAIN ST.	(413) 785-0268

RO = REGIONAL OFFICE   DO = DISTRICT OFFICE   BO = BRANCH OFFICE

SOUTH CAROLINA

TYPE	CITY	STATE	ZIP CODE	ADDRESS	PHONE NUMBER
RO	ATLANTA	GA	30367	1375 PEACHTREE ST., NE	(404) 347-2797
DO	ATLANTA	GA	30309	1720 PEACHTREE RD., NW	(404) 347-4749
DO	BIRMINGHAM	AL	35203-2398	2121 8TH AVE. N.	(205) 731-1344
DO	CHARLOTTE	NC	28202	200 N. COLLEGE ST.	(704) 344-6563
DO	COLUMBIA	SC	29201	1835 ASSEMBLY ST.	(803) 765-5376
DO	JACKSON	MS	39201	101 W. CAPITOL ST.	(601) 965-5325
DO	JACKSONVILLE	FL	32256-7504	7825 BAYMEADOWS WAY	(904) 443-1900
DO	LOUISVILLE	KY	40202	600 DR. M.L. KING JR PL	(502) 582-5976
DO	CORAL GABLES	FL	33146-2911	1320 S. DIXIE HGWY.	(305) 536-5521
DO	NASHVILLE	TN	37228-1500	50 VANTAGE WAY	(615) 736-5881
BO	GULFPORT	MS	39501-7758	1 HANCOCK PLAZA	(601) 863-4449
POD	STATESBORO	GA	30458	52 N. MAIN ST.	(912) 489-8719
POD	TAMPA	FL	33602-3945	501 E. POLK ST.	(813) 228-2594
POD	W. PALM BEACH	FL	33407-2044	5601 CORPORATE WAY	(407) 689-3922

RO = REGIONAL OFFICE   DO = DISTRICT OFFICE   BO = BRANCH OFFICE   POD = POST OF DUTY

SOUTH DAKOTA

TYPE	CITY	STATE	ZIP CODE	ADDRESS	PHONE NUMBER
RO	DENVER	CO	80202	999 18TH STREET	(303) 294-7021
DO	CASPER	WY	82602	100 EAST B STREET	(307) 261-5761
DO	DENVER	CO	80201	721 19TH STREET	(303) 844-3984
DO	FARGO	ND	58108	657 2ND AVE NORTH	(701) 239-5131
DO	HELENA	MT	59626	301 SOUTH PARK	(406) 449-5381
DO	SALT LAKE CITY	UT	84138	125 SOUTH STATE ST.	(801) 524-5800
DO	SIOUX FALLS	SD	57102	101 SOUTH MAIN AVENUE	(605) 330-4231

RO = REGIONAL OFFICE   DO = DISTRICT OFFICE

TENNESSEE

TYPE	CITY	STATE	ZIP CODE	ADDRESS	PHONE NUMBER
RO	ATLANTA	GA	30367	1375 PEACHTREE ST., NE	(404) 347-2797
DO	ATLANTA	GA	30309	1720 PEACHTREE RD., NW	(404) 347-4749
DO	BIRMINGHAM	AL	35203-2398	2121 8TH AVE. N.	(205) 731-1344
DO	CHARLOTTE	NC	28202	200 N. COLLEGE ST.	(704) 344-6563
DO	COLUMBIA	SC	29201	1835 ASSEMBLY ST.	(803) 765-5376
DO	JACKSON	MS	39201	101 W. CAPITOL ST.	(601) 965-5325
DO	JACKSONVILLE	FL	32256-7504	7825 BAYMEADOWS WAY	(904) 443-1900
DO	LOUISVILLE	KY	40202	600 DR. M.L. KING JR PL	(502) 582-5976
DO	CORAL GABLES	FL	33146-2911	1320 S. DIXIE HGWY.	(305) 536-5521
DO	NASHVILLE	TN	37228-1500	50 VANTAGE WAY	(615) 736-5881
BO	GULFPORT	MS	39501-7758	1 HANCOCK PLAZA	(601) 863-4449
POD	STATESBORO	GA	30458	52 N. MAIN ST.	(912) 489-8719
POD	TAMPA	FL	33602-3945	501 E. POLK ST.	(813) 228-2594
POD	W. PALM BEACH	FL	33407-2044	5601 CORPORATE WAY	(407) 689-3922

RO = REGIONAL OFFICE   DO = DISTRICT OFFICE   BO = BRANCH OFFICE   POD = POST OF DUTY

TEXAS

TYPE	CITY	STATE	ZIP CODE	ADDRESS	PHONE NUMBER
RO	DALLAS	TX	75235	8625 KING GEORGE DR	(214) 767-7635
DO	ALBUQUERQUE	NM	87102	625 SILVER AVENUE, SW	(505) 766-1870
DO	DALLAS	TX	75242	1100 COMMERCE STREET	(214) 767-0600
DO	EL PASO	TX	79935	10737 GATEWAY WEST	(915) 541-5676
DO	HOUSTON	TX	77054	2525 MURWORTH	(713) 660-4401
DO	LITTLE ROCK	AR	72202	2120 RIVERFRONT DRIVE	(501) 324-5278
DO	HARLINGEN	TX	78550	222 EAST VAN BUREN ST	(512) 427-8533
DO	LUBBOCK	TX	79401	1611 TENTH STREET	(806) 743-7462
DO	NEW ORLEANS	LA	70112	1661 CANAL STREET	(504) 589-2744
DO	OKLAHOMA CITY	OK	73102	200 NORTH WEST 5TH ST	(405) 231-4301
DO	SAN ANTONIO	TX	78216	7400 BLANCO ROAD	(512) 229-4535
BO	CORPUS CHRISTI	TX	78476	606 NORTH CARANCAHUA	(512) 888-3301
BO	FT. WORTH	TX	76102	819 TAYLOR STREET	(817) 334-3777
POD	AUSTIN	TX	78701	300 EAST 8TH STREET	(512) 482-5288
POD	MARSHALL	TX	75670	505 EAST TRAVIS	(903) 935-5257
POD	SHREVEPORT	LA	71101	500 FANNIN STREET	(318) 226-5196

RO = REGIONAL OFFICE   DO = DISTRICT OFFICE   BO = BRANCH OFFICE   POD = POST OF DUTY

UTAH

TYPE	CITY	STATE	ZIP CODE	ADDRESS	PHONE NUMBER
RO	DENVER	CO	80202	999 18TH STREET	(303) 294-7021
DO	CASPER	WY	82602	100 EAST B STREET	(307) 261-5761
DO	DENVER	CO	80201	721 19TH STREET	(303) 844-3984
DO	FARGO	ND	58108	657 2ND AVE NORTH	(701) 239-5131
DO	HELENA	MT	59626	301 SOUTH PARK	(406) 449-5381
DO	SALT LAKE CITY	UT	84138	125 SOUTH STATE ST.	(801) 524-5800
DO	SIOUX FALLS	SD	57102	101 SOUTH MAIN AVENUE	(605) 330-4231

RO = REGIONAL OFFICE   DO = DISTRICT OFFICE

VERMONT

TYPE	CITY	STATE	ZIP CODE	ADDRESS	PHONE NUMBER
RO	BOSTON	MA	02110	155 FEDERAL ST.	(617) 451-2023
DO	BOSTON	MA	02222-1093	10 CAUSEWAY ST.	(617) 565-5590
DO	AUGUSTA	ME	04330	40 WESTERN AVE.	(207) 622-8378
DO	CONCORD	NH	03302-1257	143 N. MAIN ST.	(603) 225-1400
DO	HARTFORD	CT	06106	330 MAIN ST.	(203) 240-4700
DO	MONTPELIER	VT	05602	87 STATE ST.	(802) 828-4422
DO	PROVIDENCE	RI	02903	380 WESTMINISTER MALL	(401) 528-4561
BO	SPRINGFIELD	MA	01103	1550 MAIN ST.	(413) 785-0268

RO = REGIONAL OFFICE   DO = DISTRICT OFFICE   BO = BRANCH OFFICE

VIRGINIA

TYPE	CITY	STATE	ZIP CODE	ADDRESS	PHONE NUMBER
RO	KING OF PRUSSIA	PA	19406	475 ALLENDALE RD.	(215) 962-3700
DO	BALTIMORE	MD	21202	10 N. CALVERT ST.	(410) 962-4392
DO	CLARKSBURG	WV	26301	168 W. MAIN ST.	(304) 623-5631
DO	KING OF PRUSSIA	PA	19406	475 ALLENDALE RD.	(215) 962-3804
DO	PITTSBURGH	PA	15222	960 PENN AVE.	(412) 644-2780
DO	RICHMOND	VA	23240	400 N. 8TH ST.	(804) 771-2400
DO	WASHINGTON	DC	20036	1111 18TH ST., N.W.	(202) 634-1500
BO	CHARLESTON	WV	25301	550 EAGAN ST.	(304) 347-5220
BO	HARRISBURG	PA	17101	100 CHESTNUT ST.	(717) 782-3840
BO	WILKES-BARRE	PA	18702	20 N. PENNSYLVANIA AVE.	(717) 826-6497
BO	WILMINGTON	DE	19801	920 N. KING ST.	(302) 573-6295

RO = REGIONAL OFFICE   DO = DISTRICT OFFICE   BO = BRANCH OFFICE

WASHINGTON

TYPE	CITY	STATE	ZIP CODE	ADDRESS	PHONE NUMBER
RO	SEATTLE	WA	98121	2615 4TH AVENUE	(206) 553-5676
DO	ANCHORAGE	AK	99513	222 WEST 8TH AVENUE	(907) 271-4022
DO	BOISE	ID	83702	1020 MAIN STREET	(208) 334-1096
DO	PORTLAND	OR	97201	222 S.W. COLUMBIA	(503) 326-5223
DO	SEATTLE	WA	98174	915 SECOND AVENUE	(206) 220-6520
DO	SPOKANE	WA	99204	WEST 601 FIRST AVE	(509) 353-2810

RO = REGIONAL OFFICE   DO = DISTRICT OFFICE

WEST VIRGINIA

TYPE	CITY	STATE	ZIP CODE	ADDRESS	PHONE NUMBER
RO	KING OF PRUSSIA	PA	19406	475 ALLENDALE RD.	(215) 962-3700
DO	BALTIMORE	MD	21202	10 N. CALVERT ST.	(410) 962-4392
DO	CLARKSBURG	WV	26301	168 W. MAIN ST.	(304) 623-5631
DO	KING OF PRUSSIA	PA	19406	475 ALLENDALE RD.	(215) 962-3804
DO	PITTSBURGH	PA	15222	960 PENN AVE.	(412) 644-2780
DO	RICHMOND	VA	23240	400 N. 8TH ST.	(804) 771-2400
DO	WASHINGTON	DC	20036	1111 18TH ST., N.W.	(202) 634-1500
BO	CHARLESTON	WV	25301	550 EAGAN ST.	(304) 347-5220
BO	HARRISBURG	PA	17101	100 CHESTNUT ST.	(717) 782-3840
BO	WILKES-BARRE	PA	18702	20 N. PENNSYLVANIA AVE.	(717) 826-6497
BO	WILMINGTON	DE	19801	920 N. KING ST.	(302) 573-6295

RO = REGIONAL OFFICE   DO = DISTRICT OFFICE   BO = BRANCH OFFICE

WISCONSIN

TYPE	CITY	STATE	ZIP CODE	ADDRESS	PHONE NUMBER
RO	CHICAGO	IL	60606-6611	300 S. RIVERSIDE PLAZA	(312) 353-5000
DO	CHICAGO	IL	60661-1093	500 W. MADISON ST.	(312) 353-4528
DO	CLEVELAND	OH	44199	1240 E. 9TH ST.	(216) 552-4180
DO	COLUMBUS	OH	43215	85 MARCONI BLVD.	(614) 469-6860
DO	DETROIT	MI	48226	477 MICHIGAN AVE.	(313) 226-6075
DO	INDIANAPOLIS	IN	46204-1873	429 N. PENNSYLVANIA	(317) 226-7272
DO	MADISON	WI	53703	212 E. WASHINGTON AVE.	(608) 264-5261
DO	MINNEAPOLIS	MN	55403-1563	100 N. 6TH ST.	(612) 370-2324
BO	CINCINNATI	OH	45202	525 VINE ST.	(513) 684-2814
BO	MILWAUKEE	WI	53203	310 W. WISCONSIN AVE	(414) 297-3941
BO	MARQUETTE	MI	49885	300 S. FRONT ST.	(906) 225-1108
BO	SPRINGFIELD	IL	62704	511 W. CAPITOL ST.	(217) 492-4416

RO = REGIONAL OFFICE   DO = DISTRICT OFFICE   BO = BRANCH OFFICE

WYOMING

TYPE	CITY	STATE	ZIP CODE	ADDRESS	PHONE NUMBER
RO	DENVER	CO	80202	999 18TH STREET	(303) 294-7021
DO	CASPER	WY	82602	100 EAST B STREET	(307) 261-5761
DO	DENVER	CO	80201	721 19TH STREET	(303) 844-3984
DO	FARGO	ND	58108	657 2ND AVE NORTH	(701) 239-5131
DO	HELENA	MT	59626	301 SOUTH PARK	(406) 449-5381
DO	SALT LAKE CITY	UT	84138	125 SOUTH STATE ST.	(801) 524-5800
DO	SIOUX FALLS	SD	57102	101 SOUTH MAIN AVENUE	(605) 330-4231

RO = REGIONAL OFFICE   DO = DISTRICT OFFICE

GUAM

No Data Available

PUERTO RICO

TYPE	CITY	STATE	ZIP CODE	ADDRESS	PHONE NUMBER
RO	NEW YORK	NY	10278	26 FEDERAL PLAZA	(212) 264-1450
DO	BUFFALO	NY	14202	111 WEST HURON ST.	(716) 846-4301
DO	NEWARK	NJ	07102	60 PARK PLACE	(201) 645-2434
DO	NEW YORK	NY	10278	26 FEDERAL PLAZA	(212) 264-2454
DO	HATO REY	PR	00918	CARLOS CHARDON AVE.	(809) 766-5572
DO	SYRACUSE	NY	13260	100 S. CLINTON ST.	(315) 423-5383
BO	ELMIRA	NY	14901	333 EAST WATER ST.	(607) 734-8130
BO	MELVILLE	NY	11747	35 PINELAWN RD.	(516) 454-0750
BO	ROCHESTER	NY	14614	100 STATE ST.	(716) 263-6700
POD	ALBANY	NY	12207	445 BROADWAY	(518) 472-6300
POD	CAMDEN	NJ	08104	2600 MT. EPHRAIN DR.	(609) 757-5183
POD	ST. CROIX	VI	00820	4200 UNITED SHOP. PLAZA	(809) 778-5380
POD	ST. THOMAS	VI	00802	VETERANS DR.	(809) 774-8530

RO = REGIONAL OFFICE   DO = DISTRICT OFFICE   BO = BRANCH OFFICE   POD = POST OF DUTY

TRUST TERRITORY OF THE PACIFIC ISLANDS

No Data Available

VIRGIN ISLANDS

TYPE	CITY	STATE	ZIP CODE	ADDRESS	PHONE NUMBER
RO	NEW YORK	NY	10278	26 FEDERAL PLAZA	(212) 264-1450
DO	BUFFALO	NY	14202	111 WEST HURON ST.	(716) 846-4301
DO	NEWARK	NJ	07102	60 PARK PLACE	(201) 645-2434
DO	NEW YORK	NY	10278	26 FEDERAL PLAZA	(212) 264-2454
DO	HATO REY	PR	00918	CARLOS CHARDON AVE.	(809) 766-5572
DO	SYRACUSE	NY	13260	100 S. CLINTON ST.	(315) 423-5383
BO	ELMIRA	NY	14901	333 EAST WATER ST.	(607) 734-8130
BO	MELVILLE	NY	11747	35 PINELAWN RD.	(516) 454-0750
BO	ROCHESTER	NY	14614	100 STATE ST.	(716) 263-6700
POD	ALBANY	NY	12207	445 BROADWAY	(518) 472-6300
POD	CAMDEN	NJ	08104	2600 MT. EPHRAIN DR.	(609) 757-5183
POD	ST. CROIX	VI	00820	4200 UNITED SHOP. PLAZA	(809) 778-5380
POD	ST. THOMAS	VI	00802	VETERANS DR.	(809) 774-8530

RO = REGIONAL OFFICE   DO = DISTRICT OFFICE   BO = BRANCH OFFICE   POD = POST OF DUTY

AMERICAN SAMOA

No Data Available

Index

Index